Hazardous Wastes
in Rural America

Hazardous Wastes in Rural America

Impacts, Implications, and Options for Rural Communities

Steve H. Murdock
Richard S. Krannich
F. Larry Leistritz
Sherrill Spies
J. D. Wulfhorst
Krissa Wrigley
Randall Sell
Steve White
Kofi Effah

ROWMAN & LITTLEFIELD PUBLISHERS, INC.
Lanham • Boulder • New York • Oxford

ROWMAN & LITTLEFIELD PUBLISHERS, INC.

Published in the United States of America
by Rowman & Littlefield Publishers, Inc.
4720 Boston Way, Lanham, Maryland 20706

12 Hid's Copse Road
Cumnor Hill, Oxford OX2 9JJ, England

British Library Cataloguing in Publication Information Available

Library of Congress Cataloging-in-Publication Data
Hazardous wastes in rural America : impacts, implications, and options
    for rural communities / Steve H. Murdock ... [et al.].
        p.   cm.
    Includes bibliographical references and index.
    ISBN 0-8476-9049-0 (cloth : alk. paper). – ISBN 0-8476-9100-4
(pbk. : alk. paper)
    1. Hazardous waste sites—Location—United States. 2. Hazardous
waste sites—Economic aspects—United States. 3. Hazardous waste
sites—Social aspects—United States. 4. Land use, Rural—United
States.   I. Murdock, Steven H.
TD1040.H372   1999
363.72'87'0973—dc21   98-53014
                                                           CIP

Printed in the United States of America

♾™ The paper used in this publication meets the minimum requirements of American
National Standard for Information Sciences—Permanence of Paper for Printed Library
Materials, ANSI Z39.48–1984.

To the residents and leaders of our study communities, and other rural communities, who are attempting to ensure that their communities remain economically viable while maintaining the quality of rural life for themselves and their descendants.

Contents

Tables and Figures

Tables

Figures

Preface

One of the most intractable problems facing technology use and development in the United States is how to dispose of the waste by-products of technology. Because of concerns about exposing large numbers of persons to the potentially hazardous effects of such wastes, the sites for their storage and/or disposal have generally been located in rural areas of the United States. The problems and controversies surrounding waste developments have thus become disproportionately problems that must be faced by rural communities. In many cases, these communities are ones that have faced decades of economic and demographic decline and thus waste-related developments represent both potential sources of economic renewal and sources of substances with potentially detrimental effects on the health and environment of rural residents. For rural community residents and leaders, the determination of the relative benefits and costs of hazardous waste developments is thus of critical importance as they consider hosting such projects.

Despite the obvious need for information about the benefits and costs of hazardous waste facilities, there is surprisingly little empirical information on the actual impacts of such projects. Although the impacts of other types of industrial developments on rural areas have been studied since the beginning of social science analyses, and the impacts of projects with potentially detrimental environmental consequences have been extensively examined for nearly three decades (since the passage of the National Environmental Policy Act), much of the debate on the impacts of waste-related projects on rural communities has been based on speculation colored by specific ideological perspectives. Even those few empirical analyses that exist have been largely examinations of single sites so that the extent to which the effects observed are a unique product of the specific siting area rather than generic consequences of such projects cannot be determined. Similarly, there have been few attempts to discern whether the impacts of waste-related projects differ significantly from those that occur in rural areas undergoing other types of industrial development or from the baseline impacts of general societal changes affecting rural areas. No prior multisite analyses that examine the effects of such projects compared to other types of developments and compared to baseline patterns of change have been completed. As a result, rural residents and community leaders have had little information, other than that provided by avid supporters and opponents of waste projects, to guide them in evaluating such projects or managing their impacts.

This volume reports the results of the most extensive multisite and multistage analysis of the impacts of hazardous waste siting in rural areas in the United States to date. Using data from fifteen communities in five states, it examines the economic, demographic, public service, fiscal, and social and special impacts of waste facility siting and operation on rural communities in the Great Plains and Intermountain West. These effects are compared to socioeconomic change in matched communities undergoing other types of industrial development and in communities experiencing only baseline patterns of socioeconomic change. Drawing on extensive secondary data and surveys of more than 1,800 community residents and leaders, it attempts to determine the actual socioeconomic impacts of waste projects from the early 1980s to the mid 1990s. The purpose of the analysis is to examine those impacts that have occurred and to identify means by which communities can address them.

The work begins with a brief introductory chapter outlining the key issues and state of knowledge related to the socioeconomic impacts of waste facility siting and operation. The second chapter and the appendix describe the methodology used in the study. These include a discussion of the resident and leader surveys, the industrial survey, the secondary data, and the service data collected for the effort. The volume then presents a series of chapters that examine specific types of socioeconomic impacts. Chapter 3 examines the economic and fiscal impacts of waste facility siting and operation. Chapter 4 evaluates the demographic and public service impacts and chapter 5, the social and special effects of waste facility siting and operation. The final chapter, chapter 6, provides a brief summary of the findings from the analysis and discusses the implications of the results for the development of the knowledge base related to socioeconomic impacts in general and effects related to waste facilities in particular. It also examines the implications for rural communities and those involved in waste facility siting.

The results of the analysis generally indicate that the economic and fiscal impacts of waste facilities have been neither substantially positive nor negative. Effects such as deterioration in business activity as a result of businesses leaving the area, substantial increases in service costs, and related negative effects often noted by the opponents of such projects are not evident. At the same time, substantial increases in the number of jobs, in business volume, and in revenues often promoted as benefits of such projects by their supporters are also not evident. In some cases, it appears that waste developments may have stabilized the economic decline in communities but such impacts are modest. What is clear, however, is that nonwaste-related developments have had larger and more positive impacts.

The results that relate to demographic and public services impacts are similar to those for the economic and fiscal impacts in that they show modest, neither substantially negative nor positive change. Overall levels of population growth in waste-impacted areas are less than in nonwaste development areas and no greater than those in baseline areas. Neither the speculated outmigration due to the fear of such projects nor extensive inmigration as a result of increased employment opportunities have materialized. Demands on services have also been modest suggesting neither a burgeoning of demand nor a loss of service capacity as a result of such projects.

Analysis of the social and special effects of such projects shows more substantial but selective impacts. First, it is evident that a majority of residents in waste-siting, waste-operation, nonwaste development, and baseline communities are opposed to the siting of waste facilities in their communities. Leaders too tend to oppose such developments. However, both residents and leaders in waste-impacted communities are less likely to oppose such projects than residents and leaders in nonwaste and baseline communities. For virtually all types of impacts, leaders and residents in waste-impacted communities perceive such projects as more economically beneficial and less environmentally threatening than residents in baseline or nonwaste development areas. Several often discussed socioeconomic effects are found to be less uniform and more complex than have often been portrayed in the literature. Levels of social conflict are perceived to have increased especially by residents in waste siting communities but are not perceived to be significantly higher in waste operating communities than in nonwaste development or baseline communities, suggesting that such impacts may dissipate over time. Perceptions of the extent to which incentives for hosting a waste-facility will increase siting acceptability show residents and leaders in waste-siting and waste-operating communities as more favorable toward such incentives than residents and leaders in other communities. This suggests either that their experience with waste facilities has shown the need for such incentives or that these residents believe that if they must host such facilities they wish to have compensation or incentives to do so. The incentive most favored is that of increasing the provisions to ensure the safety of the facility, suggesting that the appeal of incentives involves more than just a desire to improve the economic state of the community. Higher levels of perceived risk and less trust in technology are more evident among residents than among leaders, but lower levels of perceived risk are evident among leaders and residents in waste-impacted communities than in other types of communities. When multivariate analyses of the determinants of favorability toward waste siting are completed, the results show residence in a waste-impacted area, perceptions of lower risk, higher trust in technology and agencies managing technology, perceptions of more positive economic benefits from waste-related project, and positive perceptions of incentives are significantly related to increased levels of favorability toward siting.

Although the findings are clearly limited in that they are based on a limited number of sites in specific regions of the nation during a given period of time, and by data availability, the results have implications for the science of socioeconomic impact assessment, for rural community residents, and for those involved in waste facility siting. The results suggest the need for additional multisite studies and for truly longitudinal monitoring studies of waste-facility-impacted communities compared to communities experiencing other types of development. For rural communities, the results suggest that such projects should be viewed realistically, as unlikely either to be a bane or a boon, and as possessing certain risks for increasing community tensions and divisions. The results suggest that community leaders should be cautious in assuming that residents will perceive such projects or view the importance of economic development for their communities in the same manner as themselves. For those who would develop such projects, the results suggest that waste facility projects are likely to face substantial resistance in virtually all types of communities. To improve levels of community acceptance, waste facility developers must ensure that the siting process provides meaningful and equitable involvement of community residents as well as leaders, extensively educate residents as well as leaders, and address perceptions of risks through incentive and compensation programs that speak to community economic needs and increase the safety of such projects.

This volume represents the results of a single study of the socioeconomic impacts of hazardous waste facility siting and operation in rural communities in the western United States. Despite these temporal and geographic limitations, however, we believe that the analysis is useful in identifying those impacts that have occurred and those that have not. We also believe that this study increases our base of knowledge of the socioeconomic impacts likely to occur as a result of the development of such projects in rural areas. More important, we hope that it will prove useful to those for whom such projects have the most immediate and important effects, the residents and leaders of rural communities hosting or considering hosting such facilities in rural America.

Acknowledgments

We wish to express our sincere appreciation to the many organizations and individuals who have contributed to the study on which this work is based and to the completion of this volume. These organizations include the Competitive Grants Program within the National Research Initiative of the U.S. Department of Agriculture, the Department of Rural Sociology and the Texas Agricultural Experiment Station in the Texas A&M University System, the Department of Sociology and the Utah Agricultural Experiment Station at Utah State University, and the Department of Agricultural Economics and the North Dakota Agricultural Experiment Station at North Dakota State University. We wish to express our sincere appreciation to these organizations for their support of this work and for their continuing support throughout the years.

We wish to also express our appreciation to a number of individuals who contributed to the completion of the study examined in this volume. We thank Dr. Richard Stuby, our original project officer, for his faith in us and his financial support. We express special appreciation to Rita Hamm from North Dakota State University. She made numerous contributions to the design of the survey questionnaires and was instrumental in the data collection efforts at several study sites in Nebraska. We also wish to thank Theresa Morris and Tim Woods for their assistance in data collection efforts at the Oklahoma sites.

Several people made significant contributions to the completion of this volume. We express our sincere appreciation to our editor, Dean Birkenkamp, with whom we have enjoyed a continuing and supportive relationship throughout the years. We sincerely appreciate his continuing support of our work and his always helpful comments and suggestions. We wish to also thank Rebecca Hoogs for her skillful guidance of the work through the editorial process.

Several people also deserve special thanks for their assistance in the completion of this manuscript. These include Teresa Ray and Sheri Keyes, who assisted in the typing of selected parts of the project report that preceded this volume; Darrell Fannin, who assisted in the preparation of the computerized data sets used in the analysis; and Beverly Pecotte, who prepared the figures used in this volume and proofed parts of the manuscript. Special appreciation is due to Patricia Bramwell, who was instrumental in all stages of both the project that provided the data for this volume and in the preparation of the volume itself. Without her continuing efforts and dedication neither the project nor this volume would have been completed. We express our deepest appreciation to Charla Wright-Adkins, who typed and retyped numerous versions of this volume, performing in an extraordinary manner under very tight time frames to produce this volume. Her efforts and dedication are sincerely appreciated. Finally, we wish to thank our families, who endured our physical absence during periods of data collection and our neglect as we prepared the numerous drafts of this volume.

Chapter 1

Introduction

Background and Rationale of the Study

The management and storage of municipal, chemical, nuclear, and other hazardous wastes is a continuing problem for the United States, which generates more than 270 million tons of hazardous wastes each year (U.S. Environmental Protection Agency 1997a). In addition, approximately 28,000 metric tons of high-level nuclear waste in the form of spent fuel rods were being stored at commercial nuclear power reactors as of 1993, with 48,000 metric tons expected to be stored by 2003. Approximately 800,000 cubic feet of low-level radioactive wastes were being stored annually as of 1993 (Nuclear Regulatory Commission 1996). As of May 1997, the Environmental Protection Agency listed 1,204 sites in the United States on the National Priority List for cleanup under Superfund provisions, sites with wastes that will either have to be treated or removed for storage and/or disposal at other sites (U.S. Environmental Protection Agency 1997b).

Despite the obvious magnitude of the nation's waste problem, little progress has been made in addressing the need for storage or disposal sites. Controversy and uncertainty regarding the impact of wastes have resulted in the inability to resolve waste issues either nationally or regionally (Bullard 1990; Murdock et al. 1991; Portney 1991; Mazmanian and Morell 1992; Feldman et al. 1994; Albrecht et al. 1996). As of 1998, no site has finished characterization for the storage of high-level nuclear wastes. The number of low-level nuclear waste storage sites has decreased in the past several decades to three active sites and most multistate compacts have not yet selected their sites for low-level nuclear waste disposal. Finally, few hazardous waste storage and/or processing facilities have been sited in the past decade.

Among the variety of reasons for siting failure, opposition to such sites among residents in potential siting communities is a key factor (Murdock et al. 1991). This opposition is rooted in a history of past technology failure, particularly those related to waste storage and management (Mazmanian and Morell 1992); as well as concern for the environment (Albrecht et al. 1996); concerns related to equity and the health and safety of present and future generations (Murdock et al. 1983b; Spies et al. 1998); management and related auspices issues (Halstead et al. 1984; Freudenburg and Gramling 1992); concerns related to the appropriate forms and types of compensation and mitigation (Halstead et al. 1984; Krannich et al. 1997); and many other factors.

Thus, from a period of almost blind faith in technology, rural and urban citizens in the United States and other parts of the world have witnessed decades with periodic examples of technology failure. Love Canal, Chernobyl, Three-mile Island, the collapse of what were thought to be permanent salt domes in Louisiana, and the Exxon *Valdez* are only a few examples of the events that have led to a substantial decline in faith in technology. There is no longer faith that technology is generally safe or that "authorities" can be trusted to tell the truth. This disenchantment with technology has become a major force in the creation of opposition to waste facility siting.

Similarly, concern for the environment has increased substantially since the height of the postwar industrial expansion of the 1950s and 1960s. As this concern has increased, perspectives on nearly all types of developments have come to include a mixture of both economic (e.g., jobs, economic growth) and environmental (e.g., water and air pollution) factors. In this context the relative calculus related to support for or opposition to a given project has become increasingly complex.

Equity issues remain major concerns for those who are asked to host waste facilities. Because of safety issues it is technically preferable to store such wastes in less populated areas which, in turn, tends to lead to the siting of such facilities in rural areas. Rural residents are in effect being asked to host a facility that stores wastes produced primarily by businesses and populations from larger urban areas. As a result, hosting areas' residents often believe that siting such projects in their areas is unfair; that it is inequitable for them to be asked to store waste by-products that are produced in other areas. This inequity can, in turn, become the dominant force driving opposition to a project.

Fears and concerns about the health of both present and future generations have been influenced by a variety of factors and events. Epidemiological analyses that have convincingly linked past events and behaviors to current health consequences such as those brought about as a result of asbestos exposure and cigarette smoking have increasingly convinced the public that although there may be no known health consequences at the present time, such consequences may emerge in the future. Relative to waste products this creates a perception that even sincere statements by siting officials relative to known risks may not provide sufficient assurance to allow siting to go forward.

There are also concerns interrelated with each of the above about the likely responsible parties in the waste siting process. Who the siting entity or auspices is for a project has become an area of concern. In a period in which corporate mergers and acquisitions lead to rapid shifts in corporate ownership and related responsibility, there is often a concern about who will be responsible if there is an accident or other mishap at a waste disposal site. When the siting process for a project involves multiple state and federal agencies as well as private institutions, residents often fear that no one will be responsible if difficulties arise.

Finally, there are often concerns about the appropriateness, forms, and levels of incentives, compensation, and mitigation related to such projects. If siting entities offer various forms of mitigation or compensation, they are often accused of attempting to "bribe" the area's leaders or citizens, while failure to offer such incentives may label the siting entity as one that is unwilling to recognize that its facility is likely to create problems for a local jurisdiction. Similarly, local residents often do not know what level of compensation is appropriate because it is often difficult to assess the short-term and long-term risks related to such projects. As a result, issues related to incentives, compensation, and mitigation often come to cloud already ambiguous perceptions about the appropriateness of waste facility siting in an area.

In sum then, a variety of factors have come to serve as sources of concern and causes for increasingly pervasive local opposition in waste siting communities that are predominantly rural. Providing objective information on issues that give rise to such concerns is thus an important first step toward assisting rural communities to make informed decisions regarding such projects and in addressing the general issues surrounding the waste storage problem in the United States.

Despite the fact that rural communities have been and will continue to be the likely sites of such facilities, surprisingly little is known about the actual impacts of the siting process or of the impacts of operating waste facilities on rural communities in the United States. Although several attempts have been made to summarize the state of knowledge in socioeconomic impact assessment and of the impacts of waste siting (see for example Murdock et al. 1986, 1991; Freudenburg 1986; Freudenburg and Jones 1991), no systematic inventory of the social and economic effects of waste sites and of community response and management of such sites is available for any region of the nation. As a result, the knowledge base available to assist local community leaders in evaluating the implications of such facilities prior to their siting or to help leaders manage and monitor sites already in existence is very limited.

Relatively limited information is available to address such important questions as:

1. What are the social, economic, demographic, public service, fiscal, and other impacts of waste facilities and of the process of siting such facilities on rural communities? How do such impacts vary with the location and presiting conditions of the community?

2. Who is likely to favor and oppose the siting of waste facilities? What are the differences in characteristics, perceptions, concerns, and priorities of those favoring and those opposing siting?

3. What actions of the developer and community leaders influence residents' perceptions and actions taken toward siting?

4. What are the effects of successful and unsuccessful siting processes on communities?

5. What actions can be taken by communities either to oppose unwanted developments or to ensure that they are appropriately safeguarded and compensated for accepting desired projects?

These and similar questions can be answered only by examining the actual impacts of such facilities on rural communities, and by comparing changes in these communities to those in communities experiencing other types of development as well as changes in communities without development other than those occurring in the general society and economy. However, with the exception of some attempts to examine the social disruption hypothesis as it was applied to resource development boom growth episodes (Krannich et al. 1989; Brown et al. 1989; Wilkinson and Camasso 1987; Freudenburg and Jones 1991) and some attempts to assess the accuracy of impact assessments (Murdock et al. 1982; Albrecht et al. 1985; Freudenburg and Jones 1991), nearly all assessments of community impacts have been derived from presiting analyses of nonwaste projects.

In the absence of analyses that establish the actual impacts of such projects, local residents in potential siting areas must make decisions regarding the appropriateness of such projects for their local areas on the bases of what have been largely suppositions and opinions of both proponents and opponents of such projects. If rural community residents and leaders and the larger society are to manage the increasing waste inventory, it is critical that they know what is likely or unlikely to occur as a result of such projects. Rural residents and society can only know how to respond to such projects, how to increase their positive and decrease their negative impacts, and what levels of compensation and mitigation are necessary and appropriate if information on actual, rather than simply presumed, impacts is obtained. Thus analyses such as that presented in this volume that utilize multimethod approaches to examine the impacts of such projects at multiple sites are essential to establishing factual bases for local decision making and for resolving the waste problem in the United States.

Goals and Objectives

The analysis reported here is an attempt to address the need for multi-community assessments of the impacts of waste siting attempts and of the operation of waste storage facilities in rural communities in the western United States. Current conditions and patterns of recent socioeconomic change in communities affected by waste facility siting and development are compared to those in communities that have experienced other types of developments and to communities that have experienced only baseline patterns of change. Although limited to an analysis of fifteen communities in five western states, it represents one of the first attempts to complete such a multisite analysis.

The study from which this volume is derived was funded by the National Research Initiative Competitive Grants Program in the U.S. Department of Agriculture. The study's objectives were to:

1. assess the level of support for several premises prevalent in literature related to the impacts of siting, construction, operation, and management of facilities handling hazardous waste materials. (These premises often maintain that the health, safety, and other concerns related to projects involving waste products make their impacts relatively unique and siting-area opposition pervasive);

2. establish the determinants of social responses to waste siting and management processes including such factors as the forms of consensus and conflict that emerge during the siting process;

3. determine the duration of impacts from both the processes of siting and storage or disposal of wastes on the economic, demographic, community service, fiscal, and social structure of rural areas, including the impacts of siting on such factors as the level of in or outmigration, community services, the fiscal status of rural governments, and the degree of social cohesion evident in the impacted communities;

4. develop a set of general principles and recommended actions for rural community leaders and residents to follow to ensure community input into the siting and management processes and obtain appropriate responses to the concerns of residents of communities hosting such sites.

General Study Design

As indicated in chapter 2, which describes the methodology used in the study, these objectives were achieved through the collection of secondary as well as primary data for each of the major socioeconomic dimensions as defined in impact analysis efforts—that is, for economic, demographic, public service, fiscal, and social (including special) impacts. (For a delineation of the components of such dimensions see Murdock and Leistritz 1979; Leistritz and Murdock 1981; and Murdock et al. 1991.)

Such data were collected for four different types of communities in three separate siting regions in five states in the western United States. The community types included: (1) waste facility study communities impacted through a successful or unsuccessful siting process; (2) waste facility communities impacted by waste facility development and operation; (3) communities that had experienced other types of nonwaste related economic development projects; and (4) control communities experiencing only baseline trends. The intent was to determine not only whether involvement with different phases of waste-related developments changed communities, but also how such changes differed from those occurring in communities not experiencing significant new economic development activities and those experiencing other forms of economic development.

First, siting regions with specific waste facilities or siting experiences were selected, and then development and control or baseline communities in close proximity to the siting area, waste-impacted communities were determined. The areas examined included an operating waste storage facility and an ongoing waste siting project in Nebraska, a waste operating facility in Oklahoma, an area with a failed waste facility siting attempt in Texas, a complex of waste operating facilities in Utah, and an ongoing waste siting project in Colorado. Nonwaste development and baseline (control) areas were located in Nebraska, Oklahoma, Texas, and Utah. To protect the identities of the study communities they are referred to simply by their state name and their community type (e.g., Nebraska waste operating community, Nebraska baseline community, Nebraska nonwaste development community, Texas waste siting community, etc.).

Following the selection of communities, secondary data were collected from applicable local and state agencies and the federal decennial census of population. Primary data were obtained from in-area surveys of a random sample of community residents and a sample of community leaders in each community, and from surveys of service providers and commercial facility operators.

Although described in greater detail in chapter 2 and in the substantive chapters that follow, the general analytic methods used are comparative. That is, demographic, economic, and social changes and conditions evident in the areas experiencing waste-related impacts are compared to those in other development areas and those in areas experiencing only baseline conditions in order to identify which impacts can be specifically attributed to waste projects, to developmental change in general, and to general socioeconomic change occurring in the study region.

In general, the site selection phase of the study took place during 1993-94. In-area surveys were completed in 1994-95; secondary data were collected in 1995 and 1996; and the analysis completed during 1996 and 1997.

Organization of the Volume

The results of the analysis of these data are presented in this volume in five additional chapters. Chapter 2 provides an overview of the methodology used in the study including a description of each of the study sites. Chapters 3 through 5 provide detailed discussions of specific types of impacts. Chapter 3 examines the economic and fiscal impacts of waste facilities; chapter 4, the demographic and public service impacts; and chapter 5, the social and special effects of waste projects. Chapter 6 is an overview of generalized impacts and study findings regarding the impacts of each of the types described in chapters 3 through 5. The impacts discussed are those we believe to have particular salience for understanding the socioeconomic impacts of waste siting and special importance for rural communities in managing the effects of such projects. Chapter 6 also presents a set of recommendations regarding further analyses of this topic.

Limitations of the Volume

This work, like all analysis, is limited in several regards. First, it examines only some of the socioeconomic impacts of waste-related facilities in only a selected set of communities in one region of the nation. Thus, generalizations from the study's results to other types of impacts, other regions and other communities are limited. In addition, the analysis is limited in that it took place at a specific point in time. Although the mid-1990s witnessed no major waste disposal accidents or other known events that could be expected to affect the results obtained, all time periods have factors that are likely to affect the results obtained in unknown ways.

The analysis is also limited by the fact that project resource constraints limited the number of waste storage sites and facilities that could be included in the study. As described in chapter 2, the process of site selection was one that required extensive analysis and tradeoffs between obtaining the best waste sites and sites that provided appropriate comparison areas in sufficiently close proximity to allow for adequate and efficient processes of data collection. Similarly, it was impossible to obtain sites that were all at exactly the same stage of either operation or siting.

The study is also limited by the fact that the quality of secondary data that could be obtained varied widely from one area to another. Results derived from primary data are also limited by relatively substantial differences in the willingness of respondents to participate in the study in different areas. For example, in one study community, researchers met with relatively open hostility to any analysis of waste siting, since any study was perceived as being a likely precursor to having a project sited in the area. On the other hand, in some study communities, waste projects were considered part of the "normal" state of affairs in these areas, and opposition to the study was not experienced.

The project must thus be viewed as having results that are limited temporally, geographically, and in several other aspects. In addition, the analysis is obviously affected by the capabilities and perspectives of the authors. Although we hope that these latter factors have not negatively impacted the quality of the analysis, the reader is cautioned to utilize the results of the analysis with full realization of the limitations of the study.

Despite these limitations, this study is based on a wider and more extensive data base than has been available in prior studies of the socioeconomic impacts of hazardous waste management. As a result, we believe the findings provide important insights regarding the economic, demographic, and social and special effects of hazardous facility siting in rural areas in the United States.

Chapter 2

Study Methodology

Introduction

In this chapter we describe the methods used in the analysis. The criteria used to select study areas, the procedures used to collect secondary and primary data for each study area, the analytical methods used to analyze the data, and a description of the individual study sites are included. Although this chapter attempts to provide a relatively comprehensive description of the methods used in the study, any attempt to describe a multistate and multimethod study will be necessarily incomplete. Readers who have questions regarding the methodology used in the study should consult the original analysis from which this work is derived (Murdock et al. 1997).

Selection of Study Areas

The selection of study communities was limited to the Great Plains and Intermountain West regions of the United States. This limitation was imposed because resource constraints prevented the research team from pursuing siting areas too distant from their research bases. These regions were also selected because they are among the major regions from which much of the historical base of socioeconomic impact information is derived. They thus provide regions for which there is substantial information on the likely impact of other types of resource developments with which the impacts of waste-related facilities can be compared (for one such historical analysis, see Murdock and Leistritz 1979).

Given these general study regions, states in these regions were grouped into subareas as follows: group one included Montana, Nebraska, North Dakota, and South Dakota; group two included Colorado, Idaho, Nevada, Utah, and Wyoming; and group three included Arizona, Kansas, New Mexico, Oklahoma, and Texas. After extensive analysis of waste facility siting and operation activities in each region, four to six communities were recommended as potential sites for survey and field research within each region.

Site selection for the sample communities was guided by a quasi-experimental design. This research design was to include a comparison of four community types in each of the three subareas. These community types were to include: (1) a community currently experiencing or having recently experienced the process of siting a waste-related development project; (2) a community with an operating waste-related development project that had been sited after 1970; (3) a community with a nonwaste-related commercial or industrial development project that had been sited after 1970; and (4) a community with baseline economic growth that had experienced no significant development projects after 1970. The latter community type served as a control while the other three types represented the siting and operational phases of waste-facility development and the operational phase of nonwaste-related development projects. Projects undertaken prior to 1970 were not included for two reasons. First, it is difficult to obtain adequate development data for many community service and other characteristics prior to 1970. Second, the post-1970 period was used because the National Environmental Policy Act was not implemented until after 1970, and this act created requirements for the collection of information on certain development projects that previously had not been required and was therefore seldom available.

Ideally, the quasi-experimental design would have resulted in the selection of communities that were identical in every respect except for development events since 1970. However, because this type of community matching is impossible in sparsely populated rural areas with a limited number of communities from which to choose, the site selection process attempted to control for as many major differences between communities as possible. The objective was to match communities according to their geographical, socioeconomic, and other similarities so that the impacts of waste-related development could be identified and measured.

The initial selection process was guided by two requirements. First, the sample communities had to be rural and, second, waste-related development sites would be limited to those handling radioactive, hazardous, or medical wastes. Because municipal waste handling and storage facilities were not perceived as leading to the same types of concerns, sites handling only such wastes were omitted from consideration. Rural areas were used because of the known impact of relatively large-scale developments on rural areas and due to the fact that waste facility siting is primarily conducted in rural settings

(Murdock et al. 1991). Rural was defined as coterminous with nonmetropolitan county status as delineated in the 1990 census.

Given these initial constraints, the site selection process began with the identification of appropriate waste-related development sites. Waste-related sites were chosen using a variety of methods, including archival research and interviews with expert informants. The establishment of contacts within state and federal regulatory agencies as well as the waste management industry was a key part of the waste site selection process. These contacts provided historical documentation of existing sites as well as information about pending waste-related developments. Knowledge of the latter was especially important because waste management companies sometimes avoid any public announcement of a pending project until the formal permitting process requires that they do so. The establishment of public- and private-sector contacts helped to ensure that the list of waste-related projects likely to be involved in siting and development by the beginning of data collection was complete.

Government and industry contacts led to the identification of seventy-three waste-related developments that were either operational or in the planning stage. Further screening was done according to geographical location, facility size, and the comparability of waste types resulting in the selection of three areas with operating facilities and three areas with facilities in the siting stage. The areas with operating waste facilities involved a total of three hazardous waste incinerators and three hazardous waste landfill and storage sites. Two of the waste siting areas involved low-level nuclear wastes while the third involved hazardous wastes. These facilities were located in Colorado, Nebraska, Oklahoma, Texas, and Utah.

Communities were selected for the field research on the basis of their size and proximity to the existing and proposed waste-related development facilities. It was determined that a minimum community population of at least 500 persons would be required for sampling purposes. For example, a community of only nine residents was the closest community to one of the sites but was not large enough to be selected as a study community because it would be impossible to obtain adequate and reliable resident information from such a small area that could be generalized to other areas. Therefore, if the community nearest the waste facility location had fewer than 500 persons in the 1990 census, the next nearest community of at least 500 residents was selected. In many instances, the nearest community of sufficient size was a county seat. This expedited the collection of secondary data and, in several cases, ensured that the study communities were ones that had played integral roles in local governmental actions related to the siting of the waste-related projects.

The social and economic characteristics of the waste-related development communities were used as the screening criteria for the selection of each of the other types of communities. That is, the population size, geographical location, and other such characteristics of the host communities established the preliminary parameters for the selection of the nonwaste development and baseline control communities. Initially, geographical proximity was the primary variable used to screen potential control communities. Control communities were selected to be geographically close enough to the experimental communities to share similar sociopolitical and economic systems. At the same time, it was determined that the control communities should be far enough away from the siting communities to be relatively unaffected by the waste-related development event. Based on these criteria, control communities generally were located in a nonadjacent county within the same region of the state as the waste-related development.

In addition, the selection of the nonwaste development communities required an identification of communities with significant nonwaste business or industrial developments. To identify the pool of potential nonwaste development communities, various business and industrial directories were utilized. Typically, these directories contain information on the types of business, the date of their establishment, and their number of employees. The directories also provided an overview of the community's industrial mix, permitting one to ensure relative similarity to the waste-related developments in terms of the numbers and types of basic and service industries in the communities. These basic criteria were used to narrow the selection frame to a group of communities where nonwaste development events were deemed likely to have population and economic impacts that were comparable to those in the waste-related development communities.

Once a pool of comparable nonwaste development communities was established, a group of baseline control communities was selected. These communities were selected using the same criteria as the nonwaste development communities with the exception that for these areas it was determined that no significant development events had occurred since 1970. The latter criterion was evaluated using the business and industrial directories described above. Typically, a baseline community had a small or declining agricultural base, little or no manufacturing, and a minimal service industry infrastructure.

The list of potential nonwaste development and baseline controls was further limited using historical population and economic data. Communities were selected that had had similar levels of population and employment growth and similar industrial compositions prior to the initiation of the developments. Data at both the county and individual community level were used in this part of the selection process.

Although the selection of study communities required consideration of numerous factors and clearly involved judgmental elements, every attempt was made to objectively select sites that represented the major types of waste-related operating and siting developments impacting rural areas in the Great

Plains and Intermountain West and to obtain matching nonwaste development and baseline communities that were as similar as possible to the waste-impacted communities. Despite extensive efforts, however, it must be acknowledged that there are some dissimilarities among sites within and across siting regions that may impact the results of this analysis.

Data Collection Procedures

The data for the study were collected through a variety of methods. These included observational analysis and key informant interviews in each of the study communities, surveys of both community leaders and residents in each study community, industry surveys, and the collection of extensive secondary data from U.S. Bureau of the Census and state and local data sources on economic, demographic, and service structures in each community. Procedures utilized in the application of each method are described below.

Initial Study Area Observational Visits

After the initial screening of communities as described above, each siting area community was visited by one or more of the research team. In this initial visit, the local area was examined relative to the likely cooperation of local elected officials and other residents with a study effort. Selected officials (in all cases this included the chief elected official, the county sheriff, and local community law enforcement personnel) were contacted to describe the proposed study effort. During the discussions with local leaders, the researchers explained that the study would involve in-area surveys of residents and leaders and collection of data from local service providers. Although leaders in some areas expressed concern about the potential impacts of such studies on community interrelationships (because the siting process had caused some internal community conflict), all agreed to cooperate in the studies provided community confidentiality was maintained.

Executives at the waste-related operating facilities and in the nonwaste-related developments were also contacted during the initial visit to explain the nature of the study and to solicit their cooperation in the project. It was recognized that without such cooperation, it would be impossible to comprehensively identify the impacts of waste and other developments and to separate their impacts from other forms of socioeconomic change occurring in the communities. In all cases, these executives indicated an initial willingness to cooperate in the study effort.

In addition to informing local leaders and facility operators of the dimensions of the study effort, informal interviews were conducted with such persons, and other residents recommended by them, to obtain an indication of their views of the key issues related to waste-facility siting and operation and of other general issues affecting their communities. The site visit also served as the initial basis for identifying formal and informal leaders. Thus, after describing the study's goals and completing informal interviews, leaders such as county commissioners, mayors, church and civic leaders, and other residents were asked to identify the leaders in their community whom they would recommend for interviews during the study process. Care was taken to probe all persons interviewed about leaders who were likely to have opposing views on siting issues. This information was important to the development of the survey research instruments and the leader sample.

Finally, during each site visit, the logistical procedures for completing the remainder of the data collection efforts were planned. This included obtaining detailed area maps, establishing local area contacts (such as tax assessors and postal officials who knew the location of residences for local residents), identifying sources of sampling frames for the resident surveys, and making preliminary estimates of the time needed to complete the in-area data collection in each area.

Other observational analyses were completed as part of the survey efforts and service data collection efforts. Throughout the study effort, attempts were made to verify any observational information obtained with at least two separate sources.

Resident and Leader Surveys

The completion of the resident and leader surveys involved three major steps. These included sample selection, survey instrument development and pretesting, and survey data collection. Each of these stages are described below.

Sample Selection

One of the most difficult tasks in any study of a rural community is obtaining an adequate and representative sample of community residents and leaders. This, in turn, requires the acquisition of an appropriate sampling frame for these two groups. For leaders, it was not deemed possible to obtain a sampling frame that would represent the total list of formal and informal leaders and no predetermined number of respondents was specified. Rather, a snowball sampling technique was used in which leaders initially interviewed identified additional leaders who in turn recommended other leaders. From the initial site visits and lists of elected leaders, attempts were made to identify major formal and informal community leaders in each community. In so doing, an attempt was made to identify not only elected officials but also leaders of civic and religious organizations, industry leaders, environmental group representatives, and other leaders. In many of the communities the number of leaders was quite small. In addition, because some leaders refused to participate, the number of leader surveys completed was less than anticipated in some communities. A listing of the number of leaders interviewed in each community is shown in table 2.1.

For the resident surveys, a variety of potential sampling frames were examined. These included telephone directories, town and city directories, property tax records, and utility listings. After screening for completeness and comparability across areas, utility lists were determined to be the most appropriate for use as sampling frames.

Such lists were available for all study area communities and allowed a random sample of households to be drawn for each community. The size of the sample for each community was determined by resource limitations and the minimum numbers needed to perform multivariate analyses of the survey data. This number was set at approximately 100 households per community. A sampling procedure involving a random sample with replacement was then utilized to draw a sample for each community. The number of residents surveyed in each community is shown in table 2.1.

Questionnaire Design and Pretesting

Two survey instruments were designed, one for waste operational and siting communities and one for nonwaste development and control communities. These two instruments were very similar with differences occurring only where necessary given the different development contexts of the study area's communities. An additional schedule was also developed for community leaders. The content of the leader and resident questionnaires differed somewhat depending on whether the communities were the sites for waste operating facilities, waste siting, nonwaste development, or control (baseline) communities. A list of the general questions used in all community surveys and the unique questions used in the surveys for each community type are shown in the appendix.

The content of the questions for the survey instruments was determined by examining past questionnaires utilized by the researchers in other impact assessment efforts and from an examination of the key issues identified in the waste siting and impact literature. The questionnaire asked respondents to

Table 2.1: Number of Community Resident and Leader Survey Respondents by Community and Response Rate for Resident Survey by Community

Area	Completed Leader Surveys	Completed Resident Surveys	Completion Rate (%) for Resident Surveys
Colorado			
Waste Siting	15	118	78.7
Utah			
Waste Operating (1)	14 [a]	91	91.0
Waste Operating (2)	–	85	85.0
Nonwaste Development	15	119	79.3
Control (Baseline)	12	127	84.6
Nebraska			
Waste Operating	25	133	83.1
Waste Siting	15	122	79.7
Nonwaste Development	28	156	88.6
Control (Baseline)	27	139	85.8
Oklahoma			
Waste Operating	3	105	57.4
Nonwaste Development	8	92	62.2
Control (Baseline)	8	87	68.0
Texas			
Waste Siting	8	95	69.9
Nonwaste Development	6	106	59.6
Control (Baseline)	6	108	69.7
Total for All Study Communities	190	1,683	75.5

[a]Includes leaders in both waste operating communities in Utah.

address such issues as their evaluation of their community and its services, to describe their levels of participation in community events, to provide their assessment of the risks of waste siting, their confidence in authorities to manage hazardous materials, their evaluation of the benefits and costs of waste and other forms of developments, their evaluation of the benefits of incentives for waste siting, to provide information on their demographic characteristics, and numerous other factors. Because of the large size of the Hispanic populations in some of the study communities, both English and Spanish versions of the questionnaire were utilized.

After the questionnaire was completed, it was pretested with a sample of approximately fifty respondents in rural communities in Texas and North Dakota. It was then revised, and again pretested with a sample of approximately twenty respondents in Texas. After this second pretest was completed, the design of the questionnaire was finalized. Once the base survey instrument was completed, slight alterations in question wording were completed to adapt it to each of the study communities.

Survey Data Collection

The surveys were completed during the period from November 1994 through April 1995. The collection of survey data was accomplished using a drop-off and pick-up procedure previously utilized by the researchers for such data collection efforts (Little and Krannich 1989; Krannich et al. 1989). This procedure was utilized because project resources were not sufficient to allow personal interviews while the nature of the questionnaire and the sampling frame available made it inappropriate for use with mail or telephone survey methods. This procedure involved personally delivering the questionnaire to each respondent household, explaining the purpose and scope of the questionnaire, and then leaving the questionnaire with the respondent indicating that the questionnaire would be picked up in two days. A minimum of three attempts to personally contact each sample household selected were completed before a replacement was selected for any sample household. When questionnaires were picked up from the respondents, respondents' questions were answered and questionnaires checked for completeness. Using these procedures, questionnaires were obtained from a household member in each of approximately 100 households in each community. The person completing each questionnaire was randomly selected by asking the person in the household who was eighteen years of age or older and had most recently had a birthday to complete the questionnaire. Respondents were limited to persons eighteen years of age or older to avoid problems with obtaining parental permission for younger respondents. In addition, since much of the socioeconomic data obtained for each household pertained to the household, adults were deemed more likely to be aware of such information.

Response rates varied substantially among communities, apparently reflecting different perspectives on the desirability of responding to such surveys. As the response rates obtained using this procedure shown in table 2.1 indicate, the rates of response were highest in Utah and lowest in Texas and Oklahoma. In these latter sites, general ideals of independence and concern about government or university acquisition of household information were widespread, contributing to many residents' reluctance to participate in the study.

Industry Surveys

To determine the impacts of the waste and nonwaste development projects on the study areas, data were also collected from the waste operating/siting and nonwaste development companies. This questionnaire asked the business operator to record information on the expenditures of the business, the size of the workforce and other information to assess the magnitude and distribution of development-related impacts (copies of individual and industry survey instruments are available from the authors). Although all companies had initially indicated a willingness to cooperate in the study effort during the initial study visit, the major industrial firm at the Utah nonwaste development site refused to provide information due to divisional and other nonlocal managers' concerns about release of proprietary information.

Secondary Data Collection

Secondary data were obtained on several aspects of the study communities. These included data on demographic and economic characteristics of the siting area counties and the siting communities within them that could be derived from the appropriate decennial censuses and from post-1990 population and other estimates, as well as from state and local service agencies. Data on service provision and fiscal matters were solicited from educational, fire, police, emergency service, social service, medical and health care, other service agencies, and libraries. The items requested included information on facilities, personnel, and expenditures for 1984 through 1994. An attempt was made to obtain such information for historical periods prior to the initiation of the development project in each of the communities for service and similar data and for longer historical periods for baseline demographic and economic data. Therefore, service data were solicited for periods from 1984 through

1994, and secondary demographic and economic data for the period from 1970 to 1994. Although such information is readily available for larger communities, much of the service data proved difficult to obtain for many of the small communities in the study area. Thus, as is evident in the chapter on service impacts, the data for some services are relatively limited.

Analytic Techniques

The data were analyzed using a variety of descriptive and statistical techniques. These include basic descriptive comparisons of data for different community types (such as percentage differences, means, etc.) as well as such statistical procedures as logistic and ordinary least-squares regression and analysis of variance. Comparisons are also completed for leaders and nonleaders and for respondents taking particular views on key issues (such as favoring or not favoring siting). Given the magnitude of data obtained in this effort, any analysis must, by necessity, be incomplete. However, our intention is to provide a relatively comprehensive analysis of the impacts of waste facility siting and operation.

Description of Study Communities

In the final part of this chapter, we present a brief description of each of the study communities. Although basic descriptive data for these communities are provided in each of the other sections, the intent in this section is to provide the reader with a brief description of the history and the demographic and economic bases of each of the study communities. These descriptions are provided for each of the community types within each of the study regions; communities are not identified by name in order to protect the confidentiality of information sources.

Colorado/Utah Study Areas

Utah Waste Operating Community

The study area selected to represent a community area affected by the presence of operating waste disposal facilities in Utah is located in northwestern Utah, approximately thirty-five miles west of the nearest metropolitan center. It is comprised of two small towns, located about ten miles from one another in the northeastern section of a county that hosts several operating waste management facilities. In 1994 the estimated population of the larger town was 14,797, while the smaller town had 4,993 residents. Together, the two towns contain approximately two-thirds of the total county population, and are treated as a single functional community because of their proximity to one another and their combined role as the social, political, and economic nucleus of the county.

Prior to Anglo settlement, the area encompassed by this study community was populated by members of several Native American cultures, most notably the Goshutes, Shoshones, and Paiutes. In 1849 pioneers sent by the Church of Jesus Christ of Latter-Day Saints (commonly known as Mormons) began moving into this semiarid valley to settle the area. By the late 1800s and into the early part of the twentieth century, two primary patterns of sustenance activity had become established—livestock grazing operations and a variety of mining and mineral extraction ventures. The area remained relatively isolated and sparsely populated until the 1940s, when the federal government located an air base, an army ordinance depot, and a chemical weapons testing area in the county. For the next several decades, the military operations facilities remained the major source of employment and economic activity in the county.

Beginning in the early 1980s, a new form of economic activity involving the development of private-sector hazardous waste disposal industries emerged in some of the uninhabited portions of the county, approximately forty miles west of the study community area. A hazardous waste facility that performs waste reclamation, recycling, hazardous waste treatment, and landfill cell disposal operations was opened in 1981 in an area just north of the interstate highway that bisects the county. Employment at the facility in 1994 was approximately ninety persons.

In 1984 the Utah Department of Environmental Quality and the U.S. Department of Energy chose another area in this same uninhabited portion of the county as the site for disposal of contaminated soil and other residues from an old uranium mill site in the nearby metropolitan area. The presence of this second waste disposal site stimulated county officials to examine the potential economic development opportunities associated with waste management facilities, and in 1987 the county commission established a 140 square-mile "Hazardous Industries Area" (HIA) as a specific zoning district for hazardous waste treatment and disposal facilities. In 1988 a second commercial waste disposal facility was opened on lands adjacent to the uranium mill waste disposal site. This landfill facility accepts naturally occurring radioactive materials, low-level radioactive wastes, uranium and thorium mill tailings, and mixed wastes. The operation employs ninety people, including administrative and on-site operations personnel.

In 1989 another firm began operating a hazardous waste incinerator in the HIA zone. This facility processes mostly industrial wastes such as contaminated soils, paint thinners, acids, sludges, and dry-cleaning solvents using high-temperature thermal treatments, a secondary emissions furnace, and wet-stack gas scrubbers. Total employment is approximately 200 persons.

During the early 1990s a similar hazardous waste incineration facility was constructed by the firm that opened the first landfill facility described above. This facility, a direct competitor with the first incinerator facility, was fully constructed and permitted and went into operation in 1995. At the point of trial burn operations in 1995, the facility employed 190 persons. In early 1997 the facility was purchased by the operator of the first incinerator and is currently being held on standby status due to the declining volume of waste materials being shipped for incineration.

In addition to these four commercial waste management and disposal facilities, the Utah waste operating study community has also recently experienced the effects of construction and operation of a large-scale military incineration facility designed to destroy chemical weapons, located approximately twenty miles south of the study community. This facility first began to operate on a trial basis in August of 1996, and became fully operational in early 1997. It is charged with the task of destroying the approximately for 45 percent of the nation's chemical weapons stockpile that is currently stored at the nearby army depot facilities.

Population trends for the study area communities and the county indicate that the area experienced a period of substantial growth during the 1970s, attributable in part to increased levels of activity at area mining operations as well as continued high levels of employment at military facilities. The county as a whole and the towns comprising the study community area experienced relatively little population change during the 1980s, due in part to declining employment at several large mining operations. However, during the 1990s the area has experienced a resurgence of population growth, despite the partial closure and substantial downsizing of military base operations in the county. Some of this renewed growth may be linked to the growth of waste management industry operations in the county. However, much of the recent growth is a result of increased residential development associated with the study community's proximity to a rapidly growing metropolitan center.

Colorado Waste Siting Community

The study area selected to represent an area affected by the ongoing siting of a hazardous waste disposal facility is located in southwestern Colorado, approximately sixty miles south of the nearest major urban center. Like the Utah waste operating study area, the waste siting study community comprises two adjacent small towns, located approximately five miles from one another in the southwestern corner of a relatively large (2,240 square miles) and largely rural (approximately 28,000 total residents) county. Together these towns had approximately 1,200 residents. Known locally as the "West End," this study area is isolated by both topography and distance from more populous portions of the county to the east.

Originally populated by Native Americans, the study area was first settled by Anglos beginning in the 1860s and 1870s. Although early settlers engaged primarily in cattle grazing and small-scale farming, by the mid-1870s the economy of the area was dominated by gold and copper mining operations. Subsequently the area became known as a major reserve for radioactive minerals. Carnotite (a source of radium, vanadium, and uranium) was first mined in the late 1800s, and mining for vanadium, used to harden steel, continued in the region through the mid-1980s. Beginning in the 1940s, the area experienced a boom associated with the development of large-scale uranium mining and milling operations. Uranium production flourished in the area during the 1950s and 1960s, but declined substantially during the 1970s and 1980s. Uranium mining and milling operations located in the vicinity of the study area were closed by the early 1980s. In 1985 the State of Colorado mandated that a major uranium mill site located approximately fifteen miles from the study community be cleaned up, at which time the dismantling of buildings and land reclamation activities began.

The existing operation involves disposal of on-site uranium tailings, dismantling and disposal of the company town site and the mill facilities, as well as remedial activities involving treatment of ponds and wetlands at the lower end of the site. In addition, the facility is licensed to accept limited types and quantities of in-state radioactive wastes. The current facility employs about forty persons. However, at the time of this study the facility operator was actually pursuing efforts to secure permits to expand the operation into a substantially larger commercial hazardous and low-level radioactive waste facility that could accept wastes from both in-state and out-of-state sources.

The decline of the uranium industry and the absence of major alternative employers, along with the isolated location of the study community, have contributed to uneven patterns of economic and demographic growth over the past several decades. During the 1970s the population of the larger of the two towns comprising this study community increased slightly, while the population of the smaller town was essentially unchanged. During the 1980s both towns experienced substantial population declines—the combined study community population dropped by over 40 percent between 1980 and 1990. Although the community has experienced modest population growth since 1990, the area remains economically depressed despite substantial local efforts to pursue economic development opportunities.

Utah Nonwaste Development Community

The Utah nonwaste development community is located in southwestern Utah, approximately 23 miles north of the Arizona border and 250 miles south of Salt Lake City. With an estimated 1994 population of 5,510, the study community is the largest of several small towns in one of Utah's fastest-growing nonmetropolitan counties.

Anglo settlement of the valley containing the study community began in the late 1800s, when Mormon church leaders sent a group of families to settle in the area and evaluate the prospects for an agricultural enterprise. Establishment of the town itself was delayed until 1906, following the completion of a major irrigation diversion canal that allowed full agricultural development of the valley. Agriculture and livestock operations dominated the local economy through midcentury. However, in more recent decades the area has experienced growth and economic diversification associated with its close proximity to two major national parks, its location near a major interstate highway, and the increasing popularity of the surrounding region as both a tourist destination and as a residential retirement location.

Development has been stimulated by the recent establishment of a planned commercial/industrial/residential area located within the city limits but nine miles west of the town's center, at the intersection of the interstate highway and a state highway. Currently, the nucleus of this new development is its first occupant, a large regional distribution center operated by a major national retail discount chain. Built in 1993, the distribution center facility represented the largest single building in the state of Utah, covering over one million square feet and having over twenty-five acres under roof. Constructed in just seven months at a cost of over $60 million, the facility employs approximately 450 persons, making it the fourth-largest employer in the county.

Unlike the Colorado waste siting and Utah baseline study areas, this study community and the surrounding county in which it is located have experienced sustained and substantial population growth over the past several decades. The county population increased by approximately 90 percent during the 1970s, and grew at roughly the same rate during the 1980s. The study community's population grew at a somewhat slower but still substantial rate, increasing by over two-thirds during the 1970s and by roughly the same amount again during the 1980s. Since 1990 both the county and the study community have continued to experience very rapid growth, with the county population increasing by an estimated 36 percent from 1990-94 and the town population increasing by roughly 40 percent during that same period.

Utah Baseline (Control) Community

The baseline or "control" site for the Colorado/Utah component of the project is a town of approximately 4,400 residents located in northeastern Utah, approximately 150 miles southeast of Salt Lake City. Although not the county seat, the community is the largest settlement in the county, with approximately 32 percent of the county's population concentrated there. The area surrounding this community was not settled by Anglo populations until the early 1900s, due both to the lack of suitable agricultural lands and water sources and the establishment of the Ute Indian Reservation in the area during the 1860s. Homesteading opportunities were opened on some reservation lands in 1905. The early settlers of the area established a strong agricultural base, initially with livestock grazing operations and subsequently with the development of irrigation systems to support alfalfa production.

During the 1960s this area of Utah began to be transformed by the discovery of major oil reserves and widespread well drilling and oil production activity. Oil production levels increased dramatically during the mid- to late 1970s, resulting in a period of boom growth in this community and many others in the region. However, by the mid-1980s declining oil prices and reduced production levels led to a "bust" period, accompanied by high rates of outmigration and high levels of unemployment. In 1995 the one refinery still operating in the area closed, resulting in a loss of over 100 jobs. Because of its relatively remote location and the absence of a nearby interstate highway or rail line, the area has had little success in attracting other industrial ventures.

Population trends in this study area over the past several decades mirror its status as a resource-dependent community and the resulting unevenness of its economic growth patterns. During the 1970s the town's population almost doubled, growing from just over 2,000 residents to 3,842 by 1980. During this same period the county's population increased by nearly three-fourths. However, a substantially different trend emerged during the 1980s, when growth during the first few years of the decade was followed by a period of widespread depopulation. As a result, the overall population change for the 1980-90 period revealed a very slight increase in the town's population (up just 1.9 percent over the 1980 population), and an even smaller increase for the county as a whole. Although there have been no new major economic developments to attract renewed population growth, the community and the county have experienced modest population increases since 1990.

Nebraska Study Areas

Nebraska Waste Operating Site

The Nebraska community that was selected to represent a community with a hazardous waste site (incinerator) currently in operation is located in the southwestern corner of Nebraska. The economic base of the local area is dominated by agriculture (specifically range livestock and winter wheat) and petroleum production. The county is among Nebraska's leading counties in petroleum production. The manufacturing sector has recently become a growing component of the local economic base. The area has experienced trends of depopulation and a reduction in its economic base typical of rural areas in the northern Great Plains during the past several decades.

The area's economy has traditionally been based on the oil industry and agriculture. Manufacturing entered into the mix in more recent years. During the 1950s the county was an oil boom area. The population went from 2,000 to almost 6,000 during the 1950s. Oil industry activity and population fell during the 1960s and early 1970s, but the oil industry revived during the late 1970s and early 1980s. In recent years, the oil industry has declined again, and by 1994 the county's population was about 4,000, 50 percent less than in 1970.

The early 1960s was the era of the Minuteman missile development. The community is on the eastern edge of the Minuteman missile wing which is based at the F. E. Warren Air Force Base, near Cheyenne, Wyoming. The missiles are still located in the area, but all of the personnel live in Cheyenne.

The hazardous waste incinerator facility is located several miles south of the community. Construction of the facility began in 1989, and it began operating in January of 1995. In its first year of operation the facility employed about 100 people full time, had an annual payroll of $3.3 million and gross sales of $10 million. The annual gross sales for the facility are now less than $10 million.

Nebraska Waste Siting Community

The waste siting community in Nebraska is located in northeastern Nebraska, in a county that had a population of 2,835 in 1990. The waste siting community is the county seat, and a site less than three miles west of town has been selected as a proposed low-level radioactive waste storage site. This action has caused substantial division among county residents—those who believe such a facility would help diversify the livestock production based economy versus those who believe such a site is not worth the associated risks. As of 1998 construction of the facility had not yet begun. Located adjacent to South Dakota to the north, the county is somewhat geographically isolated in that the Niobrara River forms its southern boundary and the Missouri River runs along about one-half of the northern boundary. The county is one of the smallest counties in area in Nebraska.

Originally the area north of the Niobrara River was inhabited by the Ponca Indians. These Native Americans were a sedentary tribe that depended on both agriculture and hunting for their subsistence. This county was one of the last counties in Nebraska to be organized. It was officially proclaimed as a county in 1891; however, its present-day boundaries were not established until 1909.

The study community became the county seat because it was the largest community in the county and was centrally located. The first few buildings of the original town site were located a short distance from the town's present location due to an absence of a water well at the original location. Somewhat unusual for communities that originated at this time, the railroad was not instrumental in this community's settlement. In fact, most of the communities were settled and developed prior to the railroad coming into the county. Initially homesteaders settled the area on 160-acre tracts of land. Those homesteaders who settled in the rougher lands of the county soon found that the land was not suitable for cultivation and the 160-acre tracts were too small for profitable ranching. Many of the homesteaders who settled on more tillable land were driven from the area by a series of drought years in the 1890s. The settlers who remained expanded their land holdings to more economically viable units. By the end of the 1930s, the livestock and cash grain system of farming was extensively utilized, and the area had more livestock per square mile than any other area of the state.

Although the number of farms has continued to decline, the area is still dominated by agriculture. In 1935 there were 1,114 farms in the county but that number had declined to 395 by 1992. The population has declined dramatically in recent decades, decreasing by 25 percent from 1970 to 1990. The community does not have an extensively developed retail sector. Existing businesses primarily serve the local agricultural sector.

Nebraska Nonwaste Development Community

The nonwaste development community is located in the southwest corner of Nebraska. Its history has been one of boom and bust. The oldest community in western Nebraska, it originated with the building of the Union Pacific Railroad. An army post was constructed to protect the railroad workers from warring Native American tribes. This was also a popular jumping-off point for people heading for the Black Hills in South Dakota during the gold rush. The town became a transportation hub (two separately owned rail lines join here) and service center for surrounding farms and ranches. During WWII, an ammunition depot built here employed 2,500 people. Also, during the 1950s the town benefitted from an oil boom. The army closed the ammunition depot in 1967; this represented a major economic blow to the area.

The community has experienced substantial economic growth during the past five years, primarily because of the expanding operations of a large sporting goods supplier. The sporting goods company, which came to the community in 1969, grew steadily during the 1980s primarily through catalogue sales. In 1991, the firm opened a large retail outlet adjacent to the interstate highway. In 1995, the company employed a total of 1,100 people at its facilities in the county, of which nearly 600 were employed at the retail outlet. The company also reported retail sales between $50 and $100 million in 1995.

The recent expansion of the sporting goods outlet combined with growth in the manufacturing and service sectors have helped diversify the local economic base. The county represents the only site selected in Nebraska that has recently had increasing population. Population growth has led to other economic growth within the community. The greatest challenge currently facing local developers is attracting more labor to the community.

Nebraska Baseline (Control) Community

The community selected as the control community in Nebraska is located in north central Nebraska. This county's economic base is dominated by agriculture, primarily livestock production. Irrigation is prevalent where the terrain allows, and corn is the predominant crop grown with irrigation. Large cattle feedlots are also common, and much of the area's corn production is utilized by local feedlots.

The earliest settlers to the area were cattlemen and ranchers, who came before the railroad and began to settle the area in the 1870s. The earliest ranch in the area was established in 1873. Not atypical for the time, the control community was named in honor of the man who was in charge of building the railroad. The first train arrived in the community in 1882, and the town was incorporated as a village the following year. At an election held in 1888 the control community was named the county seat.

The Kincaid Act of 1904 permitted newcomers to acquire 640 acres of land by maintaining residence on the site for five years and improving the claim to a total value of $800. This act was of great value to the county because of the number of new residents who settled because of it. Also of strategic importance to the area's development was an irrigation project, completed in 1966 by the U.S. Bureau of Reclamation. This project had the capacity to deliver 65,000 acre-feet of water and was capable of irrigating 33,960 acres. Subsequently, additional land was developed for irrigation using wells as the water source. Widespread adoption of center-pivot sprinkler systems allowed sandy soils and land with rolling topography to be irrigated.

This irrigation development was primarily responsible for the subsequent development of the area's livestock feeding industry. During the past decade some of the land that was unfit for irrigation, either because of the water/soil quality issues or a cost/price squeeze, was enrolled in the Conservation Reserve Program. This government program was designed to pay farmers a rental payment to take highly erodible, marginal land out of production for a contract period of at least ten years.

The county has experienced outmigration, depopulation, and a declining economic base typical of counties in the northern Great Plains. The basic economic activities of the community are cattle feeding, ranching, farming, retailing, and tourism. The town's primary trade area extends fifty miles north-south and approximately forty-three miles east-west. This area contains about 6,700 people; the community's 1990 population was 1,870. The community's population has declined 18 percent since 1980. Similar to other rural areas in the United States, the number of farms in the county has declined from 353 in 1982 to 332 in 1992. The total number of retail trade, wholesale trade, and service businesses in the county has also declined, from 84 in 1982 to 79 in 1992. Total employment in the county also declined by 6 percent from 1982 through 1993. The control community is the largest community in the county, and retail sales from the community typically represent more than 95 percent of the county's total retail sales.

Oklahoma/Texas Study Areas

Oklahoma Waste Operating Community

The community hosting a waste operating facility in Oklahoma is located in the Cherokee Strip area of Northwestern Oklahoma. The county in which the community is located was organized in 1900 and was originally part of the Cherokee Outlet that was taken from the Cherokee and opened for Anglo settlement in 1893.

The community was historically a major regional railroad center for the Santa Fe Railroad, but with railroad consolidation and declining area populations its railroad employment base has declined substantially. As a result, although the community had more than 1,444 residents in 1970, its 1994 population was estimated to be 933, a decrease of more than 35 percent. The area's other major resource base is in agriculture, primarily livestock production. Thus 14 percent of its workforce in 1990 (compared to 3.7 percent in the State of Oklahoma) was employed in agriculture. As is typical of agriculture in the Great Plains, however, agricultural income has been highly variable from year to year making the area desirous of other forms of development.

The waste facility is located fourteen miles south of the community and began limited operation in 1979 but did not receive its federally required Resource Conservation and Reclamation Act (RCRA) permit required for hazardous waste storage until 1988. The facility both treats and stores, including drum processing and disposal, waste stabilization and disposal, and on-site management and monitoring of several closed landfill cells. In 1994 it employed 113 persons, and had annual operating expenditures of more than $17.5 million and gross sales of more than $50 million. The facility is seen as a major employer in the area, despite its relatively small number of employees, and its continued operation is seen by local leaders as essential to the economic viability of the area.

Oklahoma Nonwaste Development Community

This community is also located in northwestern Oklahoma in an area historically occupied by the Comanches and Kiowas and later by the Cheyenne and Arapahos. It was the site of numerous conflicts between Native Americans and the U.S. Army and the area in which it is located was not formed into a county until 1892 after the 3-million-acre Cheyenne and Arapaho Indian Reservation had been opened for Anglo settlement.

The area has had a strong base in oil and gas activity. As a result, the county in which the community is located increased its population from nearly 11,800 in 1970 to more than 13,400 by 1980. With the decline in gas and oil prices in the 1980s, however, the population decreased to slightly less than 11,500 by 1990. Similarly, the study community increased from just under 3,700 in 1970 to more than 4,100 by 1980 and then declined to 3,400 by 1990. By 1994, the county's population was roughly 10,700 and the community's estimated population was less than 3,300.

The nonwaste facility located in the community is a large carpet mill that finishes carpet fibers and spins them into carpets. The facility started small but became a major facility and employer in 1986 when it expanded its facility by more than 22,500 square feet and added forty employees. Its 1994 employment was 220 persons with an estimated 170 living in the community. Its annual payroll is more than $4.1 million, its operating expenditures exceed $32.8 million, and its annual gross sales are less than $50 million. The company provides jobs that are generally seen as paying better wages than most other sources of employment in the area.

Oklahoma Baseline (Control) Community

The baseline community is also located in northwestern Oklahoma in an area that was also part of lands originally belonging to Native Americans. As with the other study areas in Oklahoma, the land it occupies was taken from Native American tribes and opened for settlement in the late 1800s. Thus, the county in which this community is located was not formed until 1907 after former reservation areas had been opened for Anglo settlement.

As with the nonwaste development community in Oklahoma, this community has been a center for gas and oil activity and has witnessed a similar rise and fall in its population. The population in the county in which it is located increased from less than 5,100 in 1970 to nearly 5,600 by 1980 and then fell to less than 4,500 by 1990 and to less than 4,300 by 1994. Similarly, the community's population increased from roughly 1,500 in 1970 to 1,760 in 1980, declined to roughly 1,450 by 1990 and to less than 1,400 by 1994.

The area's employment base reflects a current emphasis on agriculture with 21.5 percent of the county's workforce being so employed. The employment level in mining is more than twice that of the state (6.5 percent employed in mining in the county versus 3.1 percent in the state of Oklahoma). The site community is a regional trade center offering substantial medical care facilities to residents of the region. Thus, nearly 22 percent of the city's workforce was employed in health services in 1990. This latter emphasis has caused the area to have higher levels of income and lower levels of poverty than found in the rest of Oklahoma. Despite such activity, however, the area clearly fits the stereotype of a rural community with a pattern of long-term demographic and economic stagnation.

Texas Waste Siting Community

The waste siting community in Texas, located in west Texas in one of the most sparsely settled counties in the state, with a county population of fewer than 1,500 people and a population density of less than 0.4 persons per square mile in 1990. The area has shown continuous outmigration for several decades. As of 1994, roughly 1,300 persons lived there. Created in 1905 from an adjacent county, this county is primarily agricultural, with one in six workers being directly employed in agriculture (compared to less than 3 percent for the state of Texas). The area's population is very diverse with more than one-half of the population being of Hispanic origin. Median and per capita income levels are below those in the state and more than 20 percent of the population lived in poverty in 1990.

The siting event of interest was a failed attempt to locate a private hazardous waste treatment and storage facility in the area. The proposed project was projected to have a workforce of approximately 100 in 1991 with expansion to nearly 400 by mid-decade. The permit application for the facility was submitted in September of 1991, with attempts to obtain appropriate permits continuing through August of 1994, when the company announced it was withdrawing its application. Although the stated reason was a downturn in the market in the hazardous waste industry, there had also been considerable opposition to the facility, particularly among residents in other nearby communities.

Texas Nonwaste Development Community

The nonwaste development community is also located in west Texas. The county in which it is located had about 4,000 persons in 1990 with the community having roughly 500 persons then. It is also an agricultural county based primarily in livestock production, especially the production of sheep and goats.

The nonwaste development projects include four companies that are involved in the cedar pressing and oil extraction industry. One corporation is a subsidiary of a Fortune 500 fragrance and flavor corporation. They began operation in 1952 but did not build their present facility until 1974. Located eight miles outside of the community, they employ 20 to 23 people with an annual payroll in 1994 of $765,000 and annual gross sales of less than $10 million. A second company is located on the edge of the community and is locally owned. Its facility was constructed in the late 1980s and began operation in 1991. It employs sixteen people with an annual payroll of about $400,000 and annual gross sales of less than $10 million. The third firm is also locally owned. Its original facility was built in 1969 but did not reach its present capacity until the mid-1980s. Located on the edge of the community, it employs 24 persons with sales of less than $10 million per year. The fourth facility, also located eight miles from town (next to the first facility), employs about forty persons with similar sales as the other facilities. In addition to these processing facilities, company representatives estimate that between forty and seventy persons are employed in cutting cedar that is processed in these plants.

Texas Baseline (Control) Community

As with the other Texas study communities, the control community is located in west Texas in an arid, low population density area. The community had a 1990 population of about 1,300 in a county with a total population of about 2,200. The community is surrounded by rolling hills with rocky, thin soil containing numerous caves and spring-fed streams. Three major state highways intersect in the town but the nearest interstate is 49 miles away.

Prior to the mid-1800s the area was primarily occupied by warring Native American tribes. A mission was established in the area in 1857 and Anglo settlement took place primarily in the period from 1857 to 1882. The county was created in 1858 from the Bexar land area, an area in south central and west Texas.

The area has shown relative population stability over the past two decades with the community increasing its population by roughly 100 persons during that period and the county increasing by less than 150 persons. The community is the county seat and as such much of its employment is based in government. The area's private-sector economy is primarily agricultural with substantial emphasis on cattle and calf and sheep and goat production.

As with many similar communities dependent on a declining agricultural base, the community has attempted to foster various forms of economic development. However, its small population base and remote location have prevented it from recruiting new industries to the area thus far.

Conclusion

This study involves a multimethod, multisite comparative analysis of different groups within different types of communities. Overall the study communities, although varying substantially, are largely typical of the types of rural communities that characterize the Great Plains and the Intermountain West. Although every attempt was made to obtain similar communities within each of the study regions, clearly there are differences among communities that must be recognized in evaluating the impacts of waste facility operation and siting and other developments that have occurred within them.

The analysis examines relationships involving both community and individual factors. As will become evident in the following chapters, the breadth of the information that was collected necessitates a focus on only a part of the complex data available and appropriate for analysis. In addition, the limitations of any such analysis must be acknowledged. The effects discussed below have occurred in a context of areal, historical, cultural, social, economic, demographic, and other differences that could not be fully controlled in the analysis. Similarly, temporal differences in the dates when waste and nonwaste developments were initiated cannot be fully controlled. Despite this, we believe the study provides a relatively comprehensive examination of the impacts of waste facility operation and siting in the western United States.

Chapter 3

Economic and Fiscal Impacts of Waste Facility Siting in the Rural United States

When major resource or industrial development projects are proposed, decision makers are often concerned about the socioeconomic impacts that may result. The socioeconomic impacts of development projects have been categorized in a number of ways. One classification of such impacts identifies: (1) *economic* impacts, including changes in local employment, business activity, earnings, and income; (2) *demographic* impacts, including changes in the size, distribution, and composition of the population; (3) *public service* impacts, including changes in demand for, and availability of, public services and facilities; (4) *fiscal* impacts that include changes in revenues and costs among local government jurisdictions; and (5) *social* impacts such as changes in the patterns of interaction, the formal and informal relationships resulting from such interactions, and the perceptions of such relationships among various groups in a social setting (Murdock et al. 1986; Leistritz and Ekstrom 1986). In this chapter we investigate the differences in the economic and fiscal impacts between communities, and their respective counties, that had experienced economic development from the siting and operation of waste processing and disposal facilities, versus those that had experienced economic development from other types of retail, wholesale distribution, or manufacturing businesses. These communities and their respective counties are compared and contrasted to selected control communities.

In chapter 3, we also provide a background of factors that are important to determine the nature and magnitude of economic and fiscal impacts associated with a given type of development. Then we briefly delineate the major areas of economic and fiscal impacts likely to occur in the rural areas as a result of varied types of economic development projects. The differences in the economic and fiscal impacts among the community types are then discussed. Finally, we present the resident survey results related to economic changes and expectations.

Factors Determining the Nature and Magnitude of Impacts

The impacts of waste facility operation and nonwaste development in rural areas result, in part, from the substantial economic and demographic scale of these projects relative to the economies and populations of the areas where they may be located. For example, the facilities selected for detailed analysis in this study had peak construction work forces ranging from 30 to 400 workers and operational employment ranging from 39 to 1,100. Thus, in scale alone some of these projects could have significant impacts on the areas where they are located, particularly in those that are relatively sparsely populated, rural areas (see chapter 4 and table 3.1).

At the same time, the operation of waste facilities will also have unique effects because they are waste sites and thus subject to effects from public perceptions of various forms of wastes. These special effects must be identified if impact management efforts are to be successful (Leistritz et al. 1983).

The magnitude and distribution of the socioeconomic impacts of any substantial development project will be affected by many factors. Among the most important of these are the characteristics of: (1) the project; (2) the site area; and (3) the project-related inmigrants (Murdock and Leistritz 1979). The characteristics of the project play a central role in determining the impacts it creates. In particular, the facility's location, its level and type of direct employment requirements, its potential to create secondary employment, the length of its construction and operational phases, and the employment policies of the developer all may affect the levels of impacts (Leistritz and Murdock 1981).

The socioeconomic characteristics of the site area and its residents will also affect the magnitude and distribution of the socioeconomic impacts. The number of alternative settlement sites in the impact area, the skill levels of the local labor force, the availability of local labor for employment at the project, the level of development of local community service and organizational

Table 3.1: Selected Demographic and Socioeconomic Characteristics of Study Counties by Community Type

	Estimated Population 1994	Population Change (%) 1980-94	Median Household Income		Employment in Selected Industries (persons 16 and older), 1990 (%)				
			1989	1979-89	Agriculture	Extractive	Manufacturing	Wholesale and Retail Trade	Services
Colorado									
Waste Siting	27,605	13.4	27,023	-13.3	10.1	1.4	8.6	22.1	30.7
Oklahoma									
Waste Operating	8,663	-20.7	23,620	-14.6	14.0	2.9	4.2	23.5	35.8
Nonwaste Development	10,938	-18.6	24,376	-12.6	10.4	6.8	13.5	19.2	30.5
Control	4,271	-23.7	23,924	-12.3	21.5	6.5	4.0	15.5	31.1
Texas									
Waste Siting	1,309	-17.9	25,354	-18.4	17.0	2.6	2.8	14.7	25.5
Nonwaste Development	4,137	1.8	20,979	-16.6	17.8	0.4	9.9	24.9	25.0
Control	2,934	44.3	17,497	-16.9	36.5	1.6	2.7	13.2	26.9
Utah									
Waste Operating	28,782	10.6	36,069	-10.2	2.0	0.6	25.4	13.9	25.2
Nonwaste Development	66,125	153.7	29,404	6.6	3.4	1.2	9.0	28.1	33.1
Control	13,641	8.6	28,270	-20.2	12.9	8.1	6.2	19.0	29.6
Nebraska									
Waste Operating	4,063	-16.8	27,767	-9.6	14.1	9.1	9.6	14.9	31.2
Waste Siting	2,722	-18.3	19,516	2.2	37.4	0.0	1.1	16.1	26.3
Nonwaste Development	9,574	-4.8	27,968	-9.1	14.0	1.5	8.1	26.5	29.8
Control	3,626	-17.2	20,398	-8.3	25.0	0.4	2.9	22.6	25.7

Source: Bureau of the Census 1990, 1994.

structures, and the preferences of residents in local communities are among the most important of these factors.

The impact of facilities located in rural areas also depends on the characteristics of the workers and their families who move to the affected areas. Characteristics of the workers (e.g., age, marital status, education, and ethnic background) as well as characteristics of the worker's family (e.g., family size; spouse's employment status; age of dependents; and settlement, service and other preferences), all affect the nature of the impacts in an area and their distribution (Murdock et al. 1983a).

The characteristics of the project, the site area, and new populations seldom operate independently, for it is the interaction of these three sets of factors that determine the actual level of socioeconomic impacts. The complementary or contravailing nature of these factors can work to reduce or to accentuate the socioeconomic impacts likely to result from any given project.

The unique socioeconomic effects of waste facility development have received much less attention than the standard (generic) impacts, and their identification and assessment are clearly more difficult (Murdock et al. 1983b). In large part, however, these impacts result from the special characteristics of waste facilities, including: (1) the inherently hazardous nature of the materials being handled and stored, (2) project duration, (3) project-related experience, and (4) the form and duration of project management. Thus, the facts that these facilities involve the handling and storage of hazardous, radioactive, or other potentially noxious materials, that these materials will remain dangerous for hundreds or even thousands of years, that there is often no base of experience with these projects to which local residents can relate, and that these projects are often managed by out-of-state firms or nonlocal governmental agencies (albeit with the concurrence of local officials) sometimes leads to serious misgivings and concerns about waste facilities among residents.

Economic and Fiscal Impacts

For many rural communities, past economic patterns have been ones of decline, decreasing economic and population bases, and decreasing levels of business activity. Substantial new development projects offer both promises and problems for these areas. New resource and industrial development projects, including waste facility developments, are likely to lead to increased levels of employment, income, and business activity. These effects are generally regarded as among the most positive, and economic impacts are frequently cited by interests promoting local economic development efforts (Leistritz and Hamm 1994).

Therefore, if relatively large new development projects are successfully recruited to a community, substantial increases in local employment and income, along with other positive and negative impacts will likely follow. Alternatively, if development leads to substantial inmigration, rental rates may increase, which in turn may create difficulties for elderly and other people on fixed incomes (Gilmore et al. 1981). In cases where growth is substantial, local retail and service businesses may find it difficult to compete with high-volume stores that are attracted to the area (Leistritz et al. 1982).

Fiscal problems for local governments can also accompany substantial development projects. These problems lie, in large part, in the timing of revenue collection in relation to public service costs and in the distribution of costs and revenues among jurisdictions. Although local governments immediately face increased demand for services as a major development enters the construction phase, they often do not have the luxury of additional revenues from which to provide the additional services until the new development actually begins operation (Leistritz and Murdock 1988).

The interjurisdictional distribution problems may be as severe as those associated with cost and revenue timing (Leistritz 1994). The project facilities that generate most of the new public sector revenues may be located in one county while most of the project-related people live in a different school district, county, or even a different state. In addition, many tax structures distribute most of the project-related revenues to state or county governments, whereas the costs are often greatest at the municipal or school district levels.

The standard economic effects of waste facility development thus may be both positive and negative. In general, the effects are most positive for those whose interests (through business sales or employment) are most directly tied to the development. They are least positive for those who have no direct link to the development. The impacts of a waste facility on other basic sectors of the local economy could result from controls on surrounding land uses, such as prohibitions on drilling in a buffer area around the facility. Waste facilities may have special fiscal effects if the unique nature of the facility leads to additional costs for local governments beyond those normally associated with industrial and resource development projects. The assessment of special fiscal impacts must also include consideration of the waste facility's tax status (e.g., is it subject to local property taxes?). Payments in lieu of taxes and other forms of assistance to nearby communities have sometimes been proposed in connection with waste projects. Evaluation of the statutes and administrative procedures governing such payments may be important in formulating community impact management strategies.

Findings

Because of the large number of sites, communities, counties, and states included within this project and the lack of data for some areas, adjustments were required in the data for some instances. However, in the case of the non-waste development sites, the problem is not data availability but rather the dramatic increase in development and population of the area near the Utah nonwaste development site which has experienced a substantial increase in population and development as a retirement community. The population decline in two of the other three nonwaste development counties was offset by the 40,000-person increase in population for the Utah site from 1980 to 1994 (table 3.1). To alleviate the potential for skewing and/or masking the results, many of the comparisons between the community types were also done on a per capita basis. Changes in median household income were uniform across the community types. The waste operating counties had the highest median household income in 1979 and 1989 while the control counties had the lowest as well as the largest percentage declines in median income. Not surprising, the changes in employment mirrored the changes in population and income. Total employment declined in the waste operating and control communities by 2 and 15 percent, respectively (table 3.2). Total employment in the nonwaste development and waste siting counties increased by 74 and 21 percent, respectively. However, if the Utah nonwaste development site is not included, the only community type that had an increase in total employment was the waste siting community type.

A comparison of gross sales and annual payroll for the individual businesses, which ultimately was the primary factor for the community being selected (see chapter 2), reveals that all of these businesses had gross sales and an annual payroll in excess of $1 million (table 3.3). Those businesses with the largest number of employees were located in the communities categorized as nonwaste development communities in Utah and Nebraska. With the exception of the Oklahoma nonwaste site, all other communities had began operating their businesses since 1979. A comparison of annual average salary of the development businesses to median income shows that in two of the three waste operating sites the annual average salary/wage of the business exceeds the median household income for the community ($1994).

Total personal income reported per county revealed slight decreases in the waste operating and control sites and dramatic increases in the nonwaste and waste siting areas from 1984 to 1994 (table 3.4). Retail sales were compared from 1985 to 1994, rather than from 1984 to 1994, because data from the Utah sites were not available in 1984. Similar to the changes in population, employment, and total personal income, the control communities' retail sales

Table 3.2: Change in Total County Employment and Number of Unemployed Persons by
Community Type, 1984-1994

Community Type	Total Employment			Percent Change	
	1984	1993	1994	1984-1994	1993-1994
Waste Operating	18,728	18,171	18,389	-1.8	1.2
Nonwaste development	23,804	36,636	41,497	74.3	13.3
Nonwaste development [a]	12,871	11,844	12,156	-5.6	2.6
Waste Siting	12,259	13,733	14,830	21.0	8.0
Control	11,047	9,287	9,365	-15.2	0.8

Community Type	Total Unemployment			Percent Change	
	1984	1993	1994	1984-1994	1993-1994
Waste Operating	947	778	820	-13.4	5.4
Nonwaste development	1,344	1,369	1,476	9.8	7.8
Nonwaste development [a]	615	441	447	-7.3	1.4
Waste Siting	1,430	840	775	-45.8	-7.7
Control	944	650	749	-20.7	15.2

Source: Nebraska Department of Labor, Labor Market Information, Labor Force/Work Force Summary.
Oklahoma Employment Security Commission, Local Area Unemployment Statistics Research Department.
Area Labor Force and Employment Trends; Bureau of Labor Statistics-Texas. Utah Department of
Employment Security Commission, Local Area Unemployment Statistics Research Department. Area
Labor Force and Employment Trends.

[a] Nonwaste development not including the Utah site.

Table 3.3: Gross Sales, Annual Employment, and Salary for Primary Industries by Waste Operating and
Nonwaste Development Community Types, 1994

State/ Community Type	Year		Gross Sales ($ Million)	Annual Employment	Total Salary ($ Million)	Annual Average Salary ($)
	Construction	Operating				
Oklahoma						
Waste Operating	1979	1979	50-100	113	4.2	37,168
Nonwaste Development	NA	1969	10-50	220	4.2	19,091
Texas						
Nonwaste Development [a]	1989	1991	2-20	39	1.2	30,769
Utah						
Waste Operating [b]	1982	1982	10-50	84	2.7	32,143
Nonwaste Development	1992	1993	NA	450	NA	
Nebraska						
Waste Operating	1989	1995	1-10	100	3.3	33,000
Nonwaste Development [c]	1989	1990	50-100	593	NA	

[a] Sales, employment, and annual salary are shown for two of three business subsidiaries which completed entire section of survey.

[b] Sales, employment, and annual salary are shown for one waste operating businesses which completed entire section of survey.

[c] Employment at local retail outlet and administrative offices only.

Table 3.4: Mean Total Personal Income and Change in Total Personal Income by Community Type ($1994), 1984-1994

Community Type	Total Personal Income			Percent Change	
	1984	1993	1994	1984-1994	1993-1994
Waste Operating	672,459	649,301	659,415	-1.9	1.6
Nonwaste Development	835,495	1,231,535	1,325,853	58.7	7.7
Nonwaste Development [a]	457,619	421,038	418,931	-8.5	-0.5
Waste Siting	405,326	501,185	522,693	29.0	4.3
Control	371,160	345,524	346,599	-6.6	0.3

Source: Bureau of Economic Analysis 1995.
[a] Nonwaste development not including the Utah site.

Table 3.5: Change in Total Retail Sales ($1994) by County and Community Type, and Mean and Change in Mean Per Capita Total Retail Sales for Counties by Type, 1985-1994

Community Type[a]		Retail Sales			Percent Change	
		1985	1993	1994	1985-1994	1993-1994
Waste Operating	County	199,888	198,304	220,120	10.1	11.0
	Community	164,688	161,454	173,807	5.5	7.7
Nonwaste Development	County	496,970	821,731	956,026	92.4	16.3
	Community	158,731	167,107	178,460	12.4	6.8
Nonwaste Development[b]	County	109,000	116,284	117,572	7.9	1.1
	Community	124,458	125,050	126,308	2.4	1.0
Waste Siting	County	272,632	403,141	442,492	62.3	9.8
	Community	23,584	23,136	24,081	2.1	4.1
Control	County	221,176	129,309	127,664	-42.3	-1.3
	Community	153,424	97,104	96,335	-37.2	-0.8
Per Capita Total Retail Sales						
Waste Operating	County	4,692	4,849	5,303	13.0	9.4
Nonwaste Development	County	7,849	9,740	10,532	34.2	8.1
Nonwaste Development [b]	County	3,956	4,695	4,770	20.6	1.6
Waste Siting	County	9,995	16,756	18,082	80.9	7.9
Control	County	7,494	4,218	4,035	-46.2	-4.3

Sources: Nebraska Department of Revenue; Oklahoma Tax Commission, Tax Policy Division-Research, 1984-1995; Texas sites from Bulletin Board from State Comptroller's Office via Internet. http://www.window.texas.gov. Comptroller's Window on State Government BBS; Utah State Tax Commission.
[a] Retail sales data not available for Oklahoma Counties.
[b] Nonwaste development not including the Utah site.

($1994) declined from 1985 through 1994 while retail sales of the other communities increased (table 3.5). Total retail sales ($1994) increased in all counties except the control counties from 1985 to 1994, led by the nonwaste development counties. The nonwaste development communities also had the largest increase in retail sales over the same period. Comparison of per capita retail sales reveals that the waste siting counties had the highest levels of retail sales in 1985 and experienced the greatest percentage increase from 1985 to 1994. Similar to the type of change exhibited in total employment when the Utah nonwaste development site was not included, the community type that exhibited the greatest increase in total personal income and county level retail sales changed from the nonwaste development community to the waste siting community type.

Government revenue data for some sites' counties and communities were not available. A nearly complete inventory of government expenditures for all sites at the community and county level, however, was secured. As community and county government revenues are not likely to substantially exceed or fall short of expenditures over an extended number of years, the measure used to estimate change in fiscal activity by community type was total government expenditures. Government expenditures declined by nearly one-third in the control counties and by 15 percent in the control communities from 1985 to 1994 ($1994) (table 3.6). In fact, the control sites (counties and communities) were the only sites in which expenditures declined at both levels. The waste siting community (only the Colorado waste site is included because data for the Texas and Nebraska waste sites were not available) had the largest percentage increase in government expenditures—71 percent or $124,000 from 1985 to 1994. However, the waste operating communities' expenditures increased by nearly $2.5 million (30 percent) over the same period. The nonwaste development communities' government expenditures increased by even more, $3.3 million (27 percent). Exempting some year-to-year variability, the trend has been increasing community government expenditures for the nonwaste development, waste operating, and waste siting communities.

The waste operating counties had the largest percentage increases in per capita county level expenditures, followed by the waste siting counties (table 3.6). The waste siting counties had the highest level of per capita county government expenditures, at $928 per person in 1994. The county government expenditures for the waste siting and waste operating counties were two to four times the per capita expenditures for the nonwaste development and control counties. Although the difference is not as large, the per student expenditures were the highest for waste operating and waste siting school districts (table 3.7). The waste operating school districts had the most dramatic change in per student expenditures, increasing from the lowest of the community types in 1987 to within $80 per student from the highest in 1994.

Table 3.6: Total Annual Government Expenditures for City and County Governments, and Mean Per Capita Annual County Government Expenditures by Community Type ($1994), 1985-1994

Community Type		Annual Expenditures			Percent Change	
		1985	1993	1994	1985-1994	1993-1994
Waste Operating	County	15,838	22,699	26,230	65.6	15.6
	Community [a]	8,273	10,147	10,732	29.7	5.8
Nonwaste Development	County	21,243	16,713	17,926	-15.6	7.3
	Community	12,272	14,987	15,610	27.2	4.2
Waste Siting	County	17,593	19,662	22,705	29.1	15.5
	Community [b]	175	283	299	71.1	5.8
Control	Community [c]	6,556	6,917	5,571	-15.0	-19.5
		1985	1992	1993	1985-1993	1992-1993
Control	County [d]	11,804	8,354	7,889	-33.2	-5.6

Community Type		Per Capita Annual Expenditures			Percent Change	
		1985	1993	1994	1985-1994	1993-1994
Waste Operating	County	372	555	632	70.0	13.9
Nonwaste Development	County	336	198	197	-41.1	-0.3
Waste Siting	County	645	817	928	43.8	13.5
		1985	1992	1993	1985-1993	1992-1993
Control [d]	County	400	282	257	-35.7	-8.7

Source: Individual county and community auditors for Nebraska, Oklahoma, and Texas sites. Utah sites fiscal information obtained from Utah Department of Revenue.
[a] Utah waste operating community expenditures data were not available from 1984 to 1994.
[b] Texas and Nebraska community expenditures data were not available from 1984 to 1994.
[c] Texas control community expenditures data were not available for some years from 1984 to 1994.
[d] County expenditure data were not available for a Texas control community in 1994, therefore county totals and percentage changes are through 1992 to 1993.

Table 3.7: Annual Expenditures Per Student by School District and Community Type ($1994), 1987-1994

Community Type	Annual Expenditures			Percent Change	
	1987	1993	1994	1987-1994	1993-1994
Waste Operating	3,532	4,437	4,872	27.5	8.9
Nonwaste Development	4,383	3,782	4,251	-3.1	11.0
Waste Siting	5,317	5,359	4,950	-7.4	-8.3
Control	4,011	4,842	4,489	10.6	-7.9

Resident population, employment, and personal income increased in the waste siting and nonwaste development counties from 1984 to 1994, while median household income declined in all counties from 1979 to 1989. Retail sales also increased in the waste siting and nonwaste development communities from 1985 to 1994. Alternatively, the control counties had a much greater decline in total employment and total personal income than the waste operating counties. The waste operating communities had a lower decline in retail sales than the control communities.

Resident Survey Results

Respondents were asked whether six community factors related to economic and fiscal impacts were affected positively or negatively by waste-related and other developments (table 3.8). The waste siting and operating community respondents were asked specifically about recent economic activity generated as a result of the waste siting and operating activities, while the other communities were asked the question relative to recent economic development activities. The waste operating respondents replied most positively to employment, funds for public education, local public revenues, and income. The waste siting community rated local public revenues and housing costs more positively than residents in the other community types. The control communities tended to have scores on the negative side of the scale with respect to employment, income, funds for education, housing costs, and local public revenues. More than 50 percent of respondents from the waste operating communities believed that employment was the most significantly impacted of 18 items (table 3.9). Employment was believed to be the most impacted in the other community types as well, but to a lesser degree. Housing costs were the second most frequently mentioned factor impacted by recent economic development projects for the nonwaste development communities. Local public revenues was considered the second most important factor for the waste operating, and funds for public education was cited as the second most important factor for waste siting communities.

Respondents from the waste operating communities were asked if the economic benefits from the waste facility were greater than economic costs. Respondents from the waste siting communities were asked if they expected the economic benefits to be greater than the economic costs. Nearly three-quarters of respondents from both community types believed that economic benefits would outweigh economic costs. There was no statistically significant difference between these community types.

Table 3.8: Respondents' Perceptions of Recent Economic Changes on a Variety of Community Factors by Community Type

Community Factor	Waste Operating	Waste Siting	Nonwaste Development	Control
	------------------average score[1]--------------------			
Employment	2.0 [b, c, d]	2.2 [a, c, d]	2.5 [a, b, d]	3.2 [a, b, c]
Income	2.1 [c, d]	2.1 [c,d]	2.8 [a,b,d]	3.2 [a,b,c]
Funds for schools or public education	2.0 [b,c,d]	2.3 [a,c,d]	2.7 [a,b,d]	3.1 [a,b,c]
Local public revenues	2.0 [b,c,d]	2.2 [a,c,d]	2.7 [a,b,d]	3.1 [a,b,c]
Local public expenditures	2.5 [b,c,d]	2.3 [a,c,d]	2.9 [a,b]	3.0 [a,b]
Housing costs	3.1 [b]	2.7 [a,c,d]	3.2 [b]	3.1 [b]

[1] Average score from 1=very positive effect, 3=neutral, 5=very negative effect.
[a] Significant difference at p=0.05 from waste operating community. (TUKEY'S Studentized Range Test)
[b] Significant difference at p=0.05 from waste siting community. (TUKEY'S Studentized Range Test)
[c] Significant difference at p=0.05 from nonwaste development community. (TUKEY'S Studentized Range Test)
[d] Significant difference at p=0.05 from control community. (TUKEY'S Studentized Range Test)

Table 3.9: Percentage of Respondents Ranking Alternative Factors as the Community Factor Most Affected by Recent Economic Changes*

Community Factor	Waste Operating	Waste Siting	Nonwaste Development	Control
Employment	53.8	43.2	35.3	39.6
Income	4.4	3.5	8.6	9.0
Funds for schools or public education	1.0	7.0	5.7	4.5
Local public revenues	4.8	2.6	3.5	11.0
Local public expenditures	0.0	0.4	1.0	0.4
Housing costs	3.1	3.5	19.4	2.4

* Significant difference at p=0.01. Chi-square test statistic equals 242.4.

Conclusions and Implications

Although care must be exercised in generalizing from this single study, the results suggest the following conclusions: (1) the nonwaste development sites have experienced the largest increases in employment, personal income, and retail sales; (2) the waste operating sites slowed the trends of declining employment and reductions in economic base, but did not reverse those trends; (3) the waste siting communities have experienced increases in employment; (4) government expenditures have increased substantially at both the community and county level for the waste siting and operating areas; and (5) residents' perceptions of economic changes are generally positive. A couple of caveats to these conclusions must be noted. First, the Utah nonwaste development site county has experienced phenomenal growth (an increase in real retail sales of nearly 200 percent from 1985 through 1994) that may be masking or exaggerating the changes in the nonwaste development category. If the Utah nonwaste development site is excluded from the nonwaste communities, the community type with the largest increase in employment, total personal income, and retail sales at the county level is the waste siting community type. Second, waste siting areas have not experienced substantial impacts as a result of the possibility of a waste facility being constructed on site. In fact, only the Nebraska waste siting area has actually had people employed because of the possibility of developing a waste processing facility at that location. The waste siting location in Texas has been abandoned since this study was undertaken. The increase in employment associated with the proposed waste siting location in Colorado is due to the attempts to clean up and dispose of an old uranium and vanadium mining facility, on which the proposed waste site will be located.

Arguments against proposed waste facility siting and operation because they will erode the area's economic base are not supported by these findings. At the same time there is little indication that such developments have led to substantial economic growth. Total personal income declined in the waste operating counties by less than one-half the rate of decline in the control counties, -1.9 versus -6.6 percent respectively, but substantive growth did not occur. Finally, the fiscal expenditures have increased at the community and county levels for the waste siting and operating sites more than for any other community type. These increases in local government expenditures may be beneficial to areas' public infrastructures, assuming their fiscal policies do not allow for deficit spending. This increase in local government expenditures may be directly related to the waste facility being located in the area. In the case of the waste operating facility in Nebraska, the waste processing facility gave funds to the local government to purchase fire fighting and emergency response vehicles and equipment. This increase in the community's expenditures is the direct result of the waste processing facility being located in the area and the community needing the type of emergency response equipment and training that would enable it to deal with the type of emergencies that can result as a direct consequence of the waste processing facility operating in the area. Alternatively, in the Nebraska waste siting community, the waste processing company assisted the community with financial aid to enable the community to expand or improve its infrastructure to manage the indirect increases in demand for services resulting from preconstruction engineering studies and the siting of the waste facility.

A ranking of residents' perceptions of economic changes caused by recent economic development efforts tended to mirror the actual measured changes. For instance, respondents from the waste operating and waste siting communities rated the impacts 'most positive' for employment, income, funds for school development, and local public expenditures. Actual changes in these categories reveal that either the waste operating or waste siting community types led in all categories except employment—nonwaste development communities had the largest increase in employment. Similarly, nearly 75 percent of both the waste siting and operating respondents believe the economic benefits from the waste facility will exceed the economic costs.

Overall, the results suggest that neither the negative economic and fiscal impacts often indicated as likely to occur as a result of waste developments by the opponents of such developments nor the boom growth often suggested by the promoters of such developments have occurred in the study area. Waste developments have served largely to stabilize economic and fiscal conditions in the impacted communities. Relative to continued decline such effects are clearly positive. Relative to expansive growth, such effects may be seen as disappointing. The results presented here suggest that the actual economic and fiscal impacts of waste projects are likely to be ones that will neither substantially disrupt nor substantially expand the economic base of impacted communities.

Chapter 4

Demographic and Public Service Impacts

Among the positive effects often sought by communities pursuing economic development are population growth and changes in the characteristics of their population bases (Murdock and Leistritz 1979; Murdock et al. 1991; Flynn et al. 1994). Many of the communities hosting waste-related projects are remotely located relative to urban centers and have had histories of declining economic bases (as shown in chapter 3) resulting in population decline. Similarly, they have had aging populations and have shown decades of decline in their populations of young adults. For such communities, population growth from the inmigration of young adults of child-bearing age is often highly desirable.

Coupled with declines in populations have been declines in health, education, law enforcement, and other services. As with population, these declines have been in both the magnitude and characteristics of service demand and service provision. Population decline occurring primarily among young adults has resulted in disproportionate losses in persons of school age, while the proportion of the population that is elderly and requiring health and related services has shown much smaller levels of decline.

In sum, rural communities similar to those involved in waste siting have often been doubly impacted by declines in their economic bases and the resultant declines in population and services. Many of these rural communities now have fewer people who have even more limited services available.

The magnitude of population and service impacts is, as for the economic impacts described in chapter 3, a product in part of the sizes and characteristics of the development projects, the characteristics of the siting areas prior to development, and the characteristics of inmigrating workforces and populations (Murdock et al. 1986, 1991). During the era of rapid energy development during the 1970s, large (relative to the population bases of the communities) influxes of young adult construction and operational workers entered rural communities during concentrated time periods leading to what was termed "boomtown" levels of growth (Gilmore and Duff 1974). This growth in population was so extensive that it was difficult to manage.

In relative terms, however, waste developments tend to have limited impacts on employment because most individual facilities employ fewer than 150 persons. As a result, for communities being impacted by waste-related developments, one can anticipate that the population and related service impacts will be relatively small. In fact, for many areas impacted by waste-related developments, the demographic impacts are likely to be ones that serve to partially abate rates of population decline rather than leading to reversals in patterns of growth. To establish the demographic and service impacts of waste-related facilities, it is therefore essential to complete comparative analyses of waste facility and waste siting communities in relation to nonwaste development and control communities. It is not absolute growth but change relative to that in similar areas that is likely to indicate the extent to which demographic and service impacts have occurred in waste facility development areas.

In this chapter, we examine demographic and service impacts in waste-impacted communities compared to nonwaste development and control communities. We begin by providing a demographic, housing, and socioeconomic overview of the individual siting areas and then examine population and service changes in the communities grouped by development type, evaluating the extent to which the development of waste-related facilities appears to have altered patterns of growth and change over time.

Demographic Impacts of Waste Developments

Tables 4.1-4.6 provide a profile of the populations of the individual study counties and communities. Tables 4.1-4.3 present data for the counties that form the context in which the study communities function; tables 4.4-4.6 show data for the individual study communities. In describing these tables the intent is not to present a detailed analysis of the population in each community but to point out the unique demographic and socioeconomic characteristics of individual communities.

Characteristics of Study Counties

The data in table 4.1 clearly show that the study counties, with the exception of the nonwaste development county in Utah and the control community in Texas, are growing less rapidly than the states of which they are a part. The Utah site, as noted above, has become a bedroom community for a growing urban area that has also become a major regional retirement destination. The Texas site is one for which the 1994 estimates have been questioned by local officials and for which much of the growth is due to the placement of a state prison in the county in the early 1990s. What is more important for the analysis here is that there appears to be little indication that growth has been more rapid, in either the 1980s or 1990s, in the waste-related counties. Rather, it appears that it is generally the nonwaste development areas that are growing most rapidly, suggesting that economic developments of a nonwaste related form are likely to be more effective than waste-related developments in promoting population growth.

Similarly, the data in table 4.1 do not suggest that the growth in the waste areas has been due to any substantial migration of persons into these areas. As is evident in the data in table 4.1, net outmigration increased in four of the six waste-impacted counties from 1990 to 1994. In one of the other two, net migration was less than 1 percent and less than that for the state as a whole. However, net inmigration was evident in three of the four nonwaste development counties and in two of four control counties from 1990 to 1994. The patterns for the 1980s are similar. The waste-related developments in this analysis did not lead to county-wide inmigration.

Other data in table 4.1 also fail to indicate that waste-related developments have led to other significant changes in the population. For example, when one examines data on age, there is little indication that the aging of the populations noted above have abated. In a majority of waste- and nonwaste-related areas the aging of the population has continued. Similarly, there is little indication that people from different ethnic groups have entered the waste-development related counties. There are increases in the proportion of Hispanics in many of the counties but such increases reflect wider patterns of substantial increase in the Hispanic population in the United States. The data in table 4.1 do not suggest that waste-related counties have had substantially different patterns of population change than areas that have not been impacted by waste-related developments. Similarly, the data in tables 4.2 and 4.3 do not suggest that waste-impacted counties have substantially different

Table 4.1: Selected Demographic Characteristics of Counties in the Study Area by State and Development Type, 1970-1994

Variable	State of Colorado	Colorado Waste Siting County	State of Utah	Utah Counties		
				Waste Operating	Nonwaste Development	Control (Baseline)
Total Population						
1970	2,207,259	18,366	1,059,273	21,545	13,669	7,299
1980	2,889,964	24,352	1,461,037	26,033	26,065	12,565
1990	3,294,394	24,423	1,722,850	26,601	48,560	12,645
1994	3,655,714	27,605	1,907,975	28,782	66,125	13,641
Density per Square Mile						
1970	21.3	8.2	12.9	3.1	5.6	2.2
1980	27.9	10.9	17.8	3.8	10.8	3.9
1990	31.8	10.9	21.0	3.8	20.0	3.9
Change (%*)						
1970-1980	30.9	32.6	37.9	20.8	90.7	72.1
1980-1990	14.0	0.3	17.9	2.2	86.3	0.6
1990-1994	11.0	13.0	10.7	8.2	36.2	7.9
Median Age						
1970	26.2	29.1	23.1	23.2	22.8	23.4
1980	28.6	30.7	24.2	24.5	24.8	22.0
1990	32.5	37.0	26.3	28.4	28.5	25.0
1994	34.0	39.0	26.7	29.1	29.3	25.9
1990 Age Distribution (%*)						
0-4	7.7	6.4	9.8	8.7	9.4	10.7
5-19	19.8	22.3	28.3	29.0	28.9	33.7
20-24	8.8	5.0	9.8	7.6	8.0	5.6
25-34	18.6	13.1	16.0	14.8	11.8	13.9
35-59	31.4	31.7	24.3	27.6	21.2	24.7
60-64	3.7	5.1	3.0	3.7	4.4	3.0
65-74	5.9	9.5	5.1	5.5	9.8	5.0
75+	4.1	6.9	3.6	3.1	6.5	3.5

Continued on next page

Table 4.1, continued

Variable	State of Colorado	Colorado Waste Siting County	State of Utah	Utah Counties		
				Waste Operating	Nonwaste Development	Control (Baseline)
Population 65 Years and Older (%)*						
1970	8.5	10.1	7.3	5.3	12.3	8.0
1980	8.6	11.6	7.5	6.1	13.3	6.8
1990	10.0	16.4	8.7	8.6	16.3	8.5
1994	10.1	16.5	8.8	8.6	16.5	8.6
Less Than 5 Years of Age (%)**						
1970	8.4	8.2	10.6	10.8	10.2	10.6
1980	7.5	8.3	13.0	12.4	13.5	14.8
1990	7.7	6.4	9.8	8.7	9.4	10.7
1994	7.4	6.2	9.6	8.3	9.1	10.2
Female (%)*						
1970	50.6	49.9	50.6	48.8	50.4	49.5
1980	50.4	50.0	50.4	49.1	50.9	49.2
1990	50.5	51.2	50.3	49.5	50.9	49.5
1994	50.5	51.1	50.3	49.4	50.8	49.4
Black (%)*						
1970	3.0	0.1	0.6	0.6	0.0	0.0
1980	3.5	0.2	0.6	0.7	0.1	0.0
1990	4.0	0.3	0.7	0.9	0.1	0.1
1994	4.3	0.3	0.8	1.0	0.1	0.1
Hispanic (%)*						
1970	N/A	N/A	N/A	N/A	N/A	N/A
1980	11.8	9.5	4.1	9.2	1.1	1.4
1990	12.9	11.2	4.9	11.1	1.8	2.8
1994	13.5	11.9	5.5	12.3	2.0	3.1

Continued on next page

Table 4.1, continued

Variable	State of Colorado	Colorado Waste Siting County	State of Utah	Utah Counties		
				Waste Operating	Nonwaste Development	Control (Baseline)
American Indian and Other (%*)						
1970	0.4	1.6	1.1	1.3	1.2	4.4
1980	0.6	0.7	1.3	1.4	1.0	2.3
1990	0.8	0.6	1.4	1.5	1.5	5.3
1994	0.9	0.6	1.5	1.6	1.5	5.7
Rural (%*)						
1970	21.5	64.6	19.6	28.2	48.1	100.0
1980	19.4	64.2	15.6	28.0	44.6	69.4
1990	17.6	63.7	13.0	31.7	26.1	69.0
Natural Increase						
1970-1980	235,423	1,492	252,626	4,216	3,803	2,831
1980-1990	333,545	1,472	293,562	3,907	5,786	2,921
1990-1994	131,455	418	115,120	1,607	2,862	960
Natural Increase (%*)						
1970-1980	10.7	8.1	23.8	19.6	27.8	38.8
1980-1990	11.5	6.0	20.1	15.0	22.2	23.2
1990-1994	4.0	1.7	6.7	6.0	5.9	7.6
Net Migration						
1970-1980	447,282	4,494	149,138	272	8,593	2,435
1980-1990	70,885	-1,401	-31,749	-3,339	16,709	-2,841
1990-1994	229,865	2,764	70,005	574	14,703	36
Net Migration (%*)						
1970-1980	20.3	24.5	14.1	1.3	62.9	33.4
1980-1990	2.5	-5.8	-2.2	-12.8	64.1	-22.6
1990-1994	7.0	11.3	4.1	2.3	30.3	.3

Continued on next page

Table 4.1, continued

53

Variable	State of Nebraska	Nebraska Counties			
		Waste Operating	Waste Siting	Nonwaste Development	Control (Baseline)
Total Population					
1970	1,483,493	6,009	3,752	10,778	4,021
1980	1,569,825	4,882	3,331	10,057	4,377
1990	1,578,385	4,108	2,835	9,494	3,657
1994	1,623,283	4,063	2,722	9,574	3,626
Density per Square Mile					
1970	19.4	5.3	7.0	9.1	3.3
1980	20.5	5.1	6.3	8.4	3.6
1990	20.5	4.3	5.2	7.9	3.0
Change (%[*])					
1970-1980	5.8	-13.8	-11.2	-6.7	8.9
1980-1990	0.5	-15.9	-14.9	-5.6	-16.4
1990-1994	2.8	-1.1	-4.0	0.8	-0.8
Median Age					
1970	28.6	27.2	38.4	30.8	35.0
1980	29.7	32.0	41.0	32.8	33.8
1990	33.0	37.9	40.9	35.9	39.0
1994	34.2	39.2	42.4	37.1	40.5
1990 Age Distribution (%[*])					
0-4	7.6	6.9	6.2	7.3	7.0
5-19	21.0	20.9	21.6	21.5	21.0
20-24	8.4	5.6	2.7	5.5	4.0
25-34	16.3	14.2	11.5	14.3	12.7
35-59	28.2	29.3	26.7	27.6	28.7
60-64	4.3	6.1	6.1	5.9	5.2
65-74	7.5	10.6	11.8	9.6	10.7
75+	6.7	8.4	13.3	8.3	10.8

Continued on next page

Table 4.1, continued

Variable	State of Nebraska	Nebraska Counties			
		Waste Operating	Waste Siting	Nonwaste Development	Control (Baseline)
65 Years and Older (%*)					
1970	12.4	8.5	18.9	13.0	17.0
1980	13.1	13.9	22.1	15.6	18.2
1990	14.1	19.0	25.1	17.9	21.5
1994	14.1	18.8	25.0	17.9	21.9
Rural (%*)					
1970	38.5	38.8	100.0	40.6	100.0
1980	37.1	36.1	100.0	40.2	100.0
1990	33.9	37.3	100.0	37.2	100.0
Less Than 5 Years of Age (%*)					
1970	8.1	8.7	6.4	7.3	7.5
1980	7.8	7.8	7.1	7.6	7.9
1990	7.6	6.9	6.2	7.3	7.0
1994	7.1	7.0	6.1	7.0	6.3
Female (%*)					
1970	51.2	50.1	49.1	51.4	51.4
1980	51.2	50.3	48.8	50.8	51.4
1990	51.3	50.9	50.6	51.7	51.8
1994	51.2	50.9	50.3	51.7	51.6
Black (%*)					
1970	2.7	0.0	0.0	0.1	0.1
1980	3.1	0.0	0.0	0.1	0.0
1990	3.6	0.1	0.0	0.1	0.0
1994	3.8	0.1	0.0	0.2	0.0

Continued on next page

Table 4.1, continued

Variable	State of Nebraska	Nebraska Counties			
		Waste Operating	Waste Siting	Nonwaste Development	Control (Baseline)
Hispanic (%*)					
1970	N/A	N/A	N/A	N/A	N/A
1980	1.8	3.1	0.3	2.5	0.3
1990	2.3	3.6	0.2	3.3	0.6
1994	3.0	4.3	0.2	4.2	0.6
American Indian and Other (%*)					
1970	0.5	0.1	0.4	0.1	0.5
1980	0.6	0.3	0.2	0.7	0.2
1990	0.8	0.2	0.8	0.8	0.3
1994	0.8	0.2	0.8	0.9	0.3
Natural Increase					
1970-1980	97,871	564	-35	409	107
1980-1990	108,251	249	-31	437	24
1990-1994	32,514	-32	-74	59	-20
Natural Increase (%*)					
1970-1980	6.6	6.1	-0.9	3.8	2.7
1980-1990	6.9	5.1	-0.9	4.3	0.5
1990-1994	2.1	-0.8	-2.6	0.6	-0.5
Net Migration					
1970-1980	-11,539	-1,491	-386	-1,130	249
1980-1990	-99,691	-1,023	-465	-1,000	-744
1990-1994	12,384	-13	-13	21	-14
Net Migration (%*)					
1970-1980	-0.3	-24.8	-10.3	-10.5	6.2
1980-1990	-6.4	-21.0	-14.0	-9.9	-17.0
1990-1994	0.8	-0.3	-0.5	0.2	-0.4

Continued on next page

Table 4.1, continued

Variable	State of Oklahoma	Oklahoma Counties			State of Texas	Texas Counties		
		Waste Operating	Nonwaste Development	Control (Baseline)		Waste Siting	Nonwaste Development	Control (Baseline)
Total Population								
1970	2,559,229	11,920	11,794	5,129	11,196,730	1,940	3,904	2,107
1980	3,025,290	10,923	13,443	5,596	14,229,191	1,595	4,063	2,033
1990	3,145,585	9,103	11,470	4,497	16,986,510	1,410	4,122	2,266
1994	3,258,074	8,663	10,938	4,271	18,378,280	1,309	4,137	2,934
Density per Square Mile								
1970	37.2	9.2	12.9	4.1	42.7	0.8	3.1	1.0
1980	44.1	8.5	14.6	4.5	54.3	0.7	3.3	1.0
1990	45.8	7.1	12.4	3.7	64.9	0.6	3.3	1.1
Change (%*)								
1970-1980	18.2	-8.4	14.0	9.1	27.1	-17.8	4.1	-3.5
1980-1990	4.0	-16.7	-14.7	-19.6	19.4	-11.6	1.5	11.5
1990-1994	3.6	-4.8	-4.6	-5.0	8.2	-7.2	0.4	29.5
Median Age								
1970	29.4	32.1	36.0	40.6	26.4	31.2	33.9	28.4
1980	30.1	35.4	33.2	33.8	28.0	31.6	38.0	29.6
1990	33.1	37.4	35.7	39.9	30.7	36.3	40.9	32.1
1994	34.2	38.8	37.0	40.7	31.9	37.7	42.1	33.5
1990 Age Distribution (%*)								
0-4	7.2	5.6	7.2	5.5	8.2	6.4	6.5	8.1
5-19	20.9	17.9	21.8	21.9	21.9	24.5	20.4	26.4
20-24	8.7	11.2	6.1	3.6	9.6	4.2	4.3	5.6
25-34	16.2	12.4	13.7	11.5	18.2	13.3	11.1	13.8
35-59	29.1	25.5	27.0	30.0	28.4	32.1	30.0	28.8
60-64	4.4	5.1	4.8	4.7	3.7	5.4	6.4	4.8
65-74	7.5	10.8	9.6	11.2	5.9	8.0	11.4	7.1
75+	6.0	11.5	9.7	11.6	4.2	6.2	9.9	5.4

Continued on next page

56

Table 4.1, continued

Variable	State of Oklahoma	Oklahoma Counties			State of Texas	Texas Counties		
		Waste Operating	Nonwaste Development	Control (Baseline)		Waste Siting	Nonwaste Development	Control (Baseline)
65 Years and Older (%*)								
1970	11.7	16.1	17.2	17.8	8.9	10.4	16.8	11.9
1980	12.4	20.4	18.2	18.7	9.6	13.0	19.7	14.8
1990	13.5	22.4	19.3	22.8	10.1	14.2	21.2	12.5
1994	13.6	22.6	19.6	22.8	10.2	14.9	21.4	12.3
Less Than 5 Years of Age (%*)								
1970	7.7	5.7	7.0	6.2	8.9	8.4	8.5	9.8
1980	7.7	6.1	8.0	8.2	8.2	8.9	6.1	8.7
1990	7.2	5.6	7.2	5.5	8.2	6.4	6.5	8.1
1994	7.3	5.7	7.4	5.3	8.5	6.7	6.5	9.0
Female (%*)								
1970	51.3	51.0	51.8	51.7	51.0	49.8	50.4	50.4
1980	51.2	51.0	51.6	51.1	50.8	48.2	50.8	51.5
1990	51.3	52.1	52.0	51.2	50.7	47.7	51.0	49.8
1994	51.2	52.2	51.8	51.1	50.7	47.8	50.8	49.4
Black (%*)								
1970	6.7	0.6	4.8	0.0	12.5	0.1	0.1	0.3
1980	6.8	0.5	4.4	0.0	12.0	0.1	0.1	0.1
1990	7.4	0.5	4.4	0.1	11.9	0.1	0.1	0.0
1994	7.7	0.5	4.6	0.1	12.2	0.1	0.1	0.0
Hispanic (%*)								
1970	N/A	N/A	N/A	N/A	N/A	N/A	N/A	N/A
1980	1.9	1.7	1.4	1.3	21.0	43.3	17.4	47.6
1990	2.7	1.6	2.5	3.1	25.6	53.3	18.7	52.2
1994	3.1	1.6	2.8	3.3	27.3	55.9	20.0	54.5

Continued on next page

Table 4.1, continued

Variable	Oklahoma Counties					Texas Counties		
	State of Oklahoma	Waste Operating	Nonwaste Development	Control (Baseline)	State of Texas	Waste Siting	Nonwaste Development	Control (Baseline)
American Indian and Other (%*)								
1970	3.9	0.3	6.8	0.4	0.2	0.1	0.1	0.1
1980	5.6	0.6	7.2	0.6	0.3	0.1	0.1	0.6
1990	8.0	1.5	8.7	1.5	0.4	0.4	0.1	0.2
1994	8.1	1.6	8.7	1.7	0.4	0.4	0.2	0.2
Rural (%*)								
1970	32.0	37.6	68.7	100.0	20.3	100.0	32.0	100.0
1980	32.7	41.3	69.2	100.0	20.4	100.0	36.2	100.0
1990	32.3	39.7	70.3	100.0	19.7	100.0	37.6	100.0
Natural Increase								
1970-1980	172,996	-127	6	48	1,260,188	102	43	154
1980-1990	226,900	-116	416	36	1,785,168	113	99	166
1990-1994	68,450	-206	-48	-95	768,702	—	-11	70
Natural Increase (%*)								
1970-1980	6.8	-1.1	0.1	0.9	11.3	5.3	1.1	7.3
1980-1990	7.5	-1.1	3.1	0.6	12.5	7.1	2.4	8.2
1990-1994	2.2	-2.3	-0.4	2.1	4.5	—	-0.3	3.1
Net Migration								
1970-1980	293,065	-870	1,643	419	1,772,273	-447	116	-228
1980-1990	-106,605	-1,704	-2,389	-1,135	972,151	-298	-40	67
1990-1994	44,039	-234	-484	-131	623,068	-101	26	598
Net Migration (%*)								
1970-1980	11.5	-7.3	13.9	8.2	15.8	-23.0	3.0	-10.8
1980-1990	-3.5	-15.6	-17.8	-20.3	6.8	-18.7	-1.0	3.3
1990-1994	1.4	-2.6	-4.2	-2.9	3.7	-7.2	0.6	26.4

*Percentages may not equal 100.0 percent because of rounding.

N/A = Not available

Table 4.2: Selected Housing Characteristics of Counties in the Study Area by State and Development Type, 1970-1990

| | | | | | Utah Counties | |
Variable	State of Colorado	Colorado Waste Siting County	State of Utah	Waste Operating	Nonwaste Development	Control (Baseline)
Total Housing Units						
1970	757,070	6,208	315,765	6,455	4,387	2,348
1980	1,194,253	9,378	490,006	8,566	9,723	4,478
1990	1,477,349	10,353	598,388	9,510	19,523	5,860
Change in Number of Housing Units (%*)						
1970-1980	57.7	51.1	55.2	32.7	121.6	90.7
1980-1990	23.7	10.4	22.1	11.0	100.8	30.9
Owner-Occupied Housing Units (%*)						
1970	63.4	70.5	69.3	68.1	73.4	78.6
1980	64.5	75.4	70.7	73.1	76.8	80.9
1990	62.2	72.0	68.1	70.2	70.8	81.5
Vacant Housing Units (%*)						
1970	8.7	9.6	5.6	5.8	12.6	17.2
1980	11.1	10.1	8.4	7.0	19.8	21.9
1990	13.2	9.2	10.2	9.8	21.9	36.7
Median Value of Owner-Occupied Housing Units ($1994)						
1970	66,079	44,689	64,169	56,530	64,169	42,780
1980	115,284	88,486	103,054	90,285	103,953	83,630
1990	92,640	68,034	77,899	68,374	88,104	49,211
Median Gross Rent of Renter-Occupied Housing Units ($1994)						
1970	371	229	306	290	256	260
1980	401	309	336	322	318	309
1990	409	291	340	330	391	245

Continued on next page

Table 4.2, continued

Variable	State of Nebraska	Nebraska Counties			
		Waste Operating	Waste Siting	Nonwaste Development	Control (Baseline)
Total Housing Units					
1970	515,069	2,056	1,372	4,116	1,627
1980	624,829	2,032	1,457	4,473	1,996
1990	660,621	1,967	1,538	4,345	1,950
Change in Number of Housing Units (%*)					
1970-1980	21.3	-1.2	6.2	8.7	22.7
1980-1990	5.7	-3.2	5.6	-2.9	-2.3
Owner-Occupied Housing Units (%*)					
1970	66.4	66.9	78.1	71.0	71.9
1980	68.4	73.1	81.0	72.5	76.1
1990	66.5	74.5	79.3	70.4	73.6
Vacant Housing Units (%*)					
1970	8.0	10.6	9.0	14.1	14.3
1980	8.6	11.4	13.0	12.0	14.9
1990	8.8	16.1	25.4	11.4	23.1
Median Value of Owner-Occupied Housing Units ($1994)					
1970	47,363	43,161	22,536	38,578	38,578
1980	68,343	55,034	28,956	49,998	50,178
1990	57,149	40,027	19,050	40,480	33,337
Median Gross Rent of Renter-Occupied Housing Units ($1994)					
1970	294	275	164	218	206
1980	306	207	138	210	194
1990	320	222	141	226	202

Continued on next page

Table 4.2, continued

Variable	Oklahoma Counties				State of Texas	Texas Counties		
	State of Oklahoma	Waste Operating	Nonwaste Development	Control (Baseline)		Waste Siting	Nonwaste Development	Control (Baseline)
Total Housing Units								
1970	939,681	4,747	4,931	2,206	3,829,502	855	1,951	943
1980	1,237,040	4,922	5,870	2,465	5,549,352	949	2,415	1,263
1990	1,406,499	4,782	5,729	2,449	7,008,999	810	2,593	1,550
Change in Number of Housing Units (%*)								
1970-1980	31.6	3.7	19.0	11.7	44.9	11.0	23.8	33.9
1980-1990	13.7	-2.8	-2.4	-0.6	26.3	-14.6	7.4	22.7
Owner-Occupied Housing Units (%*)								
1970	69.2	71.9	75.3	79.0	64.7	64.7	68.9	66.8
1980	63.9	72.9	75.3	79.1	64.3	68.6	76.0	72.9
1990	68.1	73.0	76.1	80.3	60.9	65.5	73.8	72.2
Vacant Housing Units (%*)								
1970	9.5	12.3	16.4	13.1	10.3	27.8	29.8	31.6
1980	9.6	10.1	13.5	9.9	11.2	39.9	35.2	44.8
1990	14.2	20.5	22.9	25.4	13.4	35.3	37.4	48.7
Median Value of Owner-Occupied Housing Units ($1994)								
1970	42,398	33,231	30,557	27,501	45,835	27,119	30,175	24,827
1980	64,027	47,660	48,560	44,423	70,321	32,193	45,682	30,215
1990	54,541	37,079	38,553	33,790	67,580	30,842	44,109	35,038
Median Gross Rent of Renter-Occupied Housing Units ($1994)								
1970	244	214	168	199	290	168	168	130
1980	295	191	194	218	383	117	156	146
1990	293	195	176	186	369	170	215	181

*Percentages may not equal 100.0 percent because of rounding.

Table 4.3: Selected Socioeconomic Characteristics of Counties in the Study Area by State and Development Type, 1970-1990

Variable	State of Colorado	Colorado Waste Siting County	State of Utah	Utah Counties		
				Waste Operating	Nonwaste Development	Control (Baseline)
Median Household Income ($1994)						
1969	N/A	N/A	N/A	N/A	N/A	N/A
1979	36,858	31,177	36,072	40,177	27,572	35,406
1989	36,023	27,023	35,223	36,069	29,404	28,270
Per Capita Income ($1994)						
1969	12,591	9,590	10,915	11,383	8,488	8,242
1979	16,326	13,021	12,870	13,183	9,939	11,290
1989	17,714	13,257	13,182	12,631	11,295	9,797
Persons Below Poverty Level (%*)						
1969	12.3	19.3	11.4	7.1	18.8	16.4
1979	10.1	10.4	10.3	7.6	15.8	12.5
1989	11.7	14.2	11.4	11.5	13.3	18.7
Educational Attainment—1990 (Persons 25 and over) (%*)						
Less than 9th grade	5.6	10.3	3.4	4.7	3.7	5.4
9th to 12th, no diploma	10.0	15.2	11.5	18.0	11.8	19.8
High school graduate	26.5	35.0	27.2	36.4	29.5	35.9
Some college, no degree	24.0	18.8	27.9	23.1	28.9	21.6
Associate degree	6.9	5.3	7.8	6.6	8.4	5.5
Bachelor's degree	18.0	9.6	15.4	8.2	12.1	8.8
Graduate degree	9.0	5.8	6.8	3.1	5.6	3.0
Occupation—1990 (Employed persons 16 and over) (%*)						
Executive, administrative, and managerial	14.0	9.2	12.1	8.9	10.4	7.6
Professional	15.9	13.9	14.6	10.7	11.6	13.2
Technicians	4.3	3.2	4.1	3.7	2.5	2.0
Sales	12.3	10.2	11.9	7.5	15.2	9.0
Administrative support and clerical	16.5	13.5	16.7	16.5	13.1	12.4
Service	13.6	14.6	13.1	17.1	17.5	13.4
Farming, forestry, fishing	2.4	9.6	2.2	1.8	3.6	12.1

Continued on next page

Table 4.3, continued

Variable	State of Colorado	Colorado Waste Siting County	State of Utah	Utah Counties Waste Operating	Utah Counties Nonwaste Development	Utah Counties Control (Baseline)
Precision production, craft	9.8	12.9	11.4	17.3	11.8	14.5
Operators, fabricators, laborers	11.1	12.9	13.9	16.6	14.2	15.8
Industry—1990 (Employed persons 16 and over) (%*)						
Agriculture, forestry, fisheries	2.8	10.1	2.4	2.0	3.4	12.9
Mining	1.3	1.4	1.3	0.6	1.2	8.1
Construction	4.8	8.5	5.4	7.1	10.0	7.2
Manufacturing, nondurable	44.4	4.0	4.9	4.8	4.1	3.6
Manufacturing, durable	8.3	4.7	10.5	20.6	4.8	2.6
Transportation	4.8	2.9	4.4	2.9	4.7	4.9
Communications/public utilities	3.4	5.5	2.5	1.1	1.8	3.8
Wholesale	4.3	2.9	4.5	1.1	3.7	2.7
Retail	17.5	19.3	17.8	12.8	24.4	16.4
Finance, insurance, real estate	7.3	4.8	5.7	2.1	5.4	2.1
Business and repair services	5.7	3.7	4.9	3.1	2.8	3.4
Personal services	3.7	3.5	3.3	3.1	5.6	2.2
Entertainment/recreation service	1.6	0.7	1.5	4.5	2.6	1.2
Health services	7.5	7.7	7.0	3.8	7.3	6.2
Educational services	8.4	8.3	10.7	7.5	9.5	12.7
Other professional and related services	8.0	6.8	6.0	3.2	5.1	3.9
Public administration	5.1	5.3	7.1	19.6	3.4	6.3

Variable	State of Nebraska	Nebraska Counties Waste Operating	Nebraska Counties Waste Siting	Nebraska Counties Nonwaste Development	Nebraska Counties Control (Baseline)
Median Household Income ($1994)					
1969	N/A	N/A	N/A	N/A	N/A
1979	32,508	30,730	19,088	30,764	22,248
1989	31,094	27,767	19,516	27,968	20,398

Continued on next page

Table 4.3, continued

		Nebraska Counties			
Variable	State of Nebraska	Waste Operating	Waste Siting	Nonwaste Development	Control (Baseline)
Per Capita Income ($1994)					
1969	11,363	11,912	6,538	9,784	8,755
1979	14,158	13,358	9,272	13,891	11,194
1989	14,883	13,273	10,732	13,765	11,007
Persons Below Poverty Level (%*)					
1969	13.1	12.6	38.9	12.9	22.4
1979	10.7	12.6	23.8	12.2	19.5
1989	11.1	11.5	22.5	10.2	18.8
Educational Attainment—1990 (Persons 25 and over) (%*)					
Less than 9th grade	8.0	10.9	17.7	9.0	10.9
9th to 12th, no diploma	10.2	15.3	10.2	10.7	9.3
High school graduate	34.7	36.3	40.3	35.1	45.4
Some college, no degree	21.1	18.1	16.2	21.4	18.0
Associate degree	7.1	6.8	5.7	8.6	5.1
Bachelor's degree	13.1	8.2	8.3	11.4	8.8
Graduate degree	5.9	4.5	1.6	3.6	2.5
Occupation—1990 (Employed person 16 and over) (%*)					
Executive, administrative, and managerial	10.4	8.1	6.5	6.9	7.3
Professional	12.7	9.7	9.4	12.5	10.0
Technicians	3.1	0.5	2.0	1.5	1.6
Sales	11.7	7.2	6.2	8.5	9.5
Administrative support and clerical	15.8	10.6	7.9	16.7	12.7
Service	14.5	16.2	14.5	16.4	15.1
Farming, forestry, fishing	7.5	12.3	36.2	11.7	22.3
Precision production, craft	10.3	14.8	6.9	10.9	10.2
Operators, fabricators, laborers	14.1	20.5	10.5	14.9	11.3

Continued on next page

Table 4.3, continued

Continued on next page

Industry—1990

(Employed person 16 and over) (%*)

Variable	Nebraska Counties				
	State of Nebraska	Waste Operating	Waste Siting	Nonwaste Development	Control (Baseline)
Agriculture, forestry, fisheries	8.3	14.1	37.4	14.0	25.0
Mining	0.3	9.1	0.0	1.5	0.4
Construction	5.3	7.6	5.8	4.9	8.9
Manufacturing, nondurable	6.2	3.1	0.1	1.8	0.7
Manufacturing, durable	6.6	6.5	1.0	6.3	2.2
Transportation	4.8	3.7	3.7	5.6	2.9
Communications/public utilities	3.2	1.4	1.9	3.0	3.3
Wholesale	4.6	2.6	2.4	2.4	4.7
Retail	17.9	12.6	13.6	24.1	17.9
Finance, insurance, real estate	6.7	2.3	5.0	3.4	3.7
Business and repair services	4.5	4.7	2.1	2.4	3.1
Personal services	2.9	3.8	2.6	2.7	1.8
Entertainment/recreation service	1.1	1.4	1.1	0.5	1.1
Health services	8.6	8.8	9.1	6.9	7.7
Educational services	8.8	8.8	6.8	11.4	7.7
Other professional and related services	6.2	3.7	4.6	5.8	4.3
Public administration	3.9	5.7	2.9	3.3	4.7

Median Household Income ($1994)

Variable	State of Oklahoma	Oklahoma Counties			State of Texas	Texas Counties		
		Waste Operating	Nonwaste Development	Control (Baseline)		Waste Siting	Nonwaste Development	Control (Baseline)
1969	N/A	N/A	N/A	N/A	N/A	N/A	N/A	N/A
1979	30,109	27,660	27,888	27,280	34,106	31,054	25,143	21,066
1989	28,179	23,620	24,376	23,924	32,290	25,354	20,979	17,497

Table 4.3, continued

Variable	State of Oklahoma	Oklahoma Counties			State of Texas	Texas Counties		
		Waste Operating	Nonwaste Development	Control (Baseline)		Waste Siting	Nonwaste Development	Control (Baseline)
Per Capita Income ($1994)								
1969	10,996	11,109	8,783	9,918	11,347	8,759	8,948	11,949
1979	13,999	15,189	13,656	13,916	14,708	14,430	11,299	10,082
1989	14,215	14,654	11,697	12,050	15,423	12,126	13,592	9,008
Persons Below Poverty Level								
1969	464,931	1,940	3,029	867	2,046,593	480	984	954
1979	393,866	1,196	2,272	578	2,035,873	291	633	674
1989	509,854	1,354	2,241	623	3,000,515	384	789	939
Persons Below Poverty Level (%*)								
1969	18.8	17.9	26.3	17.2	18.8	23.9	25.3	47.5
1979	13.4	11.6	17.3	10.4	14.7	18.2	15.8	33.3
1989	16.7	15.8	20.0	14.1	18.1	27.4	19.5	41.7
Educational Attainment—1990 (Persons 25 and over) (%*)								
Less than 9th grade	9.8	11.6	10.8	13.6	13.5	23.8	17.3	27.6
9th to 12th, no diploma	15.6	12.3	18.0	12.6	14.4	9.9	18.1	14.1
High school graduate	30.5	26.2	39.8	37.3	25.6	32.8	32.8	25.9
Some college, no degree	21.3	23.7	15.1	20.3	21.1	16.8	16.8	12.9
Associate degree	5.0	2.7	2.9	2.2	5.2	4.7	2.7	5.8
Bachelor's degree	11.8	15.1	7.0	9.3	13.9	9.1	9.3	10.1
Graduate degree	6.0	8.4	5.4	4.7	6.5	2.9	3.1	3.6
Occupation—1990 (Employed persons 16 and over) (%*)								
Executive, administrative, and managerial	11.1	9.8	6.4	8.4	12.3	8.8	6.3	3.1
Professional	13.1	13.5	9.2	9.3	13.8	12.7	5.2	8.5
Technicians	3.6	2.0	2.6	2.7	3.9	1.0	1.2	0.8
Sales	11.8	10.1	9.4	6.2	12.5	6.6	9.9	5.5
Administrative support and clerical	15.7	13.8	12.7	13.3	16.1	12.1	14.3	12.0

Continued on next page

Table 4.3, continued

	Oklahoma Counties					Texas Counties			
Variable	State of Oklahoma	Waste Operating	Nonwaste Development	Control (Baseline)	State of Texas	Waste Siting	Nonwaste Development	Control (Baseline)
Service	14.2	16.7	18.0	13.0	13.5	14.2	18.8	14.8
Farming, forestry, fishing	3.5	12.4	10.2	20.0	2.6	17.2	17.9	35.4
Precision production, craft	12.0	10.0	13.1	12.9	11.7	12.7	11.5	8.8
Operators, fabricators, laborers	15.0	11.8	18.5	14.3	13.6	14.7	14.8	11.1
Industry—1990 (Employed persons 16 and over) (%*)								
Agriculture, forestry, fisheries	3.7	14.0	10.4	21.5	2.8	17.0	17.8	36.5
Mining	3.1	2.9	6.8	6.5	2.2	2.6	0.4	1.6
Construction	5.5	5.0	5.7	6.1	6.7	6.8	5.2	6.0
Manufacturing, nondurable	5.2	1.8	7.3	2.4	6.0	1.3	6.1	1.6
Manufacturing, durable	9.0	2.4	6.1	1.6	8.4	1.5	3.8	1.1
Transportation	4.6	2.8	3.4	3.1	4.6	13.2	4.9	2.6
Communications/public utilities	2.8	3.3	3.0	1.9	3.0	6.4	2.6	3.6
Wholesale	4.3	2.7	3.8	2.4	4.9	0.0	4.7	3.3
Retail	17.3	20.9	15.4	13.1	17.4	14.7	20.7	9.9
Finance, insurance, real estate	5.7	5.3	3.9	3.8	6.8	3.0	6.0	1.9
Business and repair services	4.5	2.2	3.7	2.1	5.5	3.5	2.5	3.7
Personal services	3.1	3.0	3.0	4.2	3.4	3.3	4.9	4.5
Entertainment/recreation service	1.2	1.3	1.2	0.8	1.2	0.5	0.4	0.5
Health services	8.5	8.7	9.3	9.9	7.3	0.0	7.4	0.7
Educational services	9.0	14.9	7.7	9.0	8.9	15.2	6.5	11.1
Other professional and related services	6.3	5.8	5.6	5.1	6.3	3.0	3.2	6.5
Public administration	6.3	3.2	3.6	6.4	4.5	7.9	2.7	4.9

*Percentages may not equal 100.0 percent because of rounding.

N/A = Not available

housing or socioeconomic characteristics than nonwaste development or baseline counties.

Characteristics of Study Communities

Because counties are larger than the communities within them extensive community-level impacts may be diluted at the county level. Tables 4.4-4.6, however, suggest that the small differences noted in demographic and housing and socioeconomic factors for counties are also evident for the study communities. In fact, except for the case of the Oklahoma waste operating site for which the decline in population growth is less than for other community (types, there is little indication that waste-related developments have positively) impacted population growth. Generally the nonwaste development communities experience the most rapid increases in population, and the most extensive changes in housing units and socioeconomic levels, while in waste-facility impacted communities, whether waste operational or waste siting, such factors have shown only modest change.

Assessing Overall Demographic Impacts

As a further means of assessing the extent to which there are differences in rates of population growth in different types of counties, the data in tables 4.7 and 4.8 are presented. These data show annualized rates of population growth and net migration for individual counties and annualized rates of population growth for communities (migration data were not available for individual communities). These data support the findings noted above that the rates of population growth and net migration for waste-impacted counties and rates of population growth for waste-impacted communities generally do not show larger increases than those for other community or county types.

The bottom panels of tables 4.7 and 4.8 show the annual rates of population growth and net migration for counties and population growth for communities in the study area by type of community. These data show little indication that waste siting and waste operating areas have experienced more rapid growth than the other types of communities. Waste siting counties experienced declines in the 1980s followed by an annual rate of increase of 2.3 percent from 1990 to 1994, and waste operating counties decreased by 0.5 percent per year from 1980 to 1990 and increased by only 1.0 percent per year from 1990 to 1994. By comparison, nonwaste development counties increased

Table 4.4: Selected Demographic Characteristics of Study Area Communities by State and Development Type, 1970-1994

Variable	Colorado Communities		Utah Communities		
	Waste Siting	Waste Siting	Waste Operating	Nonwaste Development	Control (Baseline)
Total Population					
1970	949	820	12,539	1,408	2,005
1980	1,027	819	14,335	2,361	3,842
1990	656	434	13,887	3,915	3,915
1994	717	489	14,797	5,510	4,388
Population Change (%*)					
1970-1980	8.2	-0.1	14.3	67.7	91.6
1980-1990	-36.1	-47.0	-3.1	65.8	1.9
1990-1994	9.3	12.7	6.6	40.7	12.1
Median Age					
1970	N/A	N/A	24.7	26.2	25.3
1980	25.8	26.2	25.9	26.8	22.9
1990	37.1	39.8	30.4	29.5	23.3
1990 Age Distribution (%*)					
0-4	8.5	6.9	8.1	9.5	12.2
5-19	21.5	18.9	26.9	31.3	32.9
20-24	3.5	4.4	7.0	5.2	6.9
25-34	13.3	15.0	14.6	10.8	15.0
35-59	33.5	32.9	27.9	22.0	22.1
60-64	4.6	4.4	4.5	4.2	2.5
65-74	7.9	11.3	6.8	9.5	4.5
75+	7.2	6.2	4.1	7.4	3.8
65 Years and Older (%*)					
1970	N/A	N/A	6.2	12.9	9.8
1980	6.8	7.8	7.8	15.0	7.5
1990	15.1	17.5	11.0	17.0	8.3
Less Than 5 Years of Age (%*)					
1970	N/A	N/A	10.0	N/A	N/A
1980	10.6	9.9	11.8	14.4	16.1
1990	8.5	6.9	8.1	9.5	12.2
Female (%*)					
1970	N/A	N/A	49.7	51.1	51.3
1980	48.2	48.6	50.1	49.8	50.2
1990	52.0	50.7	50.9	50.1	52.1
Black (%*)					
1970	N/A	N/A	0.0	0.0	0.0
1980	0.1	0.0	0.2	0.1	0.0
1990	0.0	0.0	0.4	0.0	0.1
Hispanic (%*)					
1970	N/A	N/A	N/A	N/A	N/A
1980	3.6	6.1	11.2	0.6	1.4
1990	3.7	5.5	11.3	1.4	2.1
American Indian and Other (%*)					
1970	N/A	N/A	0.3	N/A	N/A
1980	0.1	2.9	1.0	0.7	2.2
1990	2.0	0.0	1.1	0.8	7.5

Continued on next page

Table 4.4, continued

	Nebraska Communities			
Variable	Waste Operating	Waste Siting	Nonwaste Development	Control (Baseline)
Total Population				
1970	3,680	575	6,403	2,073
1980	3,120	529	6,010	2,256
1990	2,574	452	5,959	1,870
1994	2,535	412	6,015	1,839
Population Change (%*)				
1970-1980	-15.2	-8.0	-6.1	8.8
1980-1990	-17.5	-14.6	-0.8	-17.1
1990-1994	-1.5	-8.8	0.9	-1.7
Median Age				
1970	27.5	N/A	30.1	39.0
1980	32.0	55.1	33.4	38.5
1990	38.9	55.6	35.5	41.7
1990 Age Distribution (%*)				
0-4	6.5	4.9	7.4	5.8
5-19	20.6	15.7	21.0	20.2
20-24	3.5	2.9	6.2	3.9
25-34	13.8	7.3	14.5	12.5
35-59	28.9	22.3	27.2	26.1
60-64	5.9	7.3	5.5	5.2
65-74	10.8	13.7	8.9	11.3
75+	10.0	25.9	9.3	15.0
65 Years and Older (%*)				
1970	9.3	N/A	13.3	22.5
1980	15.4	38.6	17.1	23.3
1990	20.8	39.6	18.2	26.3
Less Than 5 Years of Age (%*)				
1970	8.7	N/A	8.1	N/A
1980	7.6	5.9	7.5	6.1
1990	6.5	4.9	7.4	5.8
Female (%*)				
1970	51.1	N/A	53.3	54.3
1980	51.7	54.1	53.1	53.1
1990	52.6	55.1	53.5	54.9
Black (%*)				
1970	0.0	N/A	0.2	0.1
1980	0.0	0.0	0.1	0.0
1990	0.1	0.0	0.1	0.1
Hispanic (%*)				
1970	N/A	N/A	N/A	N/A
1980	3.8	0.0	3.3	0.2
1990	4.5	0.0	4.4	0.6
American Indian and Other (%*)				
1970	0.1	N/A	0.1	N/A
1980	0.4	0.0	0.9	0.1
1990	0.3	0.7	0.7	0.2

Continued on next page

Table 4.4, continued

Variable	Oklahoma Communities			Texas Communities		
	Waste Operating	Nonwaste Development	Control (Baseline)	Waste Siting	Nonwaste Development	Control (Baseline)
Total Population						
1970	1,444	3,696	1,546	1,229	2,654	1,221
1980	1,377	4,139	1,759	1,241	2,593	1,317
1990	947	3,408	1,454	1,128	2,654	1,339
1994	933	3,276	1,390	--	2,605	1,671
Population Change (%*)						
1970-1980	-4.6	12.0	13.8	1.0	-2.3	7.9
1980-1990	-31.2	-17.7	-17.3	-9.1	2.4	1.7
1990-1994	-1.5	-3.9	-4.4	--	-1.8	24.8
Median Age						
1970	44.2	32.0	43.4	29.9	29.1	23.2
1980	45.2	31.1	35.0	31.6	34.8	25.0
1990	44.5	33.8	40.9	36.2	36.8	27.4
1990 Age Distribution (%*)						
0-4	5.8	8.2	5.1	6.7	7.7	9.8
5-19	17.3	22.2	21.7	25.2	22.2	29.4
20-24	5.5	6.9	3.3	4.2	4.8	6.9
25-34	11.9	14.6	11.3	12.3	12.9	14.6
35-59	23.8	25.1	27.3	30.4	27.6	25.9
60-64	4.3	4.3	4.7	5.9	4.9	3.2
65-74	14.0	8.7	11.4	8.4	9.6	5.7
75+	17.3	10.2	15.3	6.8	10.3	4.6
65 Years and Older (%*)						
1970	24.4	16.0	22.9	11.5	15.2	11.1
1980	27.7	18.5	22.7	14.3	19.1	11.5
1990	31.4	18.9	26.7	15.2	19.9	10.2
Less Than 5 Years of Age (%*)						
1970	N/A	7.5	N/A	N/A	9.9	N/A
1980	5.4	8.6	8.4	8.7	6.8	10.3
1990	5.8	8.2	5.1	6.7	7.7	9.8
Female (%*)						
1970	52.3	53.2	54.3	50.6	51.1	52.3
1980	53.4	53.3	54.0	49.7	51.7	52.7
1990	55.8	553.3	53.6	50.5	52.4	50.0
Black (%*)						
1970	0.0	10.2	0.0	0.0	0.1	0.3
1980	0.1	10.7	0.0	0.0	0.1	0.0
1990	0.1	11.7	0.0	0.1	0.0	0.0
Hispanic (%*)						
1970	N/A	N/A	N/A	N/A	N/A	N/A
1980	5.5	2.1	2.0	50.9	20.6	62.2
1990	4.1	3.2	3.9	57.0	23.0	70.9
American Indian and Other (%*)						
1970	N/A	8.3	N/A	N/A	0.1	N/A
1980	0.8	6.8	0.6	0.2	0.0	0.5
1990	2.3	9.3	1.3	0.3	0.0	0.1

*Percentages may not equal 100.0 percent because of rounding. N/A = Not available

Table 4.5: Selected Housing Characteristics of Study Area Communities by State and Development Type, 1970-1990

Variable	Colorado Communities		Utah Communities			
	Waste Siting	Waste Siting	Waste Operating	Waste Operating	Nonwaste Development	Control (Baseline)
Total Housing Units						
1970	N/A	N/A	818	3,855	441	585
1980	399	318	1,348	4,877	833	1,222
1990	338	230	1,472	5,190	1,325	1,347
Change in Number of Housing Units (%*)						
1970-1980	N/A	N/A	64.8	26.5	88.9	108.9
1980-1990	-15.3	-27.7	9.2	6.4	59.1	10.2
Owner-Occupied Housing Units (%*)						
1970	N/A	N/A	81.5	75.4	83.3	74.3
1980	75.5	75.0	80.5	78.2	82.4	77.5
1990	69.8	76.1	77.9	74.5	78.2	70.6
Vacant Housing Units						
1970	N/A	N/A	3.7	4.2	6.3	4.3
1980	12.0	13.2	6.2	5.0	12.6	7.3
1990	18.6	21.7	6.5	6.7	11.5	13.1
Median Value of Owner-Occupied Housing Units ($1994)						
1970	N/A	N/A	53,092	59,968	56,530	51,947
1980	69,602	68,588	89,925	90,105	91,364	86,688
1990	43,995	37,759	64,972	67,807	77,219	49,778
Median Gross Rent of Renter-Occupied Housing Units ($1994)						
1970	N/A	N/A	256	275	225	275
1980	360	551	284	347	286	363
1990	252	235	263	328	291	253

Continued on next page

Table 4.5, continued

<table>
<tr><th></th><th colspan="4">Nebraska Counties</th></tr>
<tr><th>Variable</th><th>Waste Operating</th><th>Waste Siting</th><th>Nonwaste Development</th><th>Control (Baseline)</th></tr>
<tr><td>Total Housing Units</td><td></td><td></td><td></td><td></td></tr>
<tr><td>1970</td><td>1,257</td><td>N/A</td><td>2,463</td><td>874</td></tr>
<tr><td>1980</td><td>1,269</td><td>230</td><td>2,638</td><td>1,035</td></tr>
<tr><td>1990</td><td>1,229</td><td>221</td><td>2,741</td><td>963</td></tr>
<tr><td>Change in Number of Housing Units (%*)</td><td></td><td></td><td></td><td></td></tr>
<tr><td>1970-1980</td><td>1.0</td><td>N/A</td><td>7.1</td><td>18.4</td></tr>
<tr><td>1980-1990</td><td>-3.2</td><td>-3.9</td><td>3.9</td><td>-7.0</td></tr>
<tr><td>Owner-Occupied Housing Units (%*)</td><td></td><td></td><td></td><td></td></tr>
<tr><td>1970</td><td>66.2</td><td>N/A</td><td>70.7</td><td>71.1</td></tr>
<tr><td>1980</td><td>70.5</td><td>78.3</td><td>73.1</td><td>74.3</td></tr>
<tr><td>1990</td><td>72.3</td><td>76.8</td><td>69.0</td><td>70.2</td></tr>
<tr><td>Vacant Housing Units (%*)</td><td></td><td></td><td></td><td></td></tr>
<tr><td>1970</td><td>8.0</td><td>N/A</td><td>13.8</td><td>10.3</td></tr>
<tr><td>1980</td><td>7.9</td><td>7.8</td><td>9.4</td><td>8.3</td></tr>
<tr><td>1990</td><td>14.3</td><td>18.1</td><td>10.4</td><td>15.1</td></tr>
<tr><td>Median Value of Owner-Occupied Housing Units ($1994)</td><td></td><td></td><td></td><td></td></tr>
<tr><td>1970</td><td>46,599</td><td>N/A</td><td>43,161</td><td>N/A</td></tr>
<tr><td>1980</td><td>57,192</td><td>32,048</td><td>54,674</td><td>54,315</td></tr>
<tr><td>1990</td><td>41,387</td><td>17,009</td><td>44,109</td><td>34,017</td></tr>
<tr><td>Median Gross Rent of Renter-Occupied Housing Units ($1994)</td><td></td><td></td><td></td><td></td></tr>
<tr><td>1970</td><td>283</td><td>N/A</td><td>225</td><td>N/A</td></tr>
<tr><td>1980</td><td>212</td><td>302</td><td>225</td><td>200</td></tr>
<tr><td>1990</td><td>230</td><td>139</td><td>239</td><td>209</td></tr>
</table>

Continued on next page

Table 4.5, continued

	Oklahoma Counties			Texas Counties		
Variable	Waste Operating	Nonwaste Development	Control (Baseline)	Waste Siting	Nonwaste Development	Control (Baseline)
Total Housing Units						
1970	660	1,483	704	492	1,014	405
1980	717	1,758	798	619	1,175	489
1990	635	1,605	821	627	1,247	536
Change in Number of Housing Units (%*)						
1970-1980	8.6	18.5	13.4	25.8	15.9	20.7
1980-1990	-11.4	-8.7	2.9	1.3	6.1	9.6
Owner-Occupied Housing Units (%*)						
1970	82.3	70.7	78.0	68.7	68.0	74.5
1980	78.6	69.5	75.0	75.0	73.5	77.3
1990	80.2	68.2	79.8	72.9	71.2	77.9
Vacant Housing Units (%*)						
1970	17.7	11.5	14.9	23.4	11.3	12.8
1980	15.3	7.1	7.6	28.9	16.3	15.3
1990	31.5	16.3	26.4	32.9	18.9	20.2
Median Value of Owner-Occupied Housing Units ($1994)						
1970	19,098	36,286	34,758	24,827	31,703	24,827
1980	24,280	55,394	52,876	31,654	46,761	29,675
1990	17,007	41,841	40,027	30,275	43,315	33,337
Median Gross Rent of Renter-Occupied Housing Units ($1994)						
1970	183	172	222	183	172	138
1980	155	227	223	131	162	158
1990	133	188	194	163	210	183

*Percentages may not equal 100.0 percent because of rounding.

N/A = Not available

Table 4.6: Selected Socioeconomic Characteristics of Study Area Communities by State and Development Type, 1990

Variable	Colorado Communities		Utah Communities			
	Waste Siting	Waste Siting	Waste Operating	Waste Operating	Nonwaste Development	Control (Baseline)
Median Household Income ($1994)	25,398	23,531	36,158	35,598	24,290	30,011
Per Capita Income ($1994)	15,914	11,172	11,721	13,255	9,979	10,450
Persons Below Poverty Level (%*)	11.3	9.3	11.7	11.9	15.9	17.4
Educational Attainment (Persons 25 and over) (%*)						
Less than 9th grade	6.6	12.0	3.1	3.4	5.6	2.9
9th to 12th, no diploma	13.6	24.6	21.4	19.2	19.4	17.8
High school graduate	40.5	46.8	35.6	39.0	30.2	31.5
Some college, no degree	24.7	12.3	21.5	21.1	25.7	24.3
Associate degree	2.6	2.8	6.5	6.0	6.8	6.1
Bachelor's degree	9.8	0.0	9.1	8.1	8.6	11.7
Graduate degree	2.2	1.4	2.6	3.1	3.8	5.6
Occupation (Employed persons 16 and over) (%*)						
Executive, administrative, and managerial	7.9	6.8	7.0	9.4	8.8	9.2
Professional	17.1	2.8	10.7	11.1	9.6	18.1
Technicians	1.2	2.3	2.1	3.6	0.9	2.6
Sales	7.5	11.3	6.8	7.2	13.9	11.3
Administrative support and clerical	15.5	11.9	15.8	17.4	11.8	14.6
Service	14.7	22.6	14.9	14.4	18.4	15.8
Farming, forestry, fishing	2.0	0.6	2.2	0.3	2.2	2.7
Precision production, craft	19.8	22.6	21.4	17.8	16.7	13.8
Operators, fabricators, laborers	14.3	19.2	19.2	18.7	17.7	11.9
Industry (Employed persons 16 and over) (%*)						
Agriculture, forestry, fisheries	2.8	0.6	1.9	0.4	2.5	3.6
Mining	4.0	9.0	0.3	0.5	0.2	7.7
Construction	11.9	11.3	8.8	6.8	17.5	4.0
Manufacturing, nondurable	0.0	0.0	6.5	4.0	4.3	4.1

Continued on next page

Table 4.6, continued

Variable	Colorado Communities		Utah Communities			
	Waste Siting	Waste Operating	Waste Siting	Waste Operating	Nonwaste Development	Control (Baseline)
Manufacturing, durable	0.8	3.4	24.5	24.0	6.1	1.5
Transportation	2.8	9.0	3.2	3.5	4.4	3.9
Communications/public utilities	9.5	7.9	0.3	1.2	1.0	4.5
Wholesale	11.5	6.8	2.3	1.0	2.8	3.1
Retail	14.3	19.8	12.3	14.1	26.1	21.3
Finance, insurance, real estate	2.8	4.0	2.0	2.2	3.3	3.1
Business and repair services	4.4	2.3	5.0	2.0	1.6	3.7
Personal services	2.4	11.3	3.2	2.4	4.1	2.1
Entertainment/recreation service	0.0	0.0	0.0	1.0	3.4	2.3
Health services	3.2	0.0	1.7	4.4	6.9	10.3
Educational services	17.1	3.4	10.1	7.4	9.8	13.3
Other professional and related services	7.1	4.5	2.3	3.0	3.6	5.1
Public administration	5.6	6.8	15.4	22.0	2.2	6.2

Nebraska Communities

Variable	Waste Operating	Waste Siting	Nonwaste Development	Control (Baseline)
Median Household Income ($1994)	28,896	18,472	28,680	20,213
Per Capita Income ($1994)	13,717	12,186	14,324	10,910
Persons Below Poverty Level (%*)	8.6	17.5	10.1	17.0
Educational Attainment (Persons 25 and over) (%*)				
Less than 9th grade	9.7	23.8	8.8	11.5
9th to 12th, no diploma	20.1	13.9	9.8	8.9
High school graduate	27.7	33.1	35.1	41.1

Continued on next page

Table 4.6, continued

Variable	Nebraska Communities			
	Waste Operating	Waste Siting	Nonwaste Development	Control (Baseline)
Some college, no degree	18.8	18.4	22.1	16.1
Associate degree	8.5	1.7	8.7	7.7
Bachelor's degree	9.3	7.9	11.4	11.9
Graduate degree	5.8	1.1	4.1	2.7
Occupation (Employed persons 16 and over) (%*)				
Executive, administrative, and managerial	9.0	11.9	7.3	10.5
Professional	12.3	13.8	14.2	13.2
Technicians	0.7	5.0	2.0	3.1
Sales	7.9	8.1	10.0	12.1
Administrative support and clerical	10.5	8.8	19.2	13.7
Service	19.7	28.1	17.4	17.7
Farming, forestry, fishing	4.2	7.5	3.9	6.5
Precision production, craft	14.9	3.1	11.2	9.7
Operators, fabricators, laborers	20.9	13.8	14.8	13.5
Industry (Employed persons 16 and over) (%*)				
Agriculture, forestry, fisheries	5.6	4.4	4.5	9.5
Mining	8.7	0.0	1.9	0.5
Construction	8.6	6.9	5.8	8.8
Manufacturing, nondurable	3.6	0.0	1.9	1.0
Manufacturing, durable	6.8	2.5	7.1	1.5
Transportation	1.5	1.3	5.4	2.2
Communications/public utilities	1.5	2.5	2.2	5.5
Wholesale	2.7	1.3	2.6	4.6
Retail	13.6	16.9	28.2	22.1
Finance, insurance, real estate	1.1	13.1	4.0	4.9
Business and repair services	6.2	6.9	2.6	4.1
Personal services	5.3	5.0	2.4	2.7

Continued on next page

Table 4.6, continued

	Nebraska Communities			
Variable	Waste Operating	Waste Siting	Nonwaste Development	Control (Baseline)
Entertainment/recreation service	1.7	1.3	0.5	0.9
Health services	9.8	15.6	9.2	8.8
Educational services	9.9	11.9	10.4	10.0
Other professional and related services	5.2	2.5	7.1	5.5
Public administration	8.1	8.1	4.0	7.3

	Oklahoma Communities			Texas Communities		
Variable	Waste Operating	Nonwaste Development	Control (Baseline)	Waste Siting	Nonwaste Development	Control (Baseline)
Median Household Income ($1994)	15,161	24,306	23,594	27,058	18,369	15,605
Per Capita Income ($1994)	11,125	12,327	12,466	12,204	12,896	7,345
Persons Below Poverty Level (%*)	24.4	19.2	9.9	27.0	22.3	49.2
Educational Attainment (Persons 25 and over) (%*)						
Less than 9th grade	20.2	10.0	18.0	22.3	19.6	38.5
9th to 12th, no diploma	14.2	19.8	8.9	11.6	21.5	12.6
High school graduate	35.3	41.6	32.9	36.2	29.7	25.0
Some college, no degree	14.8	14.0	20.4	14.6	15.4	11.2
Associate degree	4.3	3.1	3.8	4.2	2.8	4.0
Bachelor's degree	7.1	5.4	10.7	8.0	7.6	5.9
Graduate degree	4.1	6.1	5.4	3.0	3.4	2.8
Occupation (Employed persons 16 and over) (%*)						
Executive, administrative, and managerial	7.1	7.0	7.1	9.6	5.2	3.3
Professional	10.2	8.3	13.3	14.5	4.8	9.6

Continued on next page

Table 4.6, continued

Variable	Oklahoma Communities			Texas Communities		
	Waste Operating	Nonwaste Development	Control (Baseline)	Waste Siting	Nonwaste Development	Control (Baseline)
Technicians	0.6	2.7	5.1	0.8	0.4	1.4
Sales	6.5	8.5	9.8	8.2	8.1	6.9
Administrative support and clerical	9.5	11.0	15.0	12.4	17.0	12.6
Service	19.7	19.4	15.3	17.6	24.4	15.4
Farming, forestry, fishing	9.2	5.6	3.5	7.1	7.9	25.8
Precision production, craft	14.2	16.4	14.3	13.3	12.3	10.8
Operators, fabricators, laborers	23.1	21.2	16.5	16.5	19.8	14.2
Industry (Employed persons 16 and over) (%)[*]						
Agriculture, forestry, fisheries	8.9	5.6	4.9	6.7	7.8	26.4
Mining	8.3	7.2	6.6	2.0	0.6	1.4
Construction	7.4	7.5	3.9	8.4	7.5	7.3
Manufacturing, nondurable	0.6	14.1	5.1	1.6	6.8	1.6
Manufacturing, durable	6.2	1.6	1.0	0.8	4.8	1.0
Transportation	4.6	3.7	4.2	15.3	5.3	2.8
Communications/public utilities	6.2	2.6	4.0	4.9	2.8	3.9
Wholesale	0.9	4.6	2.4	0.0	4.8	4.3
Retail	15.1	14.0	21.4	17.8	23.0	13.4
Finance, insurance, real estate	2.8	5.8	3.0	3.7	5.4	3.0
Business and repair services	0.9	5.0	2.4	3.5	2.3	4.7
Personal services	5.2	3.8	2.0	3.7	5.6	3.7
Entertainment/recreation service	1.2	0.3	0.7	0.6	0.7	0.4
Health services	15.1	7.2	21.9	0.0	8.1	0.6
Educational services	10.2	5.6	8.3	17.6	6.6	13.8
Other professional and related services	2.8	8.9	3.0	3.7	3.9	5.3
Public administration	3.7	2.6	5.2	9.8	3.8	6.5

[*] Percentages may not equal 100.0 percent because of rounding.

Table 4.7: Comparison of Annualized Exponential Percentage Rates of Population Growth and Annual Rates of Net Migration in Waste-Related, Nonwaste Development and Control (Baseline) Counties and Related States, 1970-1994

Counties	Population Growth			Net Migration		
	1970-1980	1980-1990	1990-1994	1970-1980	1980-1990	1990-1994
Colorado	2.7	1.3	2.5	2.0	0.3	1.6
Waste Siting	2.8	0.0	2.9	2.5	-0.6	2.7
Total Study Area	2.8	0.0	2.9	2.5	-0.6	2.7
Utah	3.2	1.7	2.4	1.4	-0.2	1.0
Waste Operating	1.9	0.2	1.9	0.1	-1.3	0.5
Nonwaste Development	6.5	6.2	7.3	6.3	6.4	7.1
Control (Baseline)	5.4	0.1	1.8	3.3	-2.3	0.1
Total Study Area	4.2	3.1	5.0	2.7	1.6	3.3
Nebraska	0.6	0.1	0.7	-0.1	-0.6	0.2
Waste Operating	-2.1	-1.7	-0.3	-2.5	-2.1	-0.1
Waste Siting	-1.2	-1.6	-1.0	-1.0	-1.4	-0.1
Nonwaste Development	-0.7	-0.6	0.2	-1.1	-1.0	0.1
Control (Baseline)	0.8	-1.8	-0.2	0.6	-1.7	-0.1
Total Study Area	-0.8	-1.2	-0.1	-1.1	-1.4	-0.0
Oklahoma	1.7	0.4	0.8	1.2	-0.4	0.3
Waste Operating	-0.9	-1.8	-1.2	-0.7	-1.6	-0.6
Nonwaste Development	1.3	-1.6	-1.1	1.4	-1.8	-1.0
Control (Baseline)	0.9	-2.2	-1.2	0.8	-2.0	-0.7
Total Study Area	0.4	-1.8	-1.2	0.4	-1.7	-0.8
Texas	2.4	1.8	1.9	1.6	0.7	0.9
Waste Siting	-2.0	-1.2	-1.7	-2.3	-1.8	-1.7
Nonwaste Development	0.4	0.1	0.1	0.3	-0.1	0.1
Control (Baseline)	-0.4	1.1	6.1	-1.1	0.3	6.2
Total Study Area	-0.3	0.1	1.7	-0.7	-0.7	1.6
All States	0.6	-0.5	1.0	-0.5	-1.4	0.2
Waste Operating	2.0	-0.2	2.3	1.5	-0.7	2.2
Waste Siting	2.9	3.2	4.9	2.3	2.5	4.6
Nonwaste Development	2.8	-0.6	1.4	1.5	-1.9	0.5
Control (Baseline)						

Table 4.8: Comparison of Annualized Exponential Percentage Rates of Population Growth in Waste-Related, Nonwaste Development and Control (Baseline) Study Communities and Related States, 1970-1994

Counties	1970-1980	1980-1990	1990-1994
Colorado	2.7	1.3	2.4
Waste Siting	0.8	-4.5	2.1
Waste Siting	0.0	-6.4	2.8
Total Study Area	0.4	-5.3	2.4
Utah	3.2	1.7	2.4
Waste Operating	4.1	0.2	2.4
Waste Operating	1.3	-0.3	1.5
Nonwaste Development	5.2	5.1	8.0
Control (Baseline)	6.5	0.2	2.7
Total Study Area	2.8	0.5	2.9
Nebraska	0.6	0.1	0.7
Waste Operating	-1.7	-1.9	-0.4
Waste Siting	-0.8	-1.6	-2.2
Nonwaste Development	-0.6	-0.1	0.2
Control (Baseline)	0.8	-1.9	-0.4
Total Study Area	-0.7	-0.9	-0.1
Oklahoma	1.7	0.4	0.8
Waste Operating	-0.5	-3.7	-0.4
Nonwaste Development	1.1	-1.9	-0.9
Control (Baseline)	1.3	-1.9	-1.1
Total Study Area	0.8	-2.3	-0.9
Texas	2.4	1.8	1.9
Waste Siting	0.1	-1.0	--
Nonwaste Development	-0.2	0.2	-0.4
Control (Baseline)	0.8	0.2	5.2
Total Study Area	0.1	-0.1	--
All States			
Waste Operating	1.2	-0.6	1.4
Waste Siting	0.1	-3.0	1.1
Nonwaste Development	0.6	0.5	2.1
Control (Baseline)	2.9	-0.7	1.9
Total Study Area	2.2	1.4	1.8

by 3.2 percent per year in the 1980s and by 4.9 percent per year from 1990 to 1994. Control counties showed population declines of 0.6 percent per year in the 1980s and an average increase of 1.4 percent per year during the 1990 to 1994 period (table 4.7). The lack of any clear relationship between waste-related developments and population growth is even more apparent for waste-impacted communities (table 4.8). For example, the annual rate of population growth from 1990 to 1994 was 1.1 percent for waste siting communities, 1.4 percent for waste operating communities, 2.1 percent for nonwaste development communities, and 1.9 percent for control communities. Such data provide little indication that waste developments have brought population growth to the communities and counties hosting them.

Overall, the data in tables 4.1-4.8 suggest that the demographic impact of waste-related developments have been relatively modest. That is, there is little indication that such developments have led to substantial population growth in areas hosting waste-related impacts.

Impacts on Community Services

The impacts on services were difficult to determine because of severe limitations in the data available for several sites. In many of these small areas historical records were not available and for others the cost of retrieval (often requiring a local service provider to complete a review of an entire set of individual service records) was prohibitive. As a result, it was possible only to examine general indicators of service usage with data on changes in factors such as service costs being impossible to obtain in a consistent manner across sites. We believe, however, that the data available allow us to adequately address the general issue of whether service usage has been impacted by waste facility siting.

The results from the analysis of the secondary data are summarized in table 4.9. In this table annualized changes in selected service indicators have been computed for the study sites for pre- and post-1990 periods. Annualized rates have been used because, in some cases, there are missing data points that would make comparisons between specific dates impossible because of missing data for a single year. We have computed annual rates between any years of data available within the two time periods. We have examined two time periods because some of the projects were initiated in the 1980s, while others did not begin until the 1990s. The inclusion of the two periods thus avoids the use of averages for periods that may confound pre- and post-development change.

The data in table 4.9 show that, as with population, the impact on services has been generally most substantial in nonwaste development areas and least evident in baseline or control areas. When one examines the bottom panel of the table, which shows the values over all areas within community types, the largest annual rates of change are generally in nonwaste development areas and the lowest rates (often negative rates) are in the control (baseline) areas.

However, there is substantial variation by service, time period and community type. For example, for police and social services, there is some indication that waste-related impacts have occurred at least for some periods. For police services, the annual rate of growth of 20.0 percent from 1990 to 1994 in waste siting areas suggests that during the siting process the need for such services may increase. At the same time, the fact that such growth is not evident for waste operating communities may suggest that such increases in demand are temporary. For social services, the data show rates of growth of 1.8 percent in the number of food stamp recipients from 1990 to 1994 in waste operating communities, compared to annual increases of 0.6 percent, 0.9 percent and 2.1 percent for waste siting, nonwaste development and control communities respectively. Similarly, the largest increases in Medicaid recipients from 1990 to 1994 are in waste siting communities. Such changes may not be a unique product of waste developments, however, because for the 1984 to 1990 period the largest increase in the number of AFDC recipients are in nonwaste development counties while in this same period for food stamps the largest increases were in control areas.

Overall, these data fail to suggest a clear pattern of more rapid service growth in waste-impacted areas and, as with population, for some services (such as the number of physicians from 1990 to 1994) waste-impacted communities show declines in the level of services. These data suggest that if waste-related developments have impacted services, those impacts appear to have been within the normal range of variation experienced by rural communities in the study area.

Although the secondary data on services were limited, data were also available from the community resident and leader surveys on respondents' evaluations of the impacts of development on public services. Below, we examine these data for several key services including education, housing, police, fire, and local service expenditures. Although additional services were assessed, the factors examined here are among those most often delineated as being impacted by economic development projects (Murdock and Leistritz 1979), including waste-related projects (Murdock et al. 1991).

These data were derived from a questionnaire item in which respondents were asked to indicate whether waste-related developments in the waste siting and waste operating communities, the nonwaste development in the nonwaste development communities, and recent economic changes in the control communities had very positive, positive, neither positive nor negative, negative, or very negative impacts on several service dimensions. In this

Table 4.9: Annualized Percentage Rates of Change in Selected Public Services in Waste Operating, Waste Siting, Nonwaste Development, and Control (Baseline) Communities, 1984-1994

| | Fire | | Police | | Public Service Area Education | | | | | | Social Services | | | | | | Medical | |
| | Number of Firefighters | | Number of Officers | | Enrollment | | Teachers | | Student/Teacher Ratio | | AFDC Recipients | | Food Stamp Recipients | | Medicaid Recipients | | Number of Physicians | |
State/Community Type	84-90	90-94	84-90	90-94	84-90	90-94	84-90	90-94	84-90	90-94	84-90	90-94	84-90	90-94	84-90	90-94	84-90	90-94
Colorado																		
Waste Siting	7.1	5.3	—	—	0.5	2.4	134.7	-17.8	18.6	-10.2	-0.4	-2.5	-1.0	1.6	—	—	0.0	0.0
Utah																		
Waste Operating	4.0	2.5	0.8	0.5	0.1	0.9	0.0	-0.3	13.0	0.9	6.9	5.1	0.0	8.0	1.8	15.7	0.0	-2.2
Nonwaste Development	—	—	20.0	-4.4	8.1	4.9	9.6	5.5	0.5	-0.7	0.0	8.7	0.0	3.0	24.0	13.1	0.0	0.0
Control (Baseline)	1.9	1.2	2.4	-5.7	-2.0	1.4	0.2	2.0	-6.3	12.9	—	—	0.0	14.1	17.5	17.6	-2.6	6.7
Nebraska																		
Waste Operating	—	—	3.8	-5.3	-2.1	3.0	0.0	0.0	0.0	0.0	-4.9	-2.4	-1.0	-10.3	3.0	1.1	-4.8	-5.0
Waste Siting	-2.2	-3.6	0.0	20.0	4.1	-1.0	0.0	1.0	4.1	-1.9	-4.2	0.0	-2.2	-7.9	1.2	10.5	21.4	-4.0
Nonwaste Development	—	—	-2.9	-1.3	0.1	3.4	0.7	1.8	-0.6	1.4	24.2	-4.0	2.2	3.6	31.8	5.2	0.0	5.7
Control (Baseline)	0.0	0.0	0.0	0.0	-0.5	3.6	0.4	4.3	-1.0	-0.7	6.4	-0.5	9.1	3.2	14.6	8.9	-6.1	0.0
Oklahoma																		
Waste Operating	0.0	0.0	-1.0	0.0	-2.1	0.1	-2.3	-1.1	0.2	1.3	1.4	7.8	-16.2	10.7	9.3	9.2	0.0	0.0
Nonwaste Development	0.0	0.0	-1.8	0.0	-0.5	0.9	-0.7	0.7	0.2	0.3	-1.5	14.6	-8.2	7.7	5.3	5.5	—	—
Control (Baseline)	—	—	28.6	0.0	-0.9	-4.9	-0.5	-0.6	-0.4	-4.4	-5.8	2.6	-9.2	9.8	10.9	5.6	—	—
Texas																		
Waste Siting	—	—	—	—	-1.2	-3.0	3.7	-1.4	-4.0	-1.6	16.3	4.0	1.7	20.7	1.5	14.2	—	—
Nonwaste Development	5.0	-0.9	—	—	-0.7	1.4	9.7	1.9	-6.2	-0.6	28.6	-17.8	17.7	7.6	10.1	12.8	14.3	0.0
Control (Baseline)	—	—	—	—	-0.0	-1.1	6.8	2.2	-4.6	-3.1	0.4	20.6	4.6	5.2	9.7	20.6	0.0	0.0
Total Study Area																		
Waste Operating	1.3	0.9	0.4	-0.4	-0.1	0.3	-0.1	-0.1	2.2	0.3	0.8	1.7	2.0	1.8	1.1	4.2	-0.8	-1.2
Waste Siting	0.9	0.8	0.0	20.0	0.2	0.6	17.7	-5.1	2.2	-2.4	-0.1	-0.7	-0.3	0.6	0.7	5.8	4.8	-1.1
Nonwaste Development	2.2	-0.4	1.8	-1.0	1.3	1.1	1.6	1.1	-0.4	0.0	1.9	0.5	-1.3	0.9	4.5	2.6	0.6	1.2
Control (Baseline)	0.3	0.2	1.3	-1.4	-0.4	0.2	0.2	0.5	-0.9	0.3	-0.3	3.3	-0.3	2.1	3.8	3.8	-1.3	1.4

analysis, we combine very positive and positive responses and negative and very negative responses for ease of reporting. In addition, we do not show the percent responding in the neutral (neither positive nor negative) category because it can be derived by subtraction. We examine residents' and leaders' evaluations of these service areas below.

Impacts on Public Schools

The effects on schools were assessed through an item that asked respondents to evaluate the impacts of developments on public school funding. Figure 4.1 and table 4.10 show the distribution of residents' responses to this item. These data indicate that 49.7 percent of all residents believed that the developments in their area had positively impacted school funds while only 17.0 believed they had negatively impacted school funds.

Similarly, when examined relative to community type (see also table 4.10), the data suggest that the impacts on school funding were viewed more positively in waste operating and waste siting areas than in nonwaste impacted communities. In waste operating communities, 57.1 percent of residents perceived that school funds had been positively impacted and in waste siting communities 74.0 percent viewed such impacts as positive. In nonwaste development areas 44.5 percent, and in control communities 28.6 percent, perceived the impacts to be positive. It appears that the lack of development in control communities has been seen as problematic for school financing.

The data in tables 4.11 and 4.12, showing leader and resident differences, suggest that leaders perceive such impacts more positively than other residents, but that both leaders and residents in waste-impacted communities tend to perceive the impacts to be more positive than residents and leaders in nonwaste related communities. Although the differences between residents and leaders within community types are not large, and are neither statistically significant nor show strong levels of association, the patterns of resident/leader differences are pervasive.

In sum, the impacts of development projects on school funding were generally perceived as positive. This is particularly evident among residents and leaders in waste-impacted communities.

Figure 4.1: Respondents' Evaluations of Development Effects on Various Services

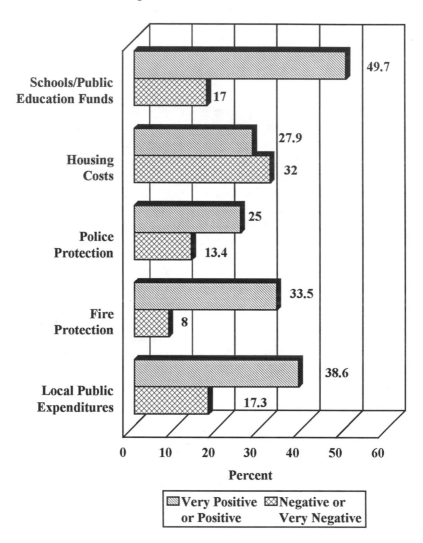

Table 4.10: Residents' Evaluations of Development Impacts on Selected Services by Community Type

Response	Waste Operating	Waste Siting	Nonwaste Development	Control (Baseline)
Schools/Public Education Funds				
Very Positive or Positive Effect	57.1	74.0	44.5	28.6
Negative Effect or Very Negative Effect	5.1	5.5	19.0	34.9
N	294	273	364	332
x^2	194.0 *			
Cramer's V	.28			
Tau-c**	.28			
Housing Costs				
Very Positive or Positive Effect	19.5	42.2	27.0	28.3
Negative Effect or Very Negative Effect	28.0	22.4	45.1	28.5
N	303	263	381	348
x^2	89.6 *			
Cramer's V	.19			
Tau-c**	.03			
Police Protection				
Very Positive or Positive Effect	8.1	36.2	27.0	29.7
Negative or Very Negative Effect	9.1	11.3	16.7	16.5
N	296	265	389	364
x^2	91.0 *			
Cramer's V	.19			
Tau-c**	-.05			
Fire Protection				
Very Positive or Positive Effect	17.5	45.0	36.0	35.2
Negative or Very Negative Effect	6.4	8.1	9.8	7.4
N	297	271	386	364
x^2	66.5 *			
Cramer's V	.12			
Tau-c**	-.03			
Local Public Expenditures				
Very Positive or Positive Effect	45.0	62.8	31.0	21.9
Negative or Very Negative Effect	7.6	6.7	23.6	27.1
N	251	239	335	288
x^2	131.4 *			
Cramer's V	.24			
Tau-c**	.24			

*$p \leq .001$

**Tau-c values were computed on uncollapsed data with more than two categories.

Table 4.11: Respondents' Evaluations of Development Impacts on Selected Services by Resident/Leader Status of Respondent

Response	Resident	Leader
Schools/Public Education Funds		
Very Positive or Positive Effect	49.7	57.2
Negative or Very Negative Effect	17.0	13.7
N	1,263	182
χ^2	13.7*	
Cramer's V	.10	
Tau-c**	-.05	
Housing Costs		
Very Positive or Positive Effect	27.8	33.9
Negative or Very Negative Effect	32.1	29.5
N	1,295	183
χ^2	9.0	
Cramer's V	.08	
Tau-c**	-.02	
Police Protection		
Very Positive or Positive Effect	25.3	22.4
Negative or Very Negative Effect	13.9	10.4
N	1,314	183
χ^2	4.1	
Cramer's V	.05	
Tau-c**	-.001	
Fire Protection		
Very Positive or Positive Effect	33.4	35.9
Negative or Very Negative Effect	8.1	7.6
N	1,318	184
χ^2	.9	
Cramer's V	.02	
Tau-c**	-.01	
Local Public Expenditures		
Very Positive or Positive Effect	38.7	48.3
Negative or Very Negative Effect	17.2	15.5
N	1,113	174
χ^2	5.9	
Cramer's V	.07	
Tau-c**	-.04	

*$p \leq .001$

**Tau-c values were computed on uncollapsed data with more than two categories.

Table 4.12: Evaluations of Development Impacts on Schools/Public Education Funds by Resident/Leader Status of Respondents and Community Type

Response	Waste Operating		Waste Siting		Nonwaste Development		Control (Baseline)	
	Resident	Leader	Resident	Leader	Resident	Leader	Resident	Leader
Schools/Public Education Funds								
Very Positive or Positive Effect	57.1	69.2	74.0	84.2	44.5	47.3	28.6	38.0
Negative or Very Negative Effect	5.1	0.0	5.5	5.3	19.0	12.7	34.9	32.0
N	294	39	273	38	364	55	332	50
χ^2	3.3		2.2		1.3		1.9	
Cramer's V	0.10		0.08		0.06		0.07	
Tau-c*	-0.06		-0.04		-0.03		-0.04	
Housing Costs								
Very Positive or Positive Effect	19.4	51.2	42.2	43.2	27.0	19.6	25.3	28.6
Negative or Very Negative Effect	28.1	9.8	22.4	21.6	45.2	51.8	28.4	26.5
N	303	41	263	37	381	56	348	49
χ^2	21.6 ****		0.0		1.5		0.3	
Cramer's V	0.25		0.01		0.06		0.03	
Tau-c*	-0.16		-0.01		0.04		-0.02	
Police Protection								
Very Positive or Positive Effect	8.1	9.8	36.2	46.0	27.0	25.0	29.7	12.2
Negative or Very Negative Effect	9.1	0.0	11.3	8.0	16.7	19.6	16.5	10.2

Continued on next page

Table 4.12, continued

Response	Waste Operating		Waste Siting		Nonwaste Development		Control (Baseline)	
	Resident	Leader	Resident	Leader	Resident	Leader	Resident	Leader
N	296	41	265	37	389	56	364	49
χ^2	4.1		1.4		0.3		10.1***	
Cramer's V	0.11		0.07		0.03		0.16	
Tau-c*	-0.04		-0.05		0.02		0.04	
Fire Protection								
Very Positive or Positive Effect	17.5	48.8	45.0	43.2	36.0	25.0	35.2	32.0
Negative or Very Negative Effect	6.4	0.0	8.1	8.1	9.8	14.3	7.4	6.0
N	297	41	271	37	386	56	364	50
χ^2	22.2****		0.0		3.0		0.4	
Cramer's V	0.26		0.01		0.08		0.03	
Tau-c*	-0.15		0.01		0.06		0.01	
Local Public Expenditures								
Very Positive or Positive Effect	45.0	51.4	62.8	60.0	31.0	50.0	21.9	35.4
Negative or Very Negative Effect	7.6	8.1	6.7	8.6	23.6	22.2	27.1	18.8
N	251	37	239	35	335	54	288	48
χ^2	0.6		0.2		8.4**		4.5	
Cramer's V	0.05		0.03		0.15		0.12	
Tau-c*	-0.03		0.02		-0.07		-0.08	

*Tau-c values were computed on uncollapsed data with more than two categories.

**$p \leq .05$ ***$p \leq .01$ ****$p \leq .001$

Impacts on Housing Costs

The effects of development projects on local housing costs are examined in figure 4.1 and tables 4.10 through 4.12. The data in the figure suggest that residents were generally more negative about the perceived impacts on housing than was evident for education. Thirty-two percent of residents perceived housing costs to have been negatively impacted compared to 27.9 percent who perceived that the impacts were positive.

When examined by community type (table 4.10), the evaluations of impacts on housing costs suggest that the most negative impacts are perceived in the nonwaste development communities (45.1 percent) with perceiving neither negative nor positive impacts being the most frequent response in waste operating (52.5 percent) and control (43.2 percent) communities, and positive evaluations (42.2 percent) being the most often noted response in waste siting communities.

The results for leaders and residents (tables 4.11 and 4.12) show quite diverse patterns across different types of communities. In general, they suggest that leaders are more positive than residents only in waste operating and waste siting communities and these resident/leader differences are only significant in waste operating areas. In nonwaste development areas, both leaders and residents are more negative than positive but residents are more likely to be positive than leaders. The results for housing are thus mixed, suggesting no general pattern of perceived impacts on housing costs.

Overall, the results for housing show fewer positive ratings and fewer clear relationships to project-related activities. It appears that other factors related to housing may affect residents' evaluations. In particular, the tendency for relatively large numbers of rural housing units to be of poor quality may be reflected in pervasive negative perceptions among residents across the study area's communities.

Impacts on Police Protection

Figure 4.1 and tables 4.10 through 4.12 also provide information on the perceived impacts of local development patterns and events on police protection. These data show (by subtraction) that a majority of residents (61.6 percent) perceive neither positive nor negative effects on police protection. Of those responding either positively or negatively, the proportion indicating that such services have been positively impacted (25.0 percent) is nearly twice as high as the proportion viewing police protection as having been negatively impacted (13.4 percent).

Data on such perceptions by community type (table 4.10) show that the modal response for all community types is to perceive such impacts as neither positive nor negative with the second most frequent response for waste siting, nonwaste development, and control communities being that the impacts have been positive. The differences by community type found for some other items are not evident in data for police protection.

The data on leaders' and residents' perceptions also fail to show patterns frequently noted in other data. That is, leader and resident differences are small overall (see table 4.11).

The data for law enforcement suggest that few residents or respondents view such services as having been impacted by recent developments. This is true whether these are waste or nonwaste related developments.

Impacts on Fire Protection

Figure 4.1 and tables 4.10 through 4.12 also show residents' and leaders' perceptions of the impact of development activities on fire protection. These data show that a majority of residents (58.5 percent) see such projects as having been neither positively nor negatively impacted, with 33.5 percent perceiving positive effects compared to 8.0 percent who perceive negative effects.

The data on perceptions by community type (see table 4.10) show similar patterns to those for police protection with the largest proportion of respondents in each community type viewing the effects on fire protection to be neither positive nor negative. However, the highest proportion of positive impact (with 45.0 percent of all residents so indicating) were perceived in waste siting communities, with nonwaste development and control communities having about equal proportions (36.0 and 35.2 percent, respectively) perceiving positive effects. More than three of every four residents (76.1 percent) in waste operating communities viewed fire protection as having been neither positively nor negatively impacted.

The data for residents and leaders (tables 4.11 and 4.12) are also similar to those for police protection in that resident and leader differences are generally small within community types. Such differences were significant only in waste operating areas where the proportion of leaders with positive perceptions was nearly three times as high as those for residents. Also, similar to the findings for police protection, perceptions are most positive among both leaders and residents in waste siting communities.

As with police protection, most residents and leaders in the study communities do not see fire protection as having been markedly impacted by waste or nonwaste related economic changes. Most view this service area as having not been impacted and perceptions on this factor are not strongly related to favorability toward siting.

Impacts on Local Public Expenditures

Impacts on public services are usually reflected in impacts on local public expenditures. Thus, in this section, we examine residents' and leaders' perceptions of the impacts of waste and other developments on public expenditures. These perceptions are again examined in figure 4.1 and tables 4.10 through 4.12.

These data show that more than twice as many respondents view the impacts on expenditures to be positive as view them negatively (38.6 percent versus 17.3 percent) but that the most often noted response (44.1 percent of all respondents) is that such expenditures have been neither positively nor negatively impacted. When examined by community type (table 4.10) the data suggest that residents in waste operating and siting communities are the most likely to perceive such impacts as positive (45.0 and 62.8 percent in waste operating and waste siting compared to 31.0 and 21.9 percent in nonwaste and control communities) and that such differences are significant and show moderate values for the measures of association.

The data on residents and leaders presented in tables 4.11 and 4.12 tend to verify the results found for other services and the findings for residents grouped by community type (in table 4.10). In general, leaders view such impacts more positively than residents and generally such perceptions are more positive in waste operating and waste siting than in nonwaste development and control communities. However, only one of the relationships is statistically significant and all have very low levels of association.

Overall, the data on perceptions of public service impacts show mixed results relative to the effects of waste-related projects. For services such as fire and police protection, the data suggest that most respondents view these services as having been neither positively nor negatively impacted by waste or other developments. Residents and leaders tend to view impacts on housing as more negative than those for other types of services but such impacts are viewed more negatively in nonwaste development and control communities than in waste-impacted communities, suggesting a general level of concern with rural housing. For educational and local government expenditures, residents tend to perceive positive impacts and such perceptions are more positive for those in waste-impacted communities than for those in nonwaste related communities. For all services, the relationships obtained are quite modest in terms of measures of association. There is no clear indication that waste-related projects have substantially affected public services as measured by residents' and leaders' perceptions and for those services perceived as having been impacted by developments, the impacts are generally perceived as positive.

Summary

The results of both the secondary data analysis and the analysis of perceptions of impacts suggest that the impacts of waste projects on populations and public services has been very modest. There is little indication in the secondary data that there have been marked increases in either populations or service demands and residents' perceptions of service impacts are either that there have been few impacts or that they have been generally positive. Neither populations nor public services in the study areas have shown the impacts sometimes noted as being likely to occur in such areas (Murdock et al. 1991). Rather, it appears that waste-related projects have had largely benign effects on population growth and community services.

In fact, the data suggest that waste projects appear to have led neither to accelerated population decline nor to rapid population growth. They do not appear to have resulted in substantial increases or decreases in public service usage. The results suggest instead that waste-related developments are likely to be of little danger to rural areas in terms of reducing population growth or overloading services. They are also unlikely to be a boon to their desires to renew population growth and improve public service availability.

Chapter 5

Social and Special Impacts of Waste Facility Siting and Operation

The social impact of any large scale industrial or resource development project include a wide array of potential changes to the social organization and social structures of affected communities. Project-induced changes in the size and characteristics of local populations, economic conditions and opportunities, public service and infrastructure conditions, land use patterns, environmental conditions, and other factors can all contribute to significant shifts in the local social context and the levels of well-being experienced by local residents. Among the major categories of social impacts resulting from various types of large-scale projects are changes in forms and patterns of interactions among residents; changes in the formal and informal institutions and organizations that allow a community to function; and changes in attitudes, values and perceptions held by residents of affected communities (Little and Krannich 1989; Murdock and Leistritz 1979; Murdock et al. 1991).

However, projects involving the processing, storage, or disposal of hazardous materials appear in most cases to be accompanied by additional, relatively unique impacts. These unique social impacts of hazardous projects and facilities, frequently referred to in the literature as "special" impacts (Murdock et al. 1983b; Murdock et al. 1991; Flynn et al. 1994), are linked to perceptions and concerns about: (1) the equity involved in having one local area host a facility to store the hazardous by-products of economic activity occurring in, and often benefitting, other areas; (2) uncertainties regarding the health and safety risks of such facilities for current and future generations; (3) the extent to which debates over facility siting and waste management safety issues generate unusually high levels of controversy and potentially corrosive conflicts in affected communities; (4) the trade-offs between potential economic benefits to the community and possible economic costs, including the prospect of local economic stigmatization; (5) uncertainties about the level of confidence that can be placed in technologies used to manage and store hazardous waste materials; and (6) varying levels of trust in the agencies and organizations that are considered responsible for assuring that hazardous wastes are safely and responsibly managed.

Individually and jointly, these social and special impact concerns can be expected to influence residents' evaluations of the acceptability and/or desirability of projects that involve the processing or disposal of hazardous wastes (Albrecht 1995). At the same time, it is likely that such perceptions will vary widely across and within local communities, for a variety of reasons. First, local responses to such projects may be affected by differential local development contexts, including experiences with the siting or operation of waste facilities or other analogous development activities (Stoffle et al. 1988). Steps taken by developers and project proponents to mitigate, compensate for, or enhance the impacts of such developments may also influence local response (Easterling and Kunreuther 1995; Halstead et al. 1993). Perceptions of and responses to such projects may also be influenced by the social ties, positions, and statuses that people occupy in the local community (Spies et al. 1998). In particular, those involved in various types of community leadership positions are likely to perceive developments somewhat differently than other residents, due in part to their unique level of knowledge and involvement in planning and decision-making activities, as well as the different interests and values that they may hold (Bailey et al. 1992; Molotch 1976; Spies et al. 1998; Takahashi and Gaber 1998).

In sum, then, assessing the social and special impacts of waste projects can be seen as determinating how changes in community relationships, organizations, and perceptions are impacted by a waste-related project's siting or operation. In situations where there is broad-based support for such development and little or no conflict over facility siting at the local level, the social and special impacts of such projects may be relatively inconsequential, especially if the scale of the project is relatively modest. However, the literature suggests that such circumstances are extremely unusual; in most cases efforts to site hazardous waste disposal facilities appear to generate substantial concern and opposition among local residents, and in many instances highly divisive conflicts between project proponents and opponents (Benford et al. 1993; Portney 1991).

Key factors in any attempt to understand and predict such effects include: attitudes and perceptions regarding the potential health and safety risks associated with such projects; levels of trust in the agencies and organizations responsible for siting and managing such facilities; trust and confidence in the technologies that are applied to hazardous waste management; views about the fairness or equity of waste facility siting; perceptions or expectations about project effects on local economic conditions; responses to possible economic or community development incentives, among others. These perceptions and responses are likely to be influenced by a variety of factors, including the social and demographic characteristics of individual local residents and the different social roles and statuses exhibited by residents and community leaders. Taken together, this complex of factors is likely to have a profound influence on the extent to which a waste facility will be accepted or opposed within an actual or potential host community.

In this chapter, we address these issues using data from the community resident and leader surveys described in chapter 2. These surveys, conducted in communities that have experienced waste facility siting and/or operation and communities not having had those experiences, represent the most systematic data collected during the course of this research effort on the social and special impacts of hazardous waste facility siting. As such, they provide the most appropriate data for examining these forms of impacts. Specifically, we examine respondents' overall acceptance of waste facility projects, as well as response patterns for an array of survey-based variables measuring attitudes and perceptions that are likely to affect views about the siting of such facilities.

For each of the measures pertaining to attitudes and perceptions about waste management issues, we present descriptive statistics and frequency distributions that summarize the overall response patterns among residents of the multiple study community settings, and compare response patterns among residents grouped by community type. We then examine differences between the perspectives of local leaders and community residents relative to each factor. Because the "favorability toward siting" item provides a crucial summary measure of residents' overall orientations toward waste projects, we also show how each of the other key factors considered in the analysis is related to responses on the favorability measure. Finally, we examine the joint predictive power of the various factors in determining favorability toward siting, using multivariate analysis techniques. In combination these multiple analytic stages are designed to provide a useful way of summarizing our findings regarding several of the most frequently cited social and special impacts of hazardous waste facility developments in rural areas.

Characteristics of Respondents by Community Type and Leadership Status

Before beginning the analysis of local responses to waste facility siting issues, it is important to identify the characteristics of survey respondents relative to demographic and socioeconomic factors that may affect their responses. In table 5.1, we examine differences in the characteristics of respondents grouped by community type and resident/leader status. In general these data suggest that across the four types of study communities, the residents who participated in the survey are quite similar overall. The major differences involve respondents' race and ethnicity, and industry of employment. The racial and ethnic differences as well as the employment sector differences are largely a function of the fact that one of the siting areas and one of the control communities are located in southwest Texas, which has a high percentage of persons of non-Anglo and Hispanic origins and persons employed in agriculture. Overall, however, the data suggest that differences in responses to waste facility siting among residents from the four types of study communities are unlikely to be a result of demographic and socioeconomic differences, since respondents are generally similar across key variables such as age, sex, marital status, educational status, employment status, home ownership, farm ownership, and income.

On the other hand, the data in table 5.1 show that local leaders and other residents are much more distinct, with significant differences in characteristics evident for all of the variables examined. Leaders are significantly more likely than resident respondents to be male, Anglo or non-Hispanic, married, highly educated, employed, own farms and homes, employed in key financial industries, and to have higher incomes than other residents. These resident/leader differences suggest that the frequently noted tendency for local community leaders to be selected from relatively unique social groups is evident for the communities included in this study (Bailey et al. 1992; Molotch 1976). Leaders' and residents' responses to waste facility issues are thus likely to reflect the influence of these differences in social and demographic characteristics, as well as other differences associated with their community roles and statuses.

Support for Siting and Operation of
Waste Facilities in the Study Area

One of the primary objectives of this study was to examine and attempt to understand variations in both residents' and leaders' levels of acceptance or resistance to the siting of hazardous waste storage or disposal facilities in

Table 5.1: Demographic and Socioeconomic Characteristics of Residents by Community Type and all Respondents by Resident/Leader Status

Characteristics (%*)	All Respondents	Community Type				Resident/Leader Status	
		Waste Operating	Waste Siting	Nonwaste Development	Control (Baseline)	Resident	Leader
Age							
<25	7.7	8.5	8.1	9.2	7.8	8.4	1.6
25-44	37.9	34.7	35.9	37.7	43.1	38.1	35.7
45-64	32.6	31.9	28.2	32.1	27.2	29.9	55.3
65+	21.8	24.9	27.8	21.0	21.9	23.6	7.4
N =	1,781	389	320	448	434	1,591	190
Sex							
Male	45.8	60.7	58.0	54.8	57.1	42.5	73.9
Female	54.2	39.3	42.0	45.2	42.9	57.5	26.1
N =	1,756	384	312	445	427	1,568	188
Race							
Anglo	85.9	91.8	80.0	88.8	77.6	84.7	95.3
Other	14.1	8.2	20.0	11.2	22.4	15.3	4.7
N =	1,781	389	320	448	434	1,591	190
Hispanic Origin	9.1	4.6	14.1	6.5	15.0	9.9	2.6
N =	1,781	18	45	29	65	1,591	190
Marital Status							
Married	70.1	64.7	65.0	71.2	68.1	67.5	91.5
Living as married	2.1	1.5	1.3	2.4	3.3	2.2	1.1
Widowed	11.0	13.3	15.6	9.5	11.4	12.1	1.6
Divorced	8.8	10.4	9.2	8.6	9.3	9.3	4.3
Separated	1.4	1.8	0.6	2.0	1.2	1.5	0.5
Never married	6.6	8.3	8.3	6.3	6.7	7.4	1.0
N =	1,761	385	314	444	430	1,573	188

Continued on next page

Table 5.1, continued

Characteristics (%*)	All Respondents	Community Type				Resident/Leader Status	
		Waste Operating	Waste Siting	Nonwaste Development	Control (Baseline)	Resident	Leader
Education Level							
<High school	11.6	10.4	14.7	11.7	15.2	12.9	—
High school or GED	32.0	34.4	39.6	32.0	32.2	34.2	13.8
Some college but no degree	30.1	34.4	28.1	31.5	27.8	30.5	26.6
College degree	18.3	16.1	13.7	18.0	17.3	16.5	33.5
Graduate degree	8.0	4.7	3.9	6.8	7.5	5.9	26.1
N =	1,757	384	313	444	428	1,569	188
Employment Status							
Unemployed	10.1	10.4	10.4	12.5	11.7	11.4	—
Retired	25.6	28.9	30.1	27.2	25.4	27.6	7.9
Employed	64.3	60.7	59.5	60.3	62.9	61.0	92.1
N =	1,656	356	289	423	410	1,478	178
Industry							
Agriculture, forestry, or fishing	7.4	5.0	10.8	6.3	8.2	7.3	7.7
Mining	5.0	6.8	6.0	2.3	7.8	5.7	1.2
Construction	6.4	5.9	7.2	10.9	5.0	7.3	1.8
Manufacturing	5.1	7.2	0.6	9.8	0.8	4.9	6.5
Transportation, communication, or utilities	7.8	4.1	16.2	3.5	10.9	8.1	5.9
Wholesale trade	1.5	1.3	0.6	3.9	0.8	1.8	—
Retail trade	14.1	14.0	9.6	18.0	11.7	13.7	16.6
Finance, insurance, and real estate	4.8	4.1	1.8	3.9	2.7	3.2	13.0
Services	35.2	34.4	38.3	32.4	42.8	37.0	26.0
Public administration	12.7	17.2	8.9	9.0	9.3	11.0	21.3
N =	1,070	221	167	256	257	901	169

Continued on next page

Table 5.1, continued

Characteristics (%)[*]	All Respondents	Community Type				Resident/Leader Status	
		Waste Operating	Waste Siting	Nonwaste Development	Control (Baseline)	Resident	Leader
Home Ownership							
Own or buying home	80.7	79.9	81.2	79.8	77.7	79.5	90.5
N =	1,741	302	251	351	330	1,552	189
Farm Ownership							
Own or operate farm	16.5	13.5	18.7	14.3	15.3	15.2	26.3
N =	1,670	49	54	62	61	1,484	186
Income							
<$15,000	21.9	23.1	29.4	21.2	25.8	24.5	1.2
$15,000-$24,999	21.8	22.2	24.3	23.4	26.1	24.0	4.9
$25,000-$34,999	18.4	18.9	17.7	20.7	17.3	18.7	15.9
$35,000-$49,999	17.9	19.4	12.9	18.1	17.0	17.1	23.6
$50,000-$59,999	7.7	9.0	4.4	7.6	7.0	7.2	11.6
$60,000-$69,999	3.4	2.3	2.9	2.9	2.0	2.5	10.4
$70,000-$79,999	2.3	1.4	4.4	1.7	1.5	2.2	3.8
$80,000 or more	6.6	3.7	4.0	4.4	3.3	3.8	28.6
N =	1,618	355	272	410	399	1,436	182

[*]Percentages may not equal 100.0 percent because of rounding.

or near their communities. The degree of acceptance or favorability toward local development of waste management facilities was measured by a question asking respondents to indicate their level of agreement with the following statement: "If an election were held today, I would vote in favor of having a waste facility located in our area"; responses were recorded on a scale ranging from 1 ("Strongly Disagree") to 5 ("Strongly Agree").

The response distributions summarized in figure 5.1 show that a majority of residents oppose the siting of a waste project in their community. Over one-half of respondents (54.8 percent) indicated that they are opposed to the siting of a waste facility in their locale (as indicated by response values of 1 or 2), while only about one-fourth (28.1 percent) favored the siting of such a facility (response values of 4 or 5). More detailed breakdowns of response patterns indicate even more clearly that resident opposition far outweighs support for such facilities. When responses were recorded on the original five-point response scale, a plurality of respondents (45 percent) indicated that they strongly disagreed with the statement that they would vote in favor of having such a facility located in the area, while only a much smaller minority (16 percent) indicated strong agreement. This suggests a general tendency for persons from a broad range of rural community settings and individual socioeconomic circumstances and statuses to oppose having a waste facility located in or near their community of residence.

The data in table 5.2 show, however, that there is a significant difference in the extent to which residents in the different types of study communities favor the local development of such facilities. Overall, respondents in waste operating and waste siting areas reported more support for waste facility

Table 5.2: Favorability Toward Siting by Community Type

Response (%*)	Waste Operating	Waste Siting	Nonwaste Development	Control (Baseline)
Oppose Siting	41.9	39.7	67.6	64.0
Neither Favor/Oppose	21.9	11.9	17.7	16.1
Favor Siting	36.2	48.4	14.7	19.9
N	384	310	442	422
χ^2	147.3 **			
Cramer's V	.22			
Tau-c	-.19			

*Percentages may not equal 100.0 percent because of rounding.

**p≤.001

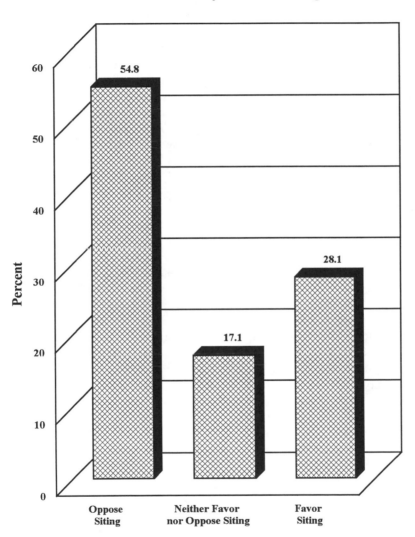

Figure 5.1: Residents' Level of
Favorability Toward Siting

siting than did respondents from either the nonwaste development or the control communities. Indeed, almost half (48.4 percent) of the respondents from the waste siting communities indicated support for the development of such facilities in their areas. At the same time, roughly 40 percent of respondents in both the waste operating and waste siting communities expressed opposition to waste facilities, while approximately two-thirds of those in the nonwaste development and control communities expressed opposition. Overall, it is clear that while there is widespread opposition to waste facilities across all four types of study areas, there also appear to be moderate to substantial bases of support, particularly in those areas where facility site selection activities and/or construction and operation have already taken place. The bimodal nature of response distributions suggests a high potential for controversy and conflict involving local residents who hold divergent perspectives about the desirability of having such facilities located in or near their communities.

Differences in levels of favorability toward waste facility siting are equally large and significant between community leaders and other local residents, with leaders being much more likely than residents to support siting. For the combined data from all study areas, one-half (50 percent) of local leaders indicated that they favored siting, while only slightly more than one-fourth (28.1 percent) of other residents expressed support. As indicated in table 5.3, this tendency for leaders to be substantially more supportive of waste facility siting holds true across all four of the community types considered in this study, with the distinction between leaders and residents being especially pronounced in the waste operating communities.

Also evident from the comparisons summarized in table 5.3 is the tendency for direct local experience with the siting and operation of a waste facility to exert a substantial influence on favorability toward siting. Among residents, those in waste operating and waste siting communities were two to three times as likely to favor siting as residents in nonwaste development and control communities. Among leaders, whereas more than 70 percent in both waste operating and waste siting communities favored siting, fewer than 38 percent of leaders favored siting in nonwaste development and control communities.

Perceptions of Risk

Levels of siting acceptance appear in many cases to be closely linked to the extent to which local residents believe they and others in their community are likely to be at risk of experiencing health and safety problems as a result of potential exposure to dangerous materials that might be released into the environment. Fitchen et al. (1987) and Freudenburg (1988) have argued that perceptions of risk are major factors in public opposition to the siting of projects involving the processing or disposal of hazardous and toxic materials, as have Desvousges et al. (1993), Albrecht et al. (1996), Krannich and Albrecht (1995), and numerous others.

Concerns about possible contamination of the environment and associated human health and safety risks are especially pronounced in the case of facilities that process or dispose of hazardous or radioactive waste materials. This is due in part to the fact that such effects are generally invisible to the casual observer, difficult to detect, and in some cases seemingly irreversible once contamination has occurred. Prior research has documented high levels of dread and perceptions of social trauma associated with the fears that many individuals express over the perceived risks of hazardous facilities, particularly those involving the processing or disposal of radioactive wastes (see Desvouges et al. 1993; Erikson 1994; Flynn et al. 1994; Slovic et al. 1993). Thus, risk perceptions represent one of the key "special effects" of hazardous facility siting and an important antecedent to levels of support or opposition to such facilities.

To measure risk perceptions, we utilized a summated index that reflects respondents' perceptions of the overall degree of risk associated with waste facilities. This measure was created by summing responses to the following statements: (1) a waste facility poses health and safety risks for future generations living in the surrounding area; and (2) environmental contamination is likely to occur as a result of a waste facility being in an area. Responses to both items were recorded on a scale with values ranging from 1 (disagree strongly) to 5 (agree strongly), resulting in index values which ranged from 2 (very low risk perception) to 10 (very high risk perception). The index had a Cronbach's reliability coefficient of 0.91, reflecting the high intercorrelation between the two component items. For purposes of summarizing results in tabular form, the index scores were recoded into low perceived risk (scores 2-4), intermediate perceived risk (scores 5-7) and high perceived risk (scores 8-10) categories.

As indicated in figure 5.2, residents generally perceive high levels of risk from waste facility siting and operation. Only 21.8 percent of residents in the aggregated sample perceived low levels of risk, while 46.7 percent perceived high levels of risk. However, risk perception levels were markedly different across the four types of study communities (table 5.4). In waste operating and waste siting communities, the proportions of residents perceiving risks as low were three to four times those observed in the nonwaste development and control communities. Similarly, the proportions perceiving high risks were 14 to 23 percent higher in the nonwaste development and control communities. Local experience with waste siting and operation apparently contributes to reduced levels of perceived risk. Although it might be argued that perceptions of lower risk in such areas simply reflect resignation to the need to adjust

Table 5.3: Favorability Toward Siting by Resident/Leader Status and Community Type

Response (%)[*]	Waste Operating		Waste Siting		Nonwaste Development		Control (Baseline)	
	Resident	Leader	Resident	Leader	Resident	Leader	Resident	Leader
Oppose Siting	41.9	9.5	39.7	21.1	67.6	54.4	64.0	47.1
Neither Favor/Oppose Siting	21.9	4.8	11.9	7.9	17.7	24.6	16.1	15.7
Favor Siting	36.2	85.7	48.4	71.0	14.7	21.0	19.9	37.2
N	384	42	310	38	442	57	422	51
χ^2	38.4***		7.0**		4.0		8.4**	
Cramer's V	0.30		0.14		0.09		0.13	
Tau-c	0.18		0.09		0.05		0.08	

*Percentages may not equal 100.0 percent because of rounding.

** $p \leq .05$, *** $p \leq .001$

Figure 5.2: Residents' Perceived Level of Risk

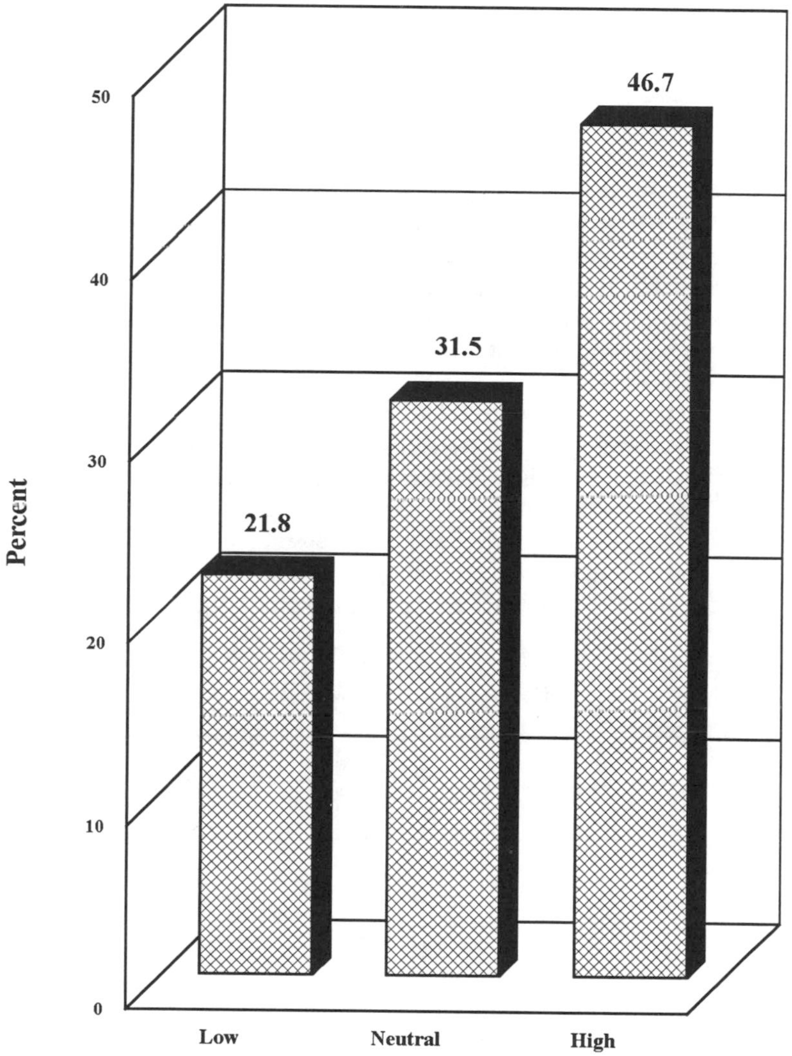

to and live with the presence of a hazardous waste facility, the fact that lower risk perceptions are evident in waste siting as well as waste operating communities suggests that other factors may be operating as well.

The general tendency for leaders to express lower levels of concern about hazardous facility siting is also evident in the data on risk perceptions. However, as is the case among residents, there are differences in leaders' responses across the four types of study communities. Thus, whereas 76.2 percent of leaders in waste operating and 57.9 percent in waste siting communities perceived low levels of risk, only 21.1 percent of leaders in nonwaste development and 30.2 percent in control communities perceived that the risks associated with hazardous waste facilities would be low. Similarly, while 30.9 percent of residents in waste operating and 40.0 percent in waste siting communities perceived low levels of risk, only 10.0 and 12.4 percent of residents in the nonwaste and control communities respectively perceived low levels of risk. Leadership status clearly accentuates differences relative to perceptions of risk, with substantial community differences evident in the response tendencies among both leaders and other residents.

The data in table 5.5 show the relationship between risk perceptions and favorability toward siting among residents of the study areas. The results in this table indicate that there is a statistically significant and relatively strong relationship between perceptions of risk and opposition to waste facility siting. Among residents who perceived high levels of risk, 79.2 percent were opposed to waste facility siting. In contrast, among those perceiving low levels of risk, only 20.7 percent were opposed to siting such facilities in or

Table 5.4: Perceived Level of Risk by Community Type

Level (%*)	Waste Operating	Waste Siting	Nonwaste Development	Control (Baseline)
Low	30.9	40.0	10.0	12.4
Neutral	30.9	25.3	32.6	35.5
High	38.2	34.7	57.4	52.1
N	389	320	448	434
χ^2	144.7 **			
Cramer's V	.21			
Tau-c	.17			

*Percentages may not equal 100.0 percent because of rounding.

**p≤.001

Table 5.5: Favorability Toward Waste Siting by Perceived Level of Risk

Response (%*)	Perceived Level of Risk		
	Low	Neutral	High
Oppose Siting	20.7	41.7	79.2
Neither Favor/Oppose	11.4	27.7	12.9
Favor Siting	67.9	30.6	7.9
N	343	480	735
χ^2	514.8 **		
Cramer's V	.41		
Tau-b	-.45		

*Percentages may not equal 100.0 percent because of rounding.
**p≤.001

near their communities. The bivariate (Pearson's) correlation between these two variables was -.59 (p<.0001), further indicating the tendency for risk perceptions to be highly associated with concerns about siting. Clearly concerns about the potential health and safety risks of waste storage and disposal facilities comprise a key social impact of such projects, and a major contributor to the high levels of controversy and local opposition that emerge in some areas where such facilities are proposed.

Factors Affected by the Waste Facility Siting Process

Albrecht et al. (1996), Murdock et al. (1983b, 1991), and Krannich and Albrecht (1995) among others have argued that how the process of siting a development project unfolds in specific siting episodes can be a key determinant of how residents perceive waste-related facilities. For example, siting processes that are viewed by local residents as being reasonably fair and equitable and that produce relatively low levels of conflict at the local level will presumably result in fewer negative community impacts, with a resulting reduction in community opposition to waste facilities. In this section, we examine the issue of equity, patterns of community conflict, and perspectives on the economic effects of waste facilities as dimensions of the waste facility siting process that may have important ramifications for the ultimate success or failure of siting efforts.

Equity/Fairness Concerns

Concerns about the equity and fairness of hazardous waste facility siting appear to underlie much of the local opposition to proposed waste facility developments. As Albrecht (1995,67) has observed, "concerns about equity have moved to center stage in the ongoing debate" over current and future directions for a variety of environmental policy issues, including hazardous waste management. Several researchers focusing specifically on hazardous and radioactive waste disposal have observed that the perceived equity of siting these types of facilities exerts substantial influence on local response (Easterling and Kunreuther 1995; Kasperson 1990; Shrader-Frechette 1993).

Equity and fairness issues can arise in response to waste facility siting for a variety of reasons. First, there is often a spatial or geographical distinction in the distribution of benefits and costs associated with waste production and waste disposal processes. The siting of any centralized hazardous waste management facility inevitably imposes potential risks and costs to a single host area targeted for the storage or disposal of hazardous byproducts from industrial processes benefitting a larger region or even an entire society. As a result, concerns about "distributional equity" can arise among host-area residents who feel that they have been unfairly asked to bear the negative consequences of industrial processes or activities that may be perceived as generating few, if any, direct benefits to the local area (Easterling and Kunreuther 1995; Gerrard 1994).

In many cases, equity concerns are also associated with the tendency for noxious and hazardous facilities to be sited in areas characterized by a concentration of minority and poor populations (see Bullard 1990). Equity concerns also emerge in response to waste management policies and processes that may be viewed as transferring the risks of hazardous materials from current to future generations (see Gerrard 1994; Kraft and Clary 1993). Finally, "procedural" equity concerns can arise in response to perceptions about the relative fairness or unfairness of the site selection and decision-making processes by which waste facility siting decisions occur (Easterling and Kunreuther 1995).

In short, concerns about equity and fairness can occur for a variety of reasons involving perceptions about inequities in the distribution of potentially negative effects of siting and operating hazardous waste management projects. While equity considerations involve a potentially complex array of specific issues and concerns, our investigation of this issue is based on a relatively general treatment. The survey questionnaires administered to community leaders and residents in the waste operating and waste siting study areas contained a question pertaining to the issue of fairness or equity in the siting of hazardous waste management facilities. A parallel question was not included in the surveys of leaders or residents in the nonwaste development and control areas, since in those areas respondents had no direct experience with the siting of a hazardous waste facility.

For both leaders and residents, survey participants were asked to respond to the following question: "Overall, do you think that the siting of (the facility) is fair to all the parties involved?" Responses were recorded on a five-point numeric scale, with values ranging from 1 (Completely Unfair) to 5 (Completely Fair). In an open-ended follow-up to this question, respondents were encouraged to provide additional qualitative information regarding their observations about the fairness of the siting process. Clearly, this measurement approach does not distinguish between the various dimensions of distributional and procedural equity noted above. Rather, it is used as a "global" indicator of the overall degree to which equity concerns may have emerged in response to hazardous waste facility siting and operation in the various study areas considered here.

Table 5.6 summarizes the joint frequency distributions for residents' responses to the fairness question across the waste operating and waste siting study areas. Response distributions indicate a broad range of opinion among local residents regarding the fairness of waste facility siting. For both waste operating and waste siting areas, about 21-22 percent of responses were on the "unfair" side of the scale midpoint (e.g., response values of 1 or 2), while about 40 percent were on the "fair" side of the scale (response values of 4 or 5). In both types of areas, the most common response was the scale midpoint, indicating substantial uncertainty or ambivalence about siting fairness. Overall, there was neither a statistically nor substantively significant difference in response patterns across the two types of study areas, and the mean response values were nearly identical (3.28 for waste operating and 3.24 for waste siting communities).

Responses to the open-ended follow-up question that asked respondents to explain their views about the fairness of facility siting included a broad range of themes, few of which were noted by more than a handful of respondents. Among the more frequently noted negative comments were concerns that the outcome of the siting decision was determined by extra local political interests, that the project would result in negative effects on the community's environment, that equity/fairness issues were never taken into account in decisions about facility siting, and various expressions of general dissatisfaction with the outcome of the siting process. Those who offered positive statements most frequently offered either general comments indicating that they considered the outcome fair or observed that the siting process had adequately addressed geological and safety criteria.

The analysis of possible differences in the perceptions of community leaders and residents regarding the fairness of waste facility siting was conducted first for the aggregated sample of respondents from the waste operating and waste siting areas, then separately within each of the study area

Table 5.6: Perceived Fairness of Waste Facility Siting by Community Type

Fairness of Siting (%*)	Waste Operating	Waste Siting
Completely Unfair (1)	10.8	16.2
(2)	10.3	6.2
Neither Unfair/Fair (3)	38.8	37.5
(4)	20.8	17.5
Completely Fair (5)	19.4	22.7
N	351	291
x^2	8.3	
Cramer's V	.11	
r^a	-.01	

*Percentages may not equal 100.0 percent because of rounding.

aBased on uncollapsed values

types. When data for both sets of study areas were combined, this comparison indicated that residents were somewhat less likely than community leaders to indicate that the siting of local waste facilities was fair. Interestingly, only a minority of either leaders (about 19 percent) or residents (about 22 percent) selected a response value on the "unfair" side of the response scale. However, the proportion of resident responses falling at the midpoint of the scale (38 percent) was more than twice as high as was the case among members of the local leader samples (15 percent), clearly indicating a higher degree of uncertainty or ambivalence on the part of residents. Leaders were substantially more likely than residents to perceive waste facility siting as having been fair; about two-thirds of leaders' responses were on the "fair" side of the response scale, while only about 40 percent of residents indicated that they thought siting of the local waste facility had been either mostly or completely fair. The mean response value for leaders (3.69) was significantly (F=8.16, p=.004) higher than that for residents (3.26).

The results summarized in table 5.7 indicate that the magnitude of leader/resident differences regarding the perceived fairness of waste facility siting does differ substantially between the waste operating and waste siting areas. Specifically, when the waste operating areas are considered separately, the difference between leaders and residents is greater than is the case for the waste siting areas. About 75 percent of the community leader respondents from the waste operating study areas considered facility siting to have been either mostly or completely fair, while only about 40 percent of residents in those study areas felt that the siting had been fair. For these waste operating

Table 5.7: Perceived Fairness of Waste Facility Siting by Resident/Leader Status of Respondent, Controlling for Community Type

Fairness of Siting (%*)	Waste Operating		Waste Siting	
	Resident	Leader	Resident	Leader
Completely Unfair (1)	10.8	9.8	16.2	8.1
(2)	10.3	2.4	6.2	18.9
Neither Unfair/Fair (3)	38.9	12.2	37.5	18.9
(4)	20.8	31.7	17.5	35.1
Completely Fair (5)	19.4	43.9	22.7	18.9
N	351	41	291	37
χ^2	21.7***		17.0**	
Cramer's V	.24		.23	
r^a	.18		.03	

*Percentages may not equal 100.0 percent because of rounding.

**p≤.01,   ***p≤.001

aBased on uncollapsed values

communities there is a statistically significant, albeit modest, overall association between the resident/leader variable and perceived fairness.

In contrast, resident/leader distinctions are attenuated somewhat in the case of the waste siting areas. For these community areas, about 54 percent of leaders and 40 percent of residents considered the siting activity to have been mostly or completely fair. Residents were still substantially more likely to express ambivalence about siting fairness, as they were twice as likely as leaders to select the response value corresponding to the scale midpoint. The small size of the community leaders sample influences statistical tests in ways that necessitate substantial caution in interpreting the results of these comparisons. However, it appears that the association between the resident/leader variable and perceived fairness is fairly weak in the case of those study areas where waste facility siting efforts were occurring but had not yet evolved into the establishment of an operating waste management facility.

As indicated in table 5.8, there is a substantial association between the views of residents in these study communities about the fairness of waste facility siting and their responses regarding the idea of voting in support of having the waste facility sited near their community. Nearly all (88.2 percent) of the respondents who considered the siting process to be "Completely Unfair" also indicated strong disagreement or opposition to the possibility of voting in favor of such a facility. In contrast, more than 80 percent of those who felt that the siting process had been "Completely Fair" indicated support for voting in favor of the facility. Overall the association between these variables is highly significant, with the Pearson's correlation (r =.56) indicating the presence of a fairly strong relationship.

The results derived from this part of the analysis clearly indicate that the perceived equity or fairness of waste facility siting is an important correlate of public support or opposition to the development and operation of such facilities. In both the waste facility siting and operating study areas, residents were generally more likely to consider the siting process to be fair as opposed to unfair. However, a substantial minority did have concerns about fairness, and an even larger proportion expressed some degree of ambivalence about the fairness of siting the facility that was affecting their community. Relatively little support for facility development was evident among those who expressed such reservations.

The results also suggest that differing views about equity and fairness in waste facility siting may contribute to substantial tensions between local residents and community leaders who are often more directly involved in discussions and negotiations with representatives from waste industries and nonlocal regulatory agencies. The tendency for local leaders to have more positive impressions than residents about the fairness of siting processes may be due to their closer involvement in actual negotiation and decision-making activities. Nevertheless, the tendency for residents to be more critical about the fairness and equity of facility siting may be one factor contributing

Table 5.8: Favorability Toward Waste Facility Siting by Response to Fairness/Equity Question

Vote/Will Build (%*)	Completely Unfair (1)	(2)	(3)	(4)	Completely Fair (5)
Oppose Siting	88.2	60.4	46.0	15.7	10.6
Neither Favor/Oppose	2.4	17.0	24.3	21.5	9.1
Favor Siting	9.4	22.6	29.7	62.8	80.3
N	85	53	239	121	132
χ^2	296.0**				
Tau-c	.49				
r^a	.56				

*Percentages may not equal 100.0 percent because of rounding.

**p≤.001

aBased on uncollapsed values

to the intracommunity conflict and tension that have often erupted in areas where such facilities are proposed or developed.

Responses to Levels of Social Conflict

Hazardous waste management is increasingly reported to be a source of social conflict for rural community areas where waste facilities exist or are proposed (Benford et al. 1993; Fitchen 1991). However, the patterns of community-level conflict over the siting and operation of facilities that are perceived to pose new or unusual risks to the well-being of local residents remain poorly understood.

One initial source of conflict in communities facing hazardous facility developments may emerge from competing efforts on the part of different groups to define or frame the issues and risks at hand (Reich 1991; Walsh, Warland, and Smith 1997). A variety of organizations external to the community—a state or federal regulatory agency, or an operating firm headquartered elsewhere for example—may have formal decision-making authority in the local area. Thus, control over organizational processes and consequences of decisions may lie beyond those most directly affected (Manning 1992). Organizations responsible for waste management and regulation often "institutionalize" risk by focusing on its more calculable elements (Reiss 1992). On the other hand, local residents tend to express concerns about risk in broader, more intuitive ways, such as by origin, distributive equity, and projected effects on future generations (Margolis 1996). Thus, conflicts between "external" organizations and the local community tend to emerge in part from different interpretations of the probabilities of harm, rather than from a lack of technical understanding on the part of local residents and organizations.

Conflict may also arise between community groups and local government entities. Kasperson et al. (1992) suggest that a growing general distrust of government along with heightened concerns about safety and environmental protection have in recent decades contributed to increased community conflict in response to hazardous facility proposals. Despite the fact that residents often have greater levels of trust in local than in nonlocal entities, local government is frequently perceived as having dual, conflicting roles in the case of hazardous facility development. Paradoxically, "internal" organizations such as the local government may be viewed simultaneously as being responsible for protecting the community from harm as well as being the party responsible for allowing or supporting exposure to a new risk (Edelstein 1988).

Social conflict related to hazardous waste management may also be manifested in relationships between communities. At one level, intercommunity conflict may result from competition for development resources and benefits, or over disputes about environmental boundaries and the dispersion of potential impacts. Media coverage of hazardous waste management and communications between groups about perceived risk may fuel conflict through the social amplification of risk (Renn et al. 1992). This process of amplification may heighten the perception of differential impacts from one community to another (Benford et al. 1993). Further, long-standing rivalries between communities may re-emerge and broaden the scope of intercommunity tensions, even if the initial tensions were essentially unrelated to hazardous waste management.

Hazardous waste management appears related to a number of other patterns of social conflict that are internal to affected communities. The proposal for a new facility or responses to concerns or problems associated with an existing operation may result in substantial divisiveness among existing as well as new community factions, contributing in some circumstances to the emergence of highly "corrosive" intracommunity effects (Kroll-Smith and Couch 1992). Technological risks may pose a threat to the social fabric of the community because they are perceived to jeopardize the collective sense of place (Fitchen 1991) and threaten the fundamental human relationship to the surrounding environment (Kroll-Smith and Couch 1991). In this context, changes in patterns of interaction involving those who hold divergent views about the acceptability of a waste facility can range from avoidance, shunning, and disregard for one another to more serious hostility, threats, and various forms of aggression (Kroll-Smith and Couch 1990; Rocky Mountain Social Science 1992). Social conflict of this caliber may also tend to have adverse effects on the collective morale of groups within a community (Edelstein 1988). Concerns about a community's identity or image may become grounds for further conflict if an area becomes stigmatized (above and beyond the perceived dangers associated with hazardous waste management) as a highly contentious place where people do not get along with one another (Wulfhorst 1997).

Survey participants were asked to respond to five measures of social conflict related to local commercial and industrial developments, in some cases including the siting and operation of hazardous waste management facilities.[1] Respondents rated the level of conflict they perceived for the following items: (1) between people in your community and local industries; (2) between people in your community and state government agencies; (3) between people in your community and the local government; (4) between people in your community and other communities; and (5) among members of your community. The response category scale for each of these five items ranged from "No Conflict" (1) to "Substantial Conflict" (5).

In addition to the individual measures of conflict, a composite index was created to provide a single, summary indicator of respondents' overall perceived level of conflict related to hazardous waste facilities or other local industrial developments. The summated index was internally consistent as verified by interitem correlations among the five individual measures (ranging between .44 and .65) and a high Cronbach's alpha coefficient (.85). Values for the index ranged from 5, indicating lower levels of conflict, to 25, indicating higher levels of conflict. To simplify presentation of the tabular results, the index response values were collapsed back to the original 1-5 scale categories, indicated by "1" (5-8, "virtually no conflict"), "2" (9-12), "3" (13-17), "4" (18-21), and "5" (22-25, "substantial conflict") for that portion of the analysis.

Figure 5.3 summarizes the combined responses of residents to the several conflict measures for all of the study areas, using the mean values of the distribution as a numeric indicator for each of the conflict measures. Ranging from 2.7 to 2.9 on a 1-5 scale, the mean values reflect very little variation across the different dimensions of conflict. At either end of this range, levels of conflict between the community and local industries appear to be the lowest, while levels of conflict between the community and state regulatory agencies appear to be the highest. The mean values indicate overall moderate levels of conflict, with a slight tendency to perceive lower rather than higher levels of conflict for each of the individual dimensions under consideration. Although none of these distributions indicate high levels of disruption and discord when considering combined responses from this set of study areas, it is important to keep in mind that this initial examination based on the aggregated data may mask the presence of divisive conflict in some of the individual communities or in particular types of study areas.

Having noted the overall similarity in response patterns for the aggregated sample of community residents, we next turn our attention to potential differences in the patterns of response to the measures of conflict across the four types of study areas considered in this project. Due to the differential development contexts characterizing the various community types, we anticipated that responses to levels of conflict related to hazardous waste management/industrial development facilities would vary across the four categories. As an example, residents in a community experiencing the siting process of a waste-related industry may be more likely to respond with higher perceived levels of conflict within the community than residents of the "control" areas that are not facing major changes that could be expected to disrupt the local social context.

To compare differences by community type, each measure of conflict was first examined separately. Overall we found that the general patterns of response differences across the four community types were very similar for each of the individual conflict measures. Given those similarities and in the

Figure 5.3: Measures of Social Conflict in the Community

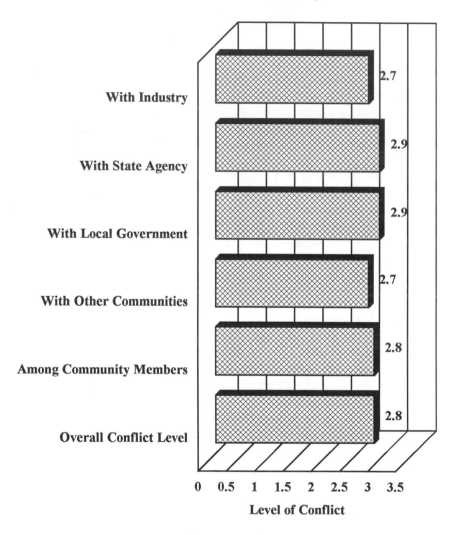

Level of Conflict

interest of streamlining the presentation of results, we have focused the comparisons presented here on the composite index as a more generalized and multidimensional measure of social conflict.

Table 5.9 summarizes differences in overall perceived levels of conflict across the four community types, as measured by the composite "conflict" index. As noted above, for tabular presentation and analysis the values for this summated index were collapsed to correspond to the original "No Conflict" (1) to "Substantial Conflict" (5) scale. The results of this comparison indicate that respondents from the communities currently experiencing a waste facility siting process appear to perceive substantially higher levels of conflict than those from nonwaste development or control areas, or those who live in communities with operating waste storage and/or disposal facilities. The degree of association between community type and level of conflict in the community is modest, but statistically significant.

This same relationship was further examined using one-way analysis of variance procedures, with the Tukey's test used to make comparisons across community types.[2] Those results indicated an overall statistically significant difference in index scores between the waste siting communities and each of the other three types of study areas. These results suggest that the process of siting a waste management facility tends to produce a substantial degree of social conflict in host communities. At the same time, the results also suggest that such conflicts are likely to dissipate once the siting process has been completed. Further support for this conclusion is provided by the absence of significant differences between the other three community categories,

Table 5.9: Response to Composite Conflict Index by Community Type

Response (%*)	Waste Operating	Waste Siting	Nonwaste Development	Control (Baseline)
No Conflict (1)	9.6	2.8	14.4	12.6
(2)	28.8	19.2	33.4	26.6
(3)	46.2	41.1	39.1	44.6
(4)	11.9	18.8	11.6	13.4
Substantial Conflict (5)	3.5	18.1	1.5	2.7
N	344	282	404	372
χ^2	144.7**			
Cramer's V	.19			

*Percentages may not equal 100.0 percent because of rounding.

**$p \leq .001$

including comparisons of both the nonwaste development and control communities with the waste operating communities. Overall, these results suggest that while substantial social conflicts often arise in host communities during the siting of waste disposal facilities, they are likely in most cases to be temporary. This may not be the case, however, if a postsiting occurrence leads to problems during operation.

The next phase of the analysis examined potential differences in residents' and community leaders' responses to the various dimensions of conflict in their communities. The resident/leader comparisons are initially based on response patterns obtained through analysis of the aggregated samples. A second analytic stage again controls for community type in order to assess whether this categorization has a conditional effect on differences between community resident and leader responses. Because this part of the analysis produced a more varied set of relationships across the five measures of conflict than was found in looking at the community-type differentiation, each individual measure along with the composite "conflict" index will be considered more thoroughly in this section.

As indicated by the first two data columns in table 5.10, community leaders are much more likely to perceive low levels of conflict between the community and local industries than is true for residents. Although residents were more likely to perceive little or no conflict (46 percent of responses were below the scale midpoint) as opposed to substantial conflict (21 percent of responses were above the midpoint), leaders overwhelmingly perceived little or no conflict (78 percent) between the operators of local industrial facilities and the community. This pattern supports the premise that community leaders are generally more supportive of commercial activity and economic development than is the general citizenry. When this resident/leader distinction in response to levels of community/industry conflict was elaborated by controlling for community type, the general tendency for leaders to perceive less conflict than residents remained evident in all four of the community categories. This relationship was especially pronounced in the waste operating and waste siting communities, with the most substantial differences in the latter. Thus, it appears that in communities impacted by the development of waste facilities, leaders are particularly likely to view the extent of conflict between industrial operations and the community as minimal.

In the case of conflict between the community and state regulatory agencies, responses of residents and leaders did differ, but less substantially (see table 5.10). Over 53 percent of leaders, compared to 33 percent of residents, perceived little or no conflict. Although this pattern held true when controlling for community type, the most substantial difference was found in

Table 5.10: Response to Levels of Conflict Between People in the Community and Other Groups by Resident/Leader Status of Respondent

Level of Conflict (%*)	Community/ Facility Conflict		Community/ State Government Conflict		Community/ Local Government Conflict		Inter-community Conflict		Intra-community Conflict		Conflict Index	
	Resident	Leader	Resident	Leader	Resident	Leader	Resident	Leader	Resident	Leader	Resident	Leader
No Conflict (1)	17.9	25.9	10.3	13.3	11.9	14.3	20.0	18.5	13.4	9.5	10.4	11.2
(2)	27.9	51.9	22.4	39.9	25.4	48.2	26.5	38.1	27.5	47.6	27.6	47.9
(3)	33.6	16.4	40.1	24.5	36.5	23.8	30.6	20.1	34.0	29.1	42.7	35.1
(4)	11.0	3.2	17.3	17.0	17.2	11.1	12.6	13.8	14.5	10.1	13.6	3.7
Substantial Conflict (5)	9.6	2.7	10.0	5.3	9.0	2.7	10.5	9.5	10.7	3.7	5.6	2.1
N	1,458	189	1,425	188	1,439	189	1,436	189	1,446	189	1,402	188
χ^2	72.3 ***		36.1 ***		51.4 ***		14.7 **		36.3 ***		42.0 ***	
Tau-c	-.13		-.07		-.10		-.02		-.06		-.10	
r^a	-.17		-.10		-.13		-.03		-.09		-.13	

*Percentages may not equal 100.0 percent because of rounding.

**p≤.01, ***p≤.001

^{a}Based on uncollapsed values.

the waste operating study areas. This finding is logical if we consider the possibility that conflict over specific ongoing regulatory issues may be greater in communities that already have an operating hazardous facility. Possibly due to a tendency to view community economic and fiscal benefits as more extensive, some leaders may be more likely than other citizens to overlook unresolved issues and citizen dissatisfaction regarding external regulators.

Results derived from the aggregated sample suggest that community residents and leaders also differ in their perceptions of conflict between the community and the local government. Again, leaders were less likely to report conflict than were residents. This general pattern held true when responses were examined controlling for community type.

Unlike other measures considered thus far, no meaningful difference existed between community residents and leaders over the issue of intercommunity conflict. Although table 5.10 shows a statistically significant difference between the two, the distributions reveal little meaningful variation despite the slight tendency for leaders to perceive less conflict overall. When this relationship was examined while controlling for community type, results for the waste operating community category indicated that leaders were noticeably more likely to perceive lower levels of intercommunity conflict than was the case among other residents. One interesting reversal occurs as well in the case of the waste siting community category, where leaders perceived higher degrees of conflict between their community and other communities than was the case among residents. This relationship could in part be a function of community leaders having more expansive ties to nonlocal networks as a result of their positions and thus being more aware of intercommunity issues and conflicts linked to deliberations about waste facility siting.

Although the distinctions are not as substantial as with some of the other measures, residents and leaders did differ somewhat in their responses about the degree of conflict among members of the community. Interestingly though, while leaders were only one-third as likely to perceive "Substantial Conflict" as residents, leaders were also slightly less likely to report "No Conflict." This same response pattern was borne out within each of the four community types. Although leaders were substantially more likely to report a low-to-moderate degree of conflict among community members, residents had higher response frequencies in the "No Conflict" category in each case. Additionally, controlling for community type indicated a difference between the waste and nonwaste community categories, at least in terms of responses in the "No Conflict" category. Both residents and leaders in the nonwaste development and baseline (control) communities were substantially more likely to respond in this category than were residents and leaders in either the waste operating or waste siting communities.

For the aggregated sample, the mean response value on the composite conflict index was 12.1 (leaders), compared to a mean of 13.9 among residents ($F=26.8$, $p \leq .001$). These values reinforce the observation that community leaders tend to be somewhat more likely than residents to respond in the little-to-no conflict range on the index, a finding that is also supported by the distributions for the collapsed index values reported in table 5.10. This pattern held true in three of the four community type categories, the exception being a less than clear pattern in the waste siting communities. Such findings correspond to the expectation that leaders will generally maintain a more positive outlook about their community, which would seem almost inevitable given their community roles. It may be in the interest of leaders to portray levels of conflict as minimal, or at least "controlled," so as not to provoke further concerns among a constituency of friends, clients, or voters and to depict their community as a viable and successful place. The differences between leaders' and residents' perceptions are less apparent in communities undergoing the process of siting a hazardous waste facility, perhaps because the uncertainties associated with anticipatory effects can exacerbate conflict among and between a variety of interest groups for both residents and leaders alike.

The final phase of this segment of the analysis involves an evaluation of the relationships between the measures of conflict in the community and the degree to which local residents either support or oppose development of a hazardous waste management facility in their area. Due to the statistical limitations on the number of community leader responses available, this portion of the analysis was based on only the community resident data.

In the interest of space, results of the comparisons between the support/opposition measure and the five individual conflict measures are not discussed in detail, largely because each of the relationships is quite similar. For each individual measure, the degree of association was found to be trivial, or very weak in the case of relationships involving the measure of intercommunity conflict and the measure of conflict between community residents and local government. The tendency across each of these measures was for more residents to strongly oppose building a waste facility in their area, regardless of the levels of conflict they perceived with respect to their communities. In general, the absence of any substantively meaningful relationships stems from the fact that those who perceived "No Conflict" were about as likely to oppose building a hazardous waste management facility as those who perceived substantial conflict. Likewise, although responses indicated much more limited support for waste facility development compared to opposition, among those who did support building such a facility, little variation in support/opposition existed between those who perceived no conflict and those reporting substantial conflict.

Table 5.11: Favorability Toward Waste Facility Siting by Response to Conflict Index

Response (%*)	No Conflict (1)	(2)	(3)	(4)	Substantial Conflict (5)
Oppose Siting	58.3	48.6	52.9	57.5	67.1
Neither Favor/Oppose	10.4	20.4	19.8	12.2	12.7
Favor Siting	31.3	31.1	27.4	30.3	20.3
N	144	383	592	188	79
χ^2	20.9 **				
Tau-c	-.04				
r^a	-.05				

*Percentages may not equal 100.0 percent because of rounding.

**p≤.01

aBased on uncollapsed values.

The overall pattern of these relationships is summarized in table 5.11, which is a joint frequency distribution between the composite conflict index and the measure of whether respondents favored or opposed building a waste facility. Again, although the differences are statistically significant, little substantive relationship exists in the patterns borne out in the distribution. However, the index distribution compared with the favorability item does illustrate a slight tendency among those who supported building a waste facility to perceive less conflict than those who were opposed; conversely, those who strongly opposed building a facility had a slight tendency to perceive higher levels of conflict than those who favored building a facility.

Community-based conflict, in some form, has often emerged in association with attempts to site and/or operate a variety of large-scale industrial projects, including hazardous waste management facilities, in rural communities. The conflict appears in some cases to have resulted in substantial change in social interaction patterns. Although results from this section of the study generally indicate a moderate rather than high degree of conflict across the four community study categories, conflict was especially evident in the waste siting communities, as a result of negotiating the location, safety standards, and operating conditions of a hazardous facility. Interestingly, the waste operating community category was consistently more similar to the nonwaste and "control" community categories across the different dimensions of conflict. Only the waste siting community category stood out as exhibiting elevated conflict levels. These findings suggest that conflict-related impacts on communities identified as potential hazardous waste sites may not be of long-term duration. However, this does not nullify or decrease the importance of attending to concerns related to the effects of siting a hazardous waste management project on local social relations and structures. Because conflicts that emerge in host community areas during the siting process may be extremely intense and divisive, attention needs to be directed where possible toward conflict management procedures and other programs designed to minimize disruptions to the local social structures and processes.

Community Economic Effects

Concerns about the instability of economic activities and opportunities are pervasive in many rural areas across the United States. Long-term patterns of decline in agriculture, extractive industries, and other traditional economic sectors have affected many rural areas, and have contributed to high rates of rural poverty, high rates of outmigration, long-term patterns of population decline, deteriorating levels of infrastructure and public services, and a general deterioration in the viability of many rural communities. Under such circumstances, there is a tendency in many rural areas for residents and leaders to support virtually any project perceived to bring with it economic development potential, even if that project might otherwise be considered undesirable in terms of possible effects on environmental quality, traditional land use patterns, or public health and safety (see Bourke 1994; Freudenburg 1992; Krannich and Luloff 1991). In many instances facilities employing even modest numbers of workers at reasonably attractive pay scales are viewed as the potential salvation of communities that have few if any other prospects for meaningful economic development. For these reasons rural areas have frequently been considered prime candidates for the siting of hazardous and noxious facilities, on the assumption that local economic development concerns will result in higher acceptability for projects that may be considered much less desirable in more stable and prosperous areas (see Cerrell Associates 1984).

At the same time, the potential for such facilities to have adverse effects on local economic conditions and future development prospects is often a strong deterrent to local acceptance of facility siting proposals (Easterling and Kunreuther 1995; Slovic et al. 1991). The risks of possible economic stigmatization effects on locally produced agricultural products can be an issue of substantial concern in areas that remain highly dependent on the marketing of locally produced crops or livestock. Similarly, stigmatization of an area as "dangerous" or "contaminated" can potentially undermine the prospects for future development involving other forms of commercial or industrial investment and growth in the local area. Although there is little evidence that such effects occur with substantial frequency (Murdock et al. 1991) to the extent that such effects do occur, affected communities may experience reduced prospects for increases in income levels and employment opportunities, and generally constrained prospects for economic growth and development.

Given these divergent perspectives and prospects regarding economic consequences of hazardous facility developments, survey respondents were asked to consider three survey items designed to address the potential economic effects of having such a facility developed in or near their communities. (1) A waste facility is economically beneficial to a community; (2) the presence of a waste facility encourages other industries to locate in the surrounding area; and (3) a waste facility results in a decrease in property values in the surrounding area. Responses were recorded on a five-point measurement scale with values ranging from 1 (disagree strongly) to 5 (agree strongly); responses to the property values question were reverse coded to correspond with the direction of responses to the other two items. These three items were then used to create a single summary measure of perceived economic impacts of hazardous waste facility siting, with response values ranging from a low of 3 (indicating extremely strong disagreement with the idea that economic effects would be positive) to 15 (indicating extremely strong agreement with the idea that economic effects would be positive). The alpha reliability coefficient for the resulting summated index was .69, reflecting an acceptable level of internal consistency in the patterns of response to the three component items. For tabular presentation these values were collapsed into five categories indicating very strong disagreement (index scores of 3-4), moderate disagreement (scores of 5-7), ambivalence (scores of 8-10), moderate agreement (scores of 11-13), and very strong agreement (scores of 14-15).

As indicated in figure 5.4, relatively few respondents expressed a belief that the overall economic effects of a hazardous waste facility on their community would be either extremely positive or extremely negative. For the aggregated sample drawn from the full set of study communities only 3 percent of residents indicated very strong disagreement with the suggestion that waste facility development would have beneficial economic effects. Likewise, only 3.1 percent expressed strong agreement. There was an overall tendency for more respondents to be optimistic rather than pessimistic about such effects: about one-third (33.4 percent) of responses fell in the moderate agreement category, more than twice the proportion that expressed moderate disagreement (15.7 percent). A plurality of response values (44.8 percent) fell in the middle portion of the index range, indicating substantial uncertainty or ambivalence about the probable economic effects of waste facility siting on local economic conditions.

Figure 5.4: Residents' Level of Agreement That a Waste Facility Would Have Beneficial Economic Effects*

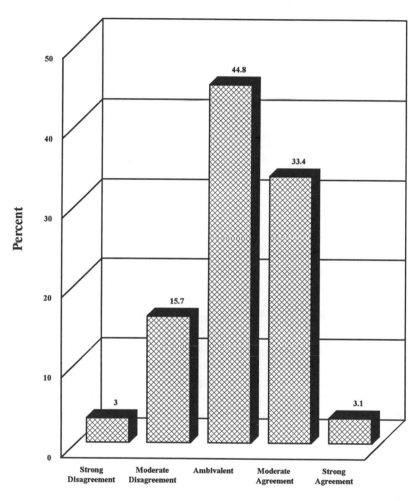

*Based on composite index values

Table 5.12: Residents' Agreement that Economic Effects of Waste Facility
Developments Are Positive, by Community Type

Response (%[*])	Waste Operating	Waste Siting	Nonwaste Development	Control (Baseline)
Strong Disagreement	1.9	3.6	3.3	3.2
Moderate Disagreement	10.9	16.7	18.5	16.5
Ambivalence	48.4	16.7	18.5	16.5
Moderate Agreement	37.2	33.8	32.3	30.8
Strong Agreement	1.6	2.0	4.5	3.7
N	376	305	421	406
χ^2	22.5**			
Cramer's V	.07			

[*]Percentages may not equal 100.0 percent because of rounding.

**$p \leq .05$

As indicated in table 5.12, there were only limited differences in
expectations about community economic effects of waste facility siting across
the four types of study communities. The highest proportion of respondents
indicating moderate to strong agreement that economic effects would be
positive occurred in the waste operating communities (38.8 percent), while
the lowest proportion of respondents indicating moderate to strong agreement
occurred in the control communities (34.5 percent). The proportions of
respondents indicating moderate to strong disagreement that economic
impacts would be positive ranged from a low of 12.8 percent in the waste
operating communities to a high of 21.8 percent in the nonwaste development
areas. In all areas the largest single response category on the summated index
was the middle category indicating uncertainty or ambivalence about
economic effects: across the four community types 41.3 percent to 48.4
percent of responses fell into that category.

Overall, there were only limited differences in the response tendencies of
residents and community leaders with respect to expectations about the
economic effects of waste facility developments. About 36.5 percent of
residents indicated moderate to strong agreement that economic effects would
be positive, compared to about 40.1 percent of community leaders. For both
groups a minority of residents (18.7 percent) and leaders (12.8 percent)
expressed strong disagreement with the premise that economic effects would
be positive. High levels of uncertainty and ambivalence were evident among
both residents (44.8 percent of responses) and leaders (47.1 percent). This

Table 5.13: Agreement that Economic Effects of Waste Facility Developments Are Positive by Resident/Leader Status and Community Type

Response (%)[*]	Waste Operating		Waste Siting		Nonwaste Development		Control (Baseline)	
	Resident	Leader	Resident	Leader	Resident	Leader	Resident	Leader
Strong Disagreement	1.9	0.0	3.6	5.3	3.3	0.0	3.2	0.0
Moderate Disagreement	10.9	9.5	16.7	10.5	18.5	12.3	16.5	14.0
Ambivalence	48.4	45.2	43.9	55.3	41.3	50.9	45.8	38.0
Moderate Agreement	37.2	45.2	33.8	26.3	32.3	35.1	30.8	46.0
Strong Agreement	1.6	0.0	2.0	2.6	4.5	1.8	3.7	2.0
N	376	42	305	38	421	57	406	50
x^2	2.73		2.67		5.11		5.92	
Cramer's V	.07		.09		.10		.11	

[*]Percentages may not equal 100.0 percent because of rounding.

general pattern was evident for the resident/leader comparisons across the four community types, although the small number of cases in the leader category requires caution in interpreting the results. As indicated in table 5.13, in nearly all cases the single largest response category for both residents and leaders included the middle range of the economic effects index, indicating uncertainty or ambivalence. Among residents, levels of agreement that economic effects of a hazardous waste facility would be positive were lowest in the control communities (34.5 percent) and highest in the waste operating communities (38.8 percent). Among leaders, agreement that economic impacts would be positive was lowest in the waste siting communities (29 percent) and highest in the control communities (48 percent).

Table 5.14 summarizes the relationship between the measure of anticipated economic effects of hazardous facility developments and the measure of favorability toward facility siting among resident respondents. Among those respondents who indicated strong disagreement that economic effects would be positive, 89 percent indicated very low favorability toward waste facility siting and none indicated very high favorability. Similarly, those who indicated moderate disagreement that economic effects would be positive tended overwhelmingly to indicate either very low (78.1 percent) or moderately low (5.1 percent) favorability. In contrast, among respondents who were moderately or strongly in agreement with the statement that the economic effects of a waste facility on their community would be positive there were higher proportions favoring siting. For example, among those who indicated moderate agreement, roughly 41 percent of responses reflected

Table 5.14: Favorability Toward Waste Facility Siting by Agreement that Economic Effects of Waste Facilities Are Positive

Response (%[*])	Strong Disagreement	Moderate Disagreement	Ambivalance	Moderate Agreement	Strong Agreement
Strongly Oppose	88.6	78.1	41.5	28.9	32.6
Moderately Oppose	0.0	5.1	11.2	12.6	8.7
Neither Favor/Oppose	9.1	7.2	19.6	19.4	17.4
Moderately Oppose	2.3	4.6	13.6	14.2	15.2
Strongly Favor	0.0	5.1	14.1	24.9	26.1
N	44	237	662	499	46
χ^2	214.35 **				
r[a]	-.32 **				

[*]Percentages may not equal 100.0 percent because of rounding.

**$p \leq .01$

[a]Based on uncollapsed values.

very low or moderately low favorability, with an almost identical percentage indicating moderately or very high favorability toward facility siting. Overall, there was a moderate correlation ($r = .32$) between the measure of anticipated economic effects and the favorability measure.

Knowledge and Attitudinal Factors Affecting Perceptions of Waste Projects

One of the factors often believed to affect perceptions of waste projects involves knowledge about waste storage technologies and waste management procedures (Desvousges et al. 1993; Kraft and Clary 1993; Portney 1991). Although it has been widely held by the waste management industry that improving public knowledge would increase levels of acceptance and change images of waste-related impacts, there is considerable debate about whether increased knowledge is associated with more or less opposition to waste siting. While Flynn et al. (1994) and Desvousges et al. (1993) indicate that increased knowledge generally contributes to higher levels of acceptance, Cotgrove (1982) and Portney (1991) indicate that increased knowledge is associated with decreased levels of acceptance. Relationships involving levels of knowledge about waste management issues are thus worthy of further examination.

In this analysis, we utilize a summated index based on answers to four questionnaire items that jointly measured several aspects of knowledge about hazardous waste management. The index scores were derived by summing the number of correct responses to the following statements:

1. Nearly all industries can achieve a level of zero waste production if they use available waste control and antipollution devices.

2. The permit that allows a waste management facility to dispose of hazardous waste also allows it to store radioactive waste.

3. In the United States, nearly all high-level radioactive waste from nuclear power plants is now being taken to be stored in a special underground facility.

4. In the United States, the federal agency with the primary responsibility for enforcing pollution laws is:
   a. Federal Emergency Management Administration (FEMA)
   b. Environmental Protection Agency (EPA)
   c. U.S. Fish and Wildlife Service
   d. Bureau of Land Management
   e. Office of Technology Assessment.

Respondents were given one point for each correct answer, resulting in possible index values ranging from 0 (no correct answers) to 4 (all correct answers). Thus respondents answering no to the first three items and indicating the Environmental Protection Agency in response to the fourth item were given a score of four. Although these were relatively simple questions for anyone familiar with waste storage, there was substantial variation in respondents' scores. As indicated in figure 5.5, levels of knowledge were generally quite low. Over one-fourth of respondents obtained scores of 0, indicating a failure to answer any of the questions correctly. An additional 37.6 percent answered only one of the four items correctly. On the other hand, only 4.2 percent of respondents answered all four questions correctly.

A comparison of response patterns across the four types of study areas suggested the presence of a weak relationship between higher levels of knowledge and community type. Thus, whereas more than 23 percent of residents in waste operating areas obtained scores of 3 or 4, the percentage of respondents obtaining such "high knowledge" scores was only 14 percent in the waste siting areas, 12.3 percent in the nonwaste development communities, and 11.3 percent in the control communities. Apparently it is primarily longer-term experience with waste facility developments that is associated with increased knowledge about waste management issues, since residents in the waste siting areas were only slightly more likely than residents in the two categories of communities not affected by waste facility projects to score 3 or 4 on the knowledge measure.

Comparisons of leader and resident responses indicated that leaders are generally more knowledgeable about waste siting and management than are other community residents. For the aggregated sample, leaders were more than twice as likely to score either 3 or 4 on the knowledge index than were residents (38.9 percent of leaders compared to 15 percent of residents). When the leader/resident comparisons were considered separately for each community type, the results indicated that higher levels of knowledge among leaders were especially pronounced in the waste operating communities and, to a lesser extent, in the waste siting communities. Over 71 percent of leaders in waste operating communities and roughly 44 percent in waste siting communities scored either 3 or 4 on the knowledge measure, compared to 23.4 percent and 14 percent of residents in those areas, respectively. In contrast, scores of 3 or 4 were obtained by 29.9 percent of leaders and 12.1 percent of residents in the nonwaste development areas, and by only 18.9 percent of leaders and 11.3 percent of residents in the control communities.

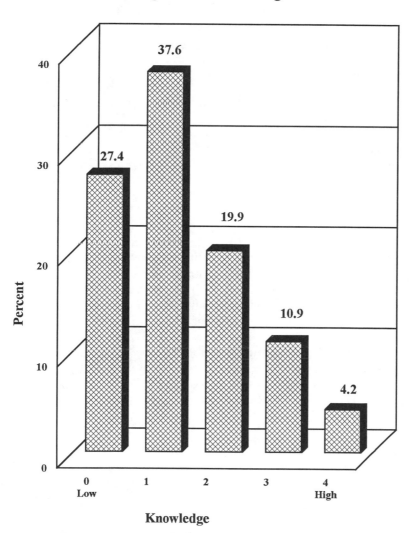

Figure 5.5: Residents' Level of General Knowledge of Waste Management

Table 5.15: Residents' Favorability Toward Siting by General Knowledge of
Waste Management

Response	Level of Knowledge				
	(Low)				(High)
(%*)	0	1	2	3	4
Oppose Siting	57.9	57.3	52.4	43.0	53.9
Neither Favor/Oppose	15.2	19.6	15.1	19.8	9.2
Favor Siting	26.9	23.1	32.5	37.2	36.9
N	420	590	311	172	65
χ^2	27.5 **				
Cramer's V	.09				
Tau-c	.07				

*Percentages may not equal 100.0 percent because of rounding.

**$p \leq .001$

The results reported in table 5.15 show that residents' levels of knowledge are not strongly related to favorability toward waste facility siting. Although 36.9 percent of those with perfect knowledge scores of 4 favored siting compared to 26.9 percent of those with low scores, the measures of association indicate that the relationship is quite weak. In addition, relative to opposition to siting, the percentage differences were very small, with 57.9 percent of those with scores of 0 opposing siting and 53.9 percent of those with scores of 4 opposing siting. However, it is noteworthy that those with the highest levels of knowledge were much less likely to have a neutral response than were other residents. This may suggest that both the strongest opponents and the strongest supporters of waste siting have obtained the highest levels of knowledge about waste management issues.

Relationships Involving Confidence in Technology

Some of the social concerns associated with proposed waste facility developments revolve around public confidence in scientific and technological solutions. Advanced industrial societies are characterized by a culture "in which technology has become not just the material basis for society, but in a real sense, its social and ideological model as well" (Segal 1994, 3). Supported by the "objectivity" of science, technological growth has contributed to a context in which the values of freedom and convenience became equated with material abundance (Piller 1991). Convenience, as the social outgrowth of technological progress, has become a core value of modernity (Tierney 1993).

At the same time, technology is viewed by many as problematic. Thayer (1994, 49) describes ambivalence toward technological systems as an emerging phenomenon of technophobia or "the suspicion, fear, aversion, and environmental guilt associated with high-technology." Public fears about technology and its consequences are paradoxical, as technology is conventionally thought of as perpetually advancing and improving (Winner 1977). But those with technophobic concerns not only critique high technology as representing false notions of perpetual progress, but also claim technology has exceeded the capacities of science to manage its consequences (Weinberg 1987, 27). These dualities often leave lay persons as well as regulators in an interpretive dilemma: technological risk lies beyond the control of the very tool used to create it—scientific explanation.

Such concerns have spurred structural shifts in the social organization and management of technical systems toward more centralized forms of control (Perrow 1984). Large-scale and/or complex technologies often require more centralized, authoritarian, or hierarchical forms of management (Thayer 1994). In modern societies, bureaucratic organizations have almost exclusive management control over technological risk. Perrow (1986) argues that the political or economic orientation of the management organizations is secondary; what matters more is the structure of increased technical complexity germane to risky systems. Especially important, however, are the overlapping linkages between these social and technical phenomena. The combination of bureaucratic organizational structures and increased technological complexity may result in decreased levels of intuitive understanding of technologies in use as well as decreased levels of direct public influence on control over those technologies. Increased exposure to sound bites about accidents or catastrophes provides more and more opportunities to observe manifestations of technological failures, with the result being heightened concerns and uncertainties about future risks associated with technologies that may fail to provide the intended levels of public protection and safety.

To address these issues, we asked survey respondents to respond to a series of four questions concerning levels of confidence in scientific and technological aspects of hazardous waste management. Respondents rated the level of confidence they perceived for the following items: (1) scientists can design a waste facility that adequately protects public health and safety; (2) engineering and construction personnel can build a waste facility that adequately protects public health and safety; (3) management and operations personnel can monitor waste conditions that might threaten public health and safety; and (4) management and operations personnel can correct problems or deficiencies that might threaten public health and safety. The response scale for each of these four items ranged from 1 for "No Confidence" to 5 for "Complete Confidence." From these four individual items a composite index was created to provide a single, summary indicator of respondents' overall perceived levels of confidence in technologies related to hazardous waste facilities. The summated index was internally consistent as verified by interitem correlations among the four individual measures (ranging between .65 to .83) and a high Cronbach's alpha coefficient (.91). Values for the index ranged from 4, indicating very low levels of confidence, to 20, indicating very high levels of confidence. To simplify presentation of the tabular results, the index response values were collapsed back to the original 1-5 scale categories, indicated by "1" (summated values of 4-6, "Virtually No Confidence"), "2" (7-10), "3" (11-13), "4" (14-17), and "5" (18-20, "Virtually Complete Confidence").

Figure 5.6 summarizes the combined responses of residents to the several confidence-in-technology measures, using the mean value of the distribution as a summary indicator for each of the measures. Ranging from 2.8 to 3.1 on a 1-5 scale, the mean values reflect very little variation across the different dimensions of confidence in technology. At either end of this range, levels of confidence in managers and operators to correct problems appear to be the lowest, while levels of confidence in scientists to design a safe facility appear to be the highest. The mean values indicate overall moderate levels of confidence, with a very slight tendency to indicate lower rather than higher levels of confidence in most cases. Although none of these distributions reveals a complete lack of confidence in the ability to design, construct, or operate a hazardous waste facility, the modest levels of confidence expressed by most respondents reflect an overall pattern of uncertainty or ambivalence toward such hazardous operations.

Having identified the overall similarities in response patterns for the aggregated sample of survey respondents, we turn next to an examination of potential differences in residents' confidence in technology across the four types of study areas. Because observed relationships were relatively uniform across each of the individual measures of confidence in technology, attention is focused here on the composite index as a summary measure of the underlying conceptual variable.

As indicated in table 5.16, residents of communities having an operating waste facility or in the process of siting one tend to express slightly higher levels of confidence in the technologies associated with waste management and disposal than residents of nonwaste development and control communities. The waste operating community category exhibited the lowest percentage of "No Confidence" responses. Results from a one-way analysis of variance with the Tukey's test for comparison across groups indicated a

Figure 5.6: Residents' Level of Confidence in Waste Management Technology

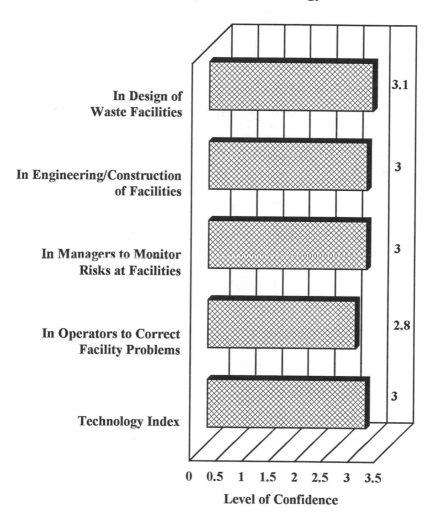

Level of Confidence

statistically significant difference in index scores between the waste communities and the nonwaste communities; no significant differences were found between either the two types of waste communities or the two types of nonwaste communities.

These results indicate that concerns over technologies used to manage hazards may be substantially different in communities facing a hazardous operation or the pending development of such a facility. Particularly in waste operating communities, residents may develop higher levels of confidence over time so long as facility operation goes smoothly. They may also exhibit increased confidence simply as a result of increased familiarity with, and adaptation to, hazards-based technologies. At the same time, it is important to note that a substantial minority of respondents in each type of study area reported either little or no confidence in waste management technologies, and roughly one-fourth to one-third of respondents expressed an intermediate level of confidence that is indicative of substantial uncertainty or ambivalence.

The next phase of the analysis examined potential differences in levels of confidence in waste management technology between residents and community leaders. The initial comparison, based on results derived from the aggregated sample for all study areas, revealed a substantial as well as statistically significant difference between community residents' and leaders' response values on the various individual measures of confidence in dimensions of technology related to hazardous waste management, as well as on the summated index scores. This pattern was also evident within each of the four community types, indicating that leaders in these varying

Table 5.16: Response to Levels of Confidence in Scientific/Technology Index by Community Type

Level of Confidence (%*)	Waste Operating	Waste Siting	Nonwaste Development	Control (Baseline)
No Confidence (1)	7.6	14.8	10.6	12.5
(2)	18.6	15.1	24.2	23.9
(3)	26.7	23.0	33.0	31.8
(4)	31.7	26.2	25.5	26.5
Complete Confidence (5)	15.3	21.0	6.7	5.4
N	419**	344	491	465
χ^2	91.3			
Cramer's V	.13			

*Percentages may not equal 100.0 percent because of rounding.

**p≤.001

development settings tend to hold different views about the uses and consequences of technologies used to manage hazards. In each case, leaders were more likely to report higher levels of confidence in technology than were residents. As is evident in table 5.17, results based on the composite index scores reveal that each community type had a substantial percentage of its leaders respond with a high degree of confidence in waste management technology: waste operating (76.2 percent), waste siting (71.0 percent), nonwaste development (50.0 percent), and control (59.7 percent). The degree of difference in the percentage of leaders and residents expressing "Complete Confidence" was largest in the waste operating and waste siting communities. Notably, and consistent with residents' response tendencies noted earlier, the nonwaste community categories yielded somewhat lower levels of confidence among local leaders than did those in the waste communities. Overall, across community types and across each of the dimensions of confidence in technology, residents were found to be only moderately confident, whereas community leaders were found to be moderately to highly confident.

The data reported in table 5.18, which summarize the relationship between favorability toward waste facility development and scores on the composite index, indicate substantial differences in levels of confidence in technology between those who oppose and those who support building a waste facility in their area. For those who oppose such a facility, a much greater proportion of respondents have "No Confidence" in technology (90 percent) than "Complete Confidence" (18.2 percent). Conversely, for those who support building such a facility a much smaller proportion of respondents have "No Confidence" in technology (6.6 percent) than "Complete Confidence" (69.6 percent). As indicated by the bivariate correlation between these two measures (r = .48), higher confidence in technology is substantially associated with a greater willingness to accept or support the building of a hazardous facility in one's community.

These findings suggest that technology-based issues may be a source of debate within areas confronted by a proposed hazardous waste operation. In such cases, local residents appear fairly likely to view the technology proposed for use at the facility as problematic. Such technical concerns may be based on claims that large-scale waste disposal facilities are "autonomous" or out of the control of any one or more individuals (Winner 1977). Fears of contamination and risks associated with the technical side of managing hazardous waste may therefore induce a qualitatively different type of social impact due to the chronic uncertainties inherent in complex systems (Kroll-Smith and Couch 1992). Worry over the soundness of technological systems may result in part from a lack of relationship to those systems, which makes risks less calculable, even if anticipated.

Table 5.17: Response to Science/Technology Index by Resident/Leader Status of Respondent, Controlling for Community Type

Level of Confidence (%*)	Waste Operating		Waste Siting		Nonwaste Development		Control (Baseline)	
	Resident	Leader	Resident	Leader	Resident	Leader	Resident	Leader
No Confidence (1)	8.5	0.0	16.4	2.6	11.0	7.1	13.3	5.8
(2)	19.4	11.9	15.1	15.8	26.2	8.9	25.7	9.6
(3)	28.4	11.9	24.6	10.5	32.9	33.9	32.7	25.0
(4)	30.5	42.9	24.9	34.2	23.9	37.5	24.0	46.2
Complete Confidence (5)	13.3	33.3	19.0	36.8	6.0	12.5	4.4	13.5
N	377	42	305	38	435	56	413	52
x^2	20.3 ***		13.5 **		13.6 **		23.7 ***	
Cramer's V	.22		.20		.17		.23	
Tau-c	.14		.12		.11		.15	
r^a	.21		.19		.15		.19	

*Percentages may not equal 100.0 percent because of rounding.

**$p \leq .01$, ***$p \leq .001$

[a]Based on uncollapsed values.

Table 5.18: Favorability Toward Waste Facility Siting by Response to Composite Science/Technology Index

Response (%*)	No Confidence (1)	(2)	(3)	(4)	Complete Confidence (5)
Oppose Siting	90.1	76.7	53.5	34.0	18.2
Neither Favor/Oppose	3.3	14.9	23.1	21.5	12.2
Favor Siting	6.6	8.4	23.4	44.5	69.6
N	182	335	454	391	148
x^2	383.8 **				
Tau-b	.42				
r^a	.48				

*Percentages may not equal 100.0 percent because of rounding.

**$p \leq .001$

[a]Based on uncollapsed values.

Trust in Agencies and Organizations (Recreancy)

Freudenburg (1988) coined the term "recreancy" to refer to a concept that is linked to the trust and technology dimensions delineated above, but extends beyond those issues to focus attention on the extent to which people have trust and confidence in various organizations and officials deemed responsible for insuring that hazardous materials and facilities are safely and responsibly managed. In a cumulative way, the patterns of trust that were once part and parcel of the social institutions of industry, government, and science are no longer taken for granted in American society. Instead, the latter half of the twentieth century has been characterized by a deterioration of trust in public and private organizations and authorities, particularly those involved in the management of risky technological systems (see Kasperson et al. 1992). Despite public support for the rhetoric of free enterprise and individualism, the profit-driven nature of industrial operations often makes business a distrusted institution (Smith 1995). The structure and actions of government also make it susceptible to public questioning and distrust (Gerrard 1994). As a result, government and industry are often perceived as inept monitors and regulators of risk in environmental systems by those who face the greatest potential for direct impact—residents of the local communities where such systems are proposed or developed (Easterling and Kunreuther 1995; Gerrard 1994).

Dimensions of recreancy involving trust in nonlocal agencies and organizations were measured using a scalar variable created by summing responses to a set of statements about eight nonlocal agencies and organizations involved in various aspects of hazardous waste facility siting and waste management. Respondents were asked to indicate their level of trust in each agency or organization on a scale ranging from 1 ("No Trust") to 5 ("Complete Trust"). The specific organizations included were:

1. U.S. Environmental Protection Agency (EPA)
2. U.S. Nuclear Regulatory Commission (NRC)
3. U.S. Department of Energy (DOE)
4. State Health Department
5. Governor's office
6. State legislature
7. State agency responsible for environmental protection
8. Private waste management companies

Resulting scale scores ranged from 8 to 40; the index had a Cronbach's alpha coefficient of 0.90, indicating substantial internal consistency. For purposes of the descriptive and crosstabular analysis reported below, we divided the range of scores into five categories (index scores of 8-14, 15-21, 22-26, 27-

33, and 34-40) corresponding roughly to the original five-point scale used in the component items.

The data shown in figure 5.7 clearly show a tendency toward low levels of recreancy, suggesting that the increasing cynicism about business and government often discussed in the popular press is evident in the study communities. Only about 21 percent of the response values on the recreancy index were in the two "higher trust" categories, with just 4.2 percent in the category corresponding to extremely high levels of trust. By contrast, 17 percent of responses fell into the category corresponding to extremely low trust, and nearly half were in the two lowest-trust response categories.

Interestingly, the data reported in table 5.19 suggest that trust in agencies and organizations responsible for waste management is slightly lower in the nonwaste development and control communities than in waste operating or waste siting communities, although the level of association between community type and the recreancy score is slight. The proportion of respondents expressing moderately high to extremely high levels of trust is about 29 percent in the waste operating communities and 24 percent in the waste siting communities, compared to about 14 percent and 19 percent of respondents in nonwaste development and control communities respectively.

Results also indicate that leaders are substantially more likely to report high levels of trust in nonlocal agencies and organizations responsible for waste management than is the case among residents. Nearly 37 percent of leaders expressed moderate to extremely high levels of trust in such organizations, compared to only about 21 percent among the resident respondents. Approximately 27 percent of leaders indicated moderately to extremely low levels of trust, while among residents, over 48 percent expressed low trust in these types of agencies and organizations. This general pattern was evident across the four community types.

As might be expected, given the similarity of the findings for recreancy to those noted for several of the variables discussed previously, there is a relatively strong relationship between residents' recreancy score and their favorability toward the siting of a hazardous waste facility in or near their community. As shown in table 5.20, whereas 77.4 percent of those with the lowest levels of trust in agencies and organizations responsible for waste management indicated strong opposition to waste facility siting in their areas, only 18.3 percent of those who reported the highest levels of trust indicated strong opposition to siting. Conversely, while only about 9 percent of those reporting extremely low levels of trust indicated that they were moderately to highly favorable toward waste facility siting, nearly 72 percent of those reporting extremely high levels of trust indicated support for siting. An overall association between recreancy levels and the measure of favorability toward waste facility siting is evident ($r = .40$, $p<.0001$).

Figure 5.7: Residents' Level of Trust in Agencies/Organizations (Recreancy)

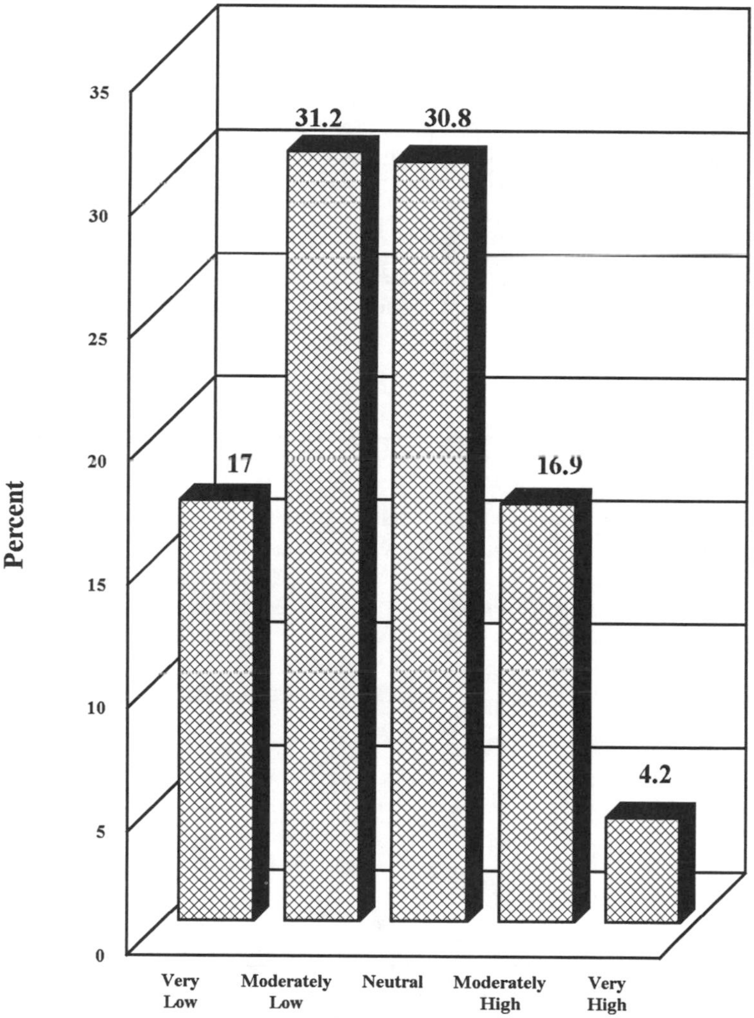

144

Table 5.19: Residents' Trust in Agencies and Organizations Responsible for Waste Management (Recreancy) by Community Type

Trust Level (%[*])	Waste Operating	Waste Siting	Nonwaste Development	Control (Baseline)
Extremely Low	12.7	18.9	19.3	17.2
Moderately Low	27.1	30.1	32.3	34.4
Neutral	31.5	27.3	34.0	29.4
Moderately High	22.7	20.3	11.6	14.7
Extremely High	6.1	3.5	2.9	4.2
N	362	286	415	401
χ^2	34.46 **			
Cramer's V	.09			

[*]Percentages may not equal 100.0 percent because of rounding.

** $p \leq .001$

Table 5.20: Favorabilility Toward Waste Facility Siting by Residents' Trust in Agencies and Organizations Responsible for Waste Management (Recreancy)

Response (%[*])	Extremely Low Trust	Moderately Low Trust	Neutral	Moderately High Trust	Extremely High Trust
Strongly Oppose	77.4	49.6	35.2	27.1	18.3
Moderately Oppose	4.1	12.6	13.4	9.0	1.7
Neither Favor/Oppose	9.5	17.6	23.4	16.4	8.3
Moderately Favor	3.7	9.7	15.0	18.0	21.7
Strongly Favor	5.4	10.6	13.2	29.5	50.0
N	243	454	441	244	60
χ^2	270.05 **				
r^a	.40				

[*]Percentages may not equal 100.0 percent because of rounding.

** $p \leq .001$

[a]Based on uncollapsed values.

Responses to Developer Incentives/Community Compensation Programs

Confronted with the likelihood of local opposition and "Not In My Backyard (NIMBY)" responses to most waste facility siting efforts (see Gervers 1987; Portney 1991), policy makers face a seemingly irresolvable dilemma in their attempts to address the societal problem of safely disposing of the ever-growing stockpile of hazardous and toxic materials. In some instances government authorities have tried to force the issue through the imposition of permitting and licensing processes that attempt to preempt the ability of local and other levels of government to intervene. However, experiences to date suggest that even in the face of such preemptive strategies, "local opposition has so far had a decided impact in thwarting the siting process" (Easterling and Kunreuther 1995, 6). Due to legal challenges, protest actions, and political pressures, attempts to impose forced-location mandates have failed to resolve the dilemmas associated with hazardous waste disposal.

In response to these circumstances, policy analysts and public officials have directed increased attention to the potential role of community compensation and incentive programs in reducing local opposition to the siting of hazardous facilities and securing higher levels of acceptability in areas where such facilities are developed (Halstead et al. 1984). Incentives and compensation programs represent attempts to provide various types of benefits to the host community in order to address at least some of the inequities and impact-related concerns that arise when local populations are asked to bear a disproportionate share of the negative impacts that result from attempts to solve a broader societal problem.

Although in many instances such benefit packages involve economic awards to host communities and/or their residents, the range of possible incentives extends well beyond the realm of direct financial awards or expenditures to support community facilities and services. For example, other approaches that have been tried or suggested include such strategies as property value guarantees or assurances of economic benefits such as employment for local residents (see Easterling and Kunreuther 1995, 175-177; Halstead et al. 1984).

Incentive-based approaches may provide a means of reducing or mitigating some of the social and economic impacts associated with the siting and operation of hazardous waste disposal facilities. As such, they may under some circumstances help to reduce local opposition to the siting of waste disposal facilities. However, to date very little empirical evidence has been presented regarding public reactions to alternative compensation and incentives programs or the circumstances under which such programs may be more or less effective as ways of increasing the acceptability of waste facilities. To address these issues, we examined the views of both residents and community leaders regarding several types of community incentives and compensation strategies that could increase the acceptability of hazardous waste disposal facilities.

Survey participants were asked to respond to six types of incentive/ compensation approaches that a waste management company could offer to a community, and asked whether such incentives would influence their views about the acceptability of such a project. The six items were: (1) waste company pays a higher level of taxes than other local industries; (2) waste company provides the community with facilities such as parks, libraries, or swimming pools; (3) waste company provides the community with equipment such as fire trucks, ambulances, etc.; (4) waste company offers to pay fair market real estate values and relocation costs for any property owners and residents negatively affected by the facility; (5) waste company has a policy to hire local residents first; and (6) waste company adopts safety standards that exceed those required by state and federal governments. For each of these individual items, response options available to the survey participants included "More Acceptable" (1), "No Effect/Don't Know" (2), and "Less Acceptable" (3).

In addition to the six individual questionnaire items, an additive index was created to provide a single, summary indicator of respondents' overall degree of receptivity to the concept of community incentive/compensation programs. The internal consistency of the resulting summary measure was verified by a pattern of substantial interitem correlations among the six individual measures (ranging between .41 and .58), and a high Cronbach's alpha reliability coefficient (.86). The resulting index assumed values ranging between 6, indicating the highest degree of receptivity to compensation/ incentive programs (e.g., a response of "more acceptable" to all six items) and 18, indicating the lowest degree of receptivity to such programs (e.g., a response of "less acceptable" to all 6 items). To simplify the presentation of results, these response values were collapsed for some portions of the analysis into 3 categories, indicating "high" receptivity to compensation/incentive programs (values of 6-8), "moderate" receptivity (values of 9-12), and "low" receptivity (values of 13-18).

Looking first at the combined responses of residents from all of the study areas, the results summarized in figure 5.8 indicate a substantial range of variation in the extent to which these compensation strategies appear likely to increase levels of acceptance for the siting of hazardous waste facilities. Strategies that involve the provision of monetary resources to local area governments appear to have only modest influence on acceptability. For example, only about one-third of respondents indicated that the siting of a hazardous waste facility would be "more acceptable" if the waste

Figure 5.8: Percent of Respondents Indicating That Various Compensation Programs Could Make the Siting of a Waste Facility in Their Community More Acceptable

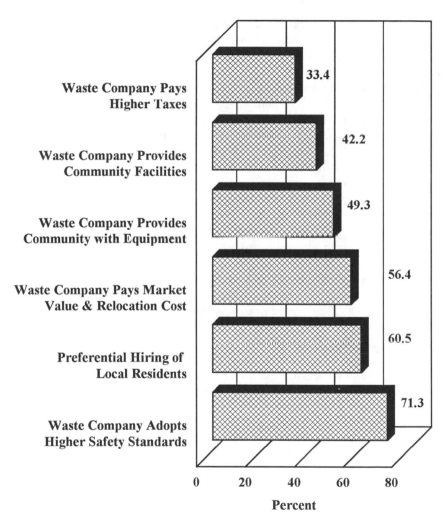

management company agreed to pay higher taxes than other local industries. Somewhat higher proportions of respondents indicated that acceptability would increase as a result of the provision of either community facilities such as parks, libraries or swimming pools (42 percent) or equipment such as fire trucks or ambulances (49 percent). The apparently modest effectiveness of these types of strategies may in part reflect a tendency for some individuals to view such financial incentives as attempts by waste management firms to "buy" local support, rather than addressing longer-term community needs and concerns (see Easterling and Kunreuther 1995; also Rocky Mountain Social Science 1992).

In contrast, strategies that more directly address longer-term issues pertaining to personal and community-level economic concerns and needs appear to have greater potential as mechanisms for increasing local acceptance of waste facility proposals. When presented with the idea that a waste company might establish a program that would pay fair market real estate values and relocation costs should property owners and residents be negatively affected by a hazardous waste facility, over one-half (56 percent) of respondents indicated that such a program would make the siting of such a facility in their community more acceptable. A similar proportion of respondents (60.5 percent) indicated that such a facility would be more acceptable if the company established a policy of preferential hiring of local residents.

Over 70 percent of respondents from the combined study areas indicated that the local siting of a hazardous waste facility would be more acceptable if the waste management company were to adopt safety standards exceeding those required by state and federal governments. While public responses to hazardous waste disposal facilities are influenced in part by interest in either personal economic opportunities and/or costs along with the potential for either positive or negative community-level economic development consequences, concerns about health and safety risks are at the center of most public opposition to such facilities (see Krannich and Albrecht 1995; Spies et al. 1998). It is therefore not surprising that the incentive or compensation strategy that appears to hold the greatest potential for increasing public acceptance of waste facility siting involves an attempt to respond directly to health and safety concerns. Of course, the waste management industry may consider existing regulatory standards to represent maximum feasible (or perhaps even excessive) limits on allowable releases of potentially harmful substances. Nevertheless, it is clear that public confidence would be substantially bolstered by industry-initiated efforts to move beyond those limits.

Having established overall response patterns for the aggregated sample of resident responses, we turn next to an examination of possible differences in the patterns of response to the compensation/incentive measures across the four types of study areas considered in this research. Attention is focused only on responses provided by members of the community resident samples; community leader responses are examined and compared with resident responses in subsequent sections of the analysis. Because the study areas exhibit substantially different levels of local experience with the siting and operation of hazardous waste management facilities, it was expected that responses to the alternative compensation strategies would vary across the four community types. For example, residents in areas that have experienced significant economic development associated with nonwaste industries may be less likely to respond positively to possible incentives for acceptance of a hazardous waste facility than residents of baseline or "control" areas, where economic conditions and prospects are generally less favorable.

Table 5.21 presents a summary of the differences in response to the various compensation/incentive programs across the four community types. Looking first at the approach involving payment of higher local property taxes than other industries, the results suggest that residents of both waste operating and waste siting areas are slightly more likely than residents of the control areas and nonwaste development areas to indicate that such a program would cause them to consider a waste management facility as "more acceptable." Only about 25 percent of respondents from the nonwaste development areas indicated that such a program would make a waste facility more acceptable, while about 38 percent of those in waste operating areas and 43 percent in waste siting areas indicated that the payment of higher taxes would increase the acceptability of such projects.

Table 5.21 also summarizes the relationship between community type and response to the compensation alternative involving provision of community facilities such as libraries or swimming pools. Once again, respondents from the waste operating and waste siting study areas were somewhat more likely than those from the nonwaste development or control areas to indicate that provision of such facilities would make the development of a waste management facility more acceptable. A similar relationship exists between community type and response to incentive programs involving provision of community equipment such as fire trucks or ambulances. As with the items discussed above, this approach to compensation generates higher levels of acceptability for waste management projects among respondents in the waste operating and waste siting study areas, while respondents from the nonwaste development areas are substantially less likely to respond positively.

The next comparison summarized in table 5.21 involves the alternative that would provide for agreements to purchase property at fair market value and cover the costs of relocation should local residents experience adverse effects from the presence of a waste management facility. The proportion of respondents who viewed such an approach positively was highest in the waste operating study areas, where nearly 70 percent of respondents indicated

Table 5.21: Percent of Resident Respondents Indicating That Community Incentives Would Make the Siting of a Hazardous Waste Facility More Acceptable, by Community Type

Type of Incentive	Waste Operating	Waste Siting	Nonwaste Development	Control (Baseline)
Company pays higher taxes	37.8	42.9	24.8	31.2
Company provides community facilities	47.5	50.4	34.1	38.9
Company provides community equipment	59.8	55.6	39.2	44.8
Company pays fair market value/relocation costs	69.8	58.1	47.1	51.9
Company hires local residents first	69.6	66.7	47.9	59.6
Company adopts higher safety standards	83.5	70.0	64.4	67.5

that such a program would make a waste facility more acceptable to them. A somewhat lower proportion of respondents (58 percent) from the waste siting areas reacted favorably to this type of compensation program. Respondents from the control areas (52 percent) and the nonwaste development areas (47 percent) were less likely to respond favorably to this compensation approach.

A similar pattern of differences across community types is evident for the incentive alternative involving a program of preferential hiring of local-area residents for work at a waste management facility. Respondents from the waste operating and waste siting study areas were slightly more likely than those in the control areas and substantially more likely than those from the nonwaste development areas to indicate that such a program would cause them to evaluate a waste management facility as more acceptable. Approximately two-thirds of respondents from the waste siting and operating areas indicated that local hiring policies would increase facility acceptability, while fewer than one-half of those from the nonwaste development areas provided such a response. It is noteworthy that for all study area types the percentage of "more acceptable" responses was substantially higher for this item than for the alternative involving payment of higher local taxes, possibly reflecting the strong emphasis that exists in many rural areas on job creation as a primary local economic development concern.

Compared to the other compensation approaches examined in the preceding discussion, responses to the approach involving having waste management companies adhere to higher safety standards than those required by state and federal agencies were notably more positive across all of the types of study areas. Once again the highest proportion of "more acceptable" responses occurred in the waste operating study areas (83.5 percent), indicating that residents of these areas where hazardous waste facilities are already operating would respond very positively to such voluntary adherence to higher safety standards. A high proportion of residents in the waste siting study areas (70 percent) also responded favorably to the idea of such a program. Even in the nonwaste development and control areas approximately two-thirds of respondents indicated that such an approach would cause them to view a waste management facility as being more acceptable.

Consistent with the pattern observed for all of the individual compensation items, the results of the comparison between community type and the composite index developed to measure overall responsiveness to compensation/incentive programs indicate that respondents from the waste operating and waste siting study areas were substantially more receptive toward such programs than are those from the nonwaste development and control areas. One-way analysis of variance procedures revealed an overall significant difference in index scores across community types. The results of the Tukey's test for comparisons across the four community types indicated that the overall degree of receptivity to compensation/incentive approaches was significantly greater (e.g., a lower average index score) in the waste operating and waste siting areas than in the nonwaste development areas.

Overall, the preceding results reveal a fairly consistent tendency across all of the compensation strategies for a higher proportion of more acceptable responses among respondents from the study areas which have experienced waste facility siting or facility operation, with generally lower values observed for responses from the nonwaste development and control areas. On most items the percentage of more acceptable responses was very similar for the control and nonwaste development areas. One exception to this involves the idea of preferential local hiring policies, where the percentage indicating that such incentives would make a waste facility more acceptable was substantially higher in the control areas than in the nonwaste development areas. This is probably a reflection of the lack of economic development activities and opportunities in the control areas, and of the higher access to employment opportunities in study areas included in the nonwaste development category.

The more favorable response among residents of the two study area categories with the most direct experience with the siting and operation of hazardous waste management facilities is consistent with a general tendency to encounter lower levels of concern with risk and reduced opposition in areas where such facilities have generated (or are expected to generate) economic opportunities. Such a positive response is especially likely in places where either prior or current local experiences with similar industries and materials have not created negative "risk perception shadows," e.g., where no major contamination or exposure problems have occurred (see Stoffle et al. 1988). In contrast, the highly negative imagery associated with radioactive and hazardous waste materials is likely to make residents of other areas without waste facility experience much less likely to view waste management facilities as acceptable, even when compensation and incentives are offered (see Slovic et al. 1993).

The next step in the analysis involved examination of possible differences in response to compensation/incentive alternatives between residents of the study areas and persons identified as community leaders. For this part of the analysis, the resident/leader comparisons are first examined for the aggregated sample (ignoring community type); these comparisons are summarized in table 5.22. Because any observed differences could be conditional depending on community type, resident/leader distinctions are also evaluated while controlling for community type.

As indicated in the first two data columns in table 5.22, for the aggregated samples community leaders were slightly more likely than residents to indicate that payment of higher taxes would make the development of a waste management facility more acceptable to them. Only about one-third of resident responses were in the more acceptable category, while approximately 45 percent of community leaders selected that response option. This pattern is consistent with the general tendency for persons in community leadership positions to be positively oriented toward projects or programs that increase local growth prospects via the provision of tax revenues, business growth opportunities, and so forth. When the resident/leader distinction in response to the higher taxes item was elaborated by controlling for community type, leaders were noticeably more likely than residents to respond favorably to this type of compensation approach only in the waste operating and control areas, where the percent of more acceptable responses was about 20 percent higher for leaders than for residents. In contrast, there were virtually no differences in leader and resident responses in the waste siting study areas.

In general, community leaders responded more positively than residents to the concept of having waste management companies provide funding for community facilities such as libraries or swimming pools. For the aggregated sample, 56 percent of leaders indicated that such a program would make a waste management facility more acceptable to them, compared to about 42 percent of residents. This same general pattern was also evident for each of the separate community type categories. The distinction between community leader and resident response distributions was especially noteworthy in the waste operating areas, where the proportion of more acceptable responses was about 20 percent greater among community leaders than among residents.

Overall, community leaders were significantly more likely than residents to indicate that provision of community equipment such as fire trucks and ambulances would make the development of a hazardous waste facility more acceptable. That same tendency was also evident in each of the community type categories. Resident/leader differences on this compensation measure were most substantial in the waste siting study areas, where almost three-fourths of leaders indicated that such a program would make a waste facility more acceptable, compared to just over half of the resident respondents. In contrast, the proportion of more acceptable responses was substantially lower, and more similar among residents and leaders, in the nonwaste development settings.

Results derived from the aggregated sample suggest that community leaders are somewhat more likely than residents to respond favorably to incentive programs involving purchase of property and payment of relocation costs in the event of adverse effects from a hazardous waste facility. However, when responses were examined for the individual community types, the tendency for more favorable responses among leaders was evident only in the waste siting and control areas. In contrast, the percentage of more acceptable responses was virtually identical for leaders and residents in the waste operating and nonwaste development study areas.

For the aggregated sample there was virtually no difference between the responses of residents and leaders regarding the effect of local hiring policies on the acceptability of a hazardous waste facility. For both groups, a substantial majority (61-65 percent) of respondents indicated that such compensation would make the development of a waste facility more acceptable. However, when this relationship was examined while controlling for the type of study community, a difference between resident and leader responses was evident in the waste operating areas. In that study community category only, leaders were significantly more likely than residents to respond favorably to a compensation program involving preferential local hiring. In all of the other types of study areas, the differences between resident and leader responses were small and not statistically significant.

The adoption of safety standards as a compensation/incentive strategy received the most favorable response on the part of both local leaders and community residents. For the aggregated sample, community leaders were more favorably disposed (81 percent more acceptable) than residents (71 percent more acceptable) to a program that would have waste management firms adopt higher safety standards than required by state and federal agencies. This same tendency was also evident within the four individual study area types. For each of the community types, leaders were slightly more receptive to this strategy than were residents, although in all cases the differences were small.

Table 5.22: Response to Community Compensation/Incentives Alternatives and Composite Incentives Index by Resident/Leader Status of Respondent

Response (%)*	Higher Taxes		Community Facilities		Community Equipment		Property Purchase/ Relocation Costs		Local Hiring Policy		Higher Safety Standards		Incentives Index	
	Resident	Leader	Resident	Leader	Resident	Leader	Resident	Leader	Resident	Leader	Resident	Leader	Resident	Leader
More Acceptable	33.4	44.6	42.2	56.0	49.3	60.7	56.4	65.0	60.5	64.8	71.3	81.1	45.9	60.3
No Effect	54.8	50.6	46.6	40.0	40.9	35.8	30.4	31.1	32.8	31.9	22.2	17.2	44.1	36.7
Less Acceptable	11.8	4.8	11.3	4.0	9.9	3.5	13.1	4.0	6.8	3.3	6.5	1.7	10.0	3.1
N	1,143	168	1,233	175	1,238	173	1,226	177	1,272	182	1,244	180	1,013	161
χ^2	12.4 **		15.9 ***		11.7 **		12.9 **		3.6		10.1 **		15.0 ***	
Tau-c	-.07		-.07		-.06		-.05		-.02		-.05		-.08	

*Percentages may not equal 100.0 percent because of rounding.

** $p \leq .01$, *** $p \leq .001$

For the aggregated sample, the mean response value on the composite incentives index was 8.5, compared to a mean of 9.4 among residents (F=13.4, p<.001). This indicates that community leaders were somewhat more likely to fall into the highly receptive range on the index than were residents, reinforcing results for the categorized index value comparisons reported in table 5.22. This pattern was also evident in all four of the community type categories, although the magnitude of the difference between residents and leaders was relatively slight in the case of the nonwaste development areas.

In virtually all of the comparisons examined in this part of the analysis, community leaders were more positive in their response to compensation and incentive programs than were rank-and-file residents of the study communities. Such distinctions are hardly surprising, for several reasons. First, many of those selected as members of the purposive sample of community leaders were persons occupying some elected or appointed local government position. Such leaders are likely to have more direct concerns about and responsibilities for the provision of local facilities and services and the adequacy of local fiscal resources than are other community members. Also, those in such official positions as well as other members of the leader samples (who in most cases were engaged in various local business enterprises) tend to be closely linked to a progrowth constituency in most communities (see Molotch 1976). As such, the types of leaders included in our samples could be expected to be more supportive of industrial development in general, including hazardous waste facility developments, particularly if such developments carry with them the promise of additional incentives that could further enhance the economic development and growth prospects of the local community.

The final step in this part of the analysis involves an evaluation of the relationship between response to compensation/incentive alternatives and levels of favorability toward the development of a hazardous waste management facility. The overall pattern of this association is effectively summarized by examination of the relationship between response on the composite incentives index and the favorability item. As indicated in table 5.23, there is a significant difference in response to the favorability item, depending on the level of receptivity to compensation/incentives measured by the index. The degree of support or opposition for facility development is distributed fairly evenly among those who indicated high receptivity to compensation/incentive programs, with nearly 30 percent indicating opposition and 45 percent indicating support. Among those who were only moderately receptive to compensation/incentives, 70 percent indicated opposition to the siting of a waste management facility, while less than 17 percent indicated support. Among the relatively small proportion of respondents who indicated that compensation/incentives would make a

Table 5.23: Favorability Toward Waste Facility Siting by Response to Composite Incentives Index

Response (%*)	More Acceptable	No Effect	Less Acceptable
Oppose Siting	29.4	70.1	90.1
Neither Favor/Oppose	25.1	13.0	4.0
Favor Siting	45.5	16.9	5.9
N	462	445	101
χ^2	213.6 **		
Tau-c	-.37		
ra	-.45		

*Percentages may not equal 100.0 percent because of rounding.

**$p \leq .001$

aBased on uncollapsed values.

waste facility less acceptable, an overwhelming majority (90.1 percent) indicated strong opposition to the development of such facilities. Overall there is a relatively strong association (r = -.45) between these variables.

The level of widespread local opposition to waste facilities (Albrecht 1995) should provide a strong impetus on the part of both policy makers and corporate interests to pursue siting processes based on the principles of voluntarism and compensation to communities that might be willing to host such projects. The results reported here suggest that there is at least some prospect that levels of acceptability for the siting of hazardous waste disposal facilities could be increased through the careful implementation of certain types of community compensation and incentive programs. However, the effectiveness of such approaches is likely to be substantially undermined if they do not clearly recognize and directly address the fundamental concerns about long-term health and safety risks and community economic development concerns that appear to be at the core of the broad-based opposition that emerges in response to most waste facility siting proposals. Programs that ignore these concerns and attempt to secure local approval through incentives that provide for mostly short-term improvements to local fiscal resources or infrastructure conditions are likely to be far less effective in securing increased acceptability, and in some cases may generate a negative backlash. In short, effective compensation approaches are unlikely to be either easy to devise and implement or inexpensive over the long term.

Summary of Descriptive and Crosstabular Findings

The findings reported thus far suggest several general patterns and conclusions. One highly consistent finding involves the presence of marked resident/leader differences, which are evident for nearly all of the social effects variables that have been examined. Compared to other residents, community leaders were substantially less likely to perceive conflicts and other difficulties during siting, more likely to have higher levels of knowledge about waste storage and management, more likely to perceive lower levels of risk and to express greater trust in technology and waste management organizations, more likely to view incentives and community compensation programs positively, and more likely to favor the siting of a hazardous waste facility in their local areas.

Also evident were substantial differences across the types of study areas included in the analysis. When compared to respondents from the nonwaste study areas (nonwaste development and control communities), both residents and leaders in waste operating and waste siting communities were less likely to perceive siting process dimensions as problematic, and more likely to have higher levels of knowledge about waste management, to perceive lower levels of concern about environmental and health risks, to express confidence in technology and trust in waste management organizations, to view incentives programs positively, and to favor siting a waste facility in their local area.

Among the variety of factors considered thus far in the analysis, several stand out as having relatively substantial associations with the measure of favorability toward the siting of hazardous waste facilities. Specifically, the measures addressing levels of perceived risk, trust and confidence in science and technology, trust in responsible authorities and organizations (recreancy), perceived fairness of the facility siting process, anticipated economic effects of waste facility developments, and receptivity to developer incentives all exhibited moderate to fairly strong relationships with the favorability measure. In contrast, the measures addressing overall levels of community conflict and levels of knowledge about waste management exhibited generally weak associations with respondents' favorability toward waste facility siting.

A substantial proportion of respondents were strongly opposed to facility siting and expressed high levels of concern about the effects of such facilities on the social and economic well-being of their communities. At the same time the results also indicate that, as was the case for the economic, demographic, public service, and fiscal impacts examined in earlier chapters, the social and special impacts perceived by residents and leaders in waste siting and operating communities are generally less substantial than might be anticipated, especially given the virtual gridlock that has emerged nationally over efforts to site new hazardous waste facilities. In addition, the results suggest that the experience of living in a community that has already been affected by the siting and/or development of a waste management facility is linked to a tendency for both residents and leaders to express higher levels of acceptance and to perceive fewer problems resulting from such projects. While this does not imply that impacts have not been substantial in at least some of the study areas, many of the areas included in this study fail to demonstrate the intensity of disruptive impacts that the existing literature has often associated with waste facility siting.

These findings provide only a partial picture of the social consequences of hazardous facility siting. There are a number of additional social impact dimensions not considered here that need to be taken into account, as well as other key explanatory variables that merit consideration in future research. While our results suggest that the reactions of both residents and leaders and the impacts on community conditions are generally indicative of relatively modest social effects, additional research is needed to develop a better understanding of the factors that may help to account for those cases where local reactions are more volatile and impacts more severe.

In addition, it is important to keep in mind that the individual dimensions of social response to hazardous facility siting outlined above operate as part of a complex of interrelated processes and responses. To further explore the complexity of those processes, we turn our attention to a multivariate analysis of relationships involving the array of variables that have been addressed in the preceding pages.

A Multivariate Analysis of Determinants of Risk and Favorability toward Siting

While the analyses reported above provide a useful examination of some of the key relationships between individual sets of waste related factors, they do not allow us to determine the extent to which the multiple variables included in this study are able to jointly predict such key factors as the level of support for waste siting; this requires a multivariate analysis. Therefore, in this section we examine the extent to which variables included in the analysis reported above are able to predict responses for two key dimensions of social response to hazardous waste management: levels of perceived risk associated with hazardous waste facilities, and levels of favorability toward the local-area siting of such facilities. As noted above, one of the major goals of this study was an attempt to understand what factors determine favorability toward the siting of hazardous waste facilities in rural areas. In addition, the results reported above indicate that concerns about environmental contamination and associated health and safety risks are among the key impacts of waste facility siting, and that risk perceptions appear to play a key role in determining favorability. For each of these dependent variables we examine the relationships between selected independent variables and the dependent variable, first for residents alone and then for all respondents (residents and leaders combined). We do so using Ordinary Least-Squares (OLS) multiple regression procedures, with dummy variables included in both the residents-only and all-respondents models for community type, and in the all-respondents model for resident/leader status as well. In addition, a parallel analysis using logistic regression procedures is included for the regression of favorability on the independent variables, because the favorability variable was originally measured on a five-category ordinal scale that does not fully satisfy the measurement requirements of OLS regression. For the logistic regressions the measure of favorability is dichotomized into "favor siting" (response values of 4 or 5) and "do not favor siting" (response values of 1-3).

The independent variables initially examined included forms of each of the variables described above (other than the equity variable, because that variable was measured only for the waste siting and operating study areas). Also included as independent variables were measures of respondents' levels of localized social interactions and local property ownership, along with several sociodemographic variables (age, educational attainment, sex, household income, length of residence in the local community, and the presence of children in the home) that have been shown in prior research to be associated with various environmental attitudes and perceptions, including responses to hazardous facilities and events. All independent variables were assessed for multicollinearity using tolerance and variance inflation factors and only one variable from each set of several highly intercorrelated variables was selected for inclusion in the analysis. The variables remaining after such exclusions are evident in the analytical tables shown below. A complete list of the variables considered for the analysis as well the operational definitions for each are presented in table 5.24

Multivariate Analysis of Perceived Risks of Hazardous Waste Facilities

Because of its clear importance as an impact of waste facility siting or operation as well as a factor affecting favorability toward waste siting, we

Table 5.24: Description of Variables Used in the Multivariate Analysis

Variable	Description
Favorability Toward Siting	A variable that indicates respondent's level of agreement or disagreement with the statement: "If an election were held today, I would vote in favor of having a waste facility located in our area." Response is expressed on a scale of 1 to 5, 1 being "strongly disagree" and 5 being "strongly agree." For logistic regressions the variable was recoded with values 4 and 5 coded as 1 "for favor" and all other responses coded 0 for "do not favor."
Risk Perception	A scalar variable which measures respondent's perceived risk associated with waste facilities. It was created by summing responses to the following statements which were expressed on a scale of 1 (disagree strongly) to 5 (agree strongly): (1) a waste facility poses health and safety risks for future generations living in the surrounding area; and (2) environmental contamination is likely to occur as a result of a waste facility being in an area. Values on the resulting index ranged from a low of 2 to a high of 10. The Cronbach's alpha coefficient was 0.91.
Community Conflict	A scalar variable created by summing responses to five questions indicating the levels of conflict existing: (1) between the community and local industries; (2) the community and state government; (3) people in the community and local government; (4) the community and other communities; and (5) among members of the local community. Responses were recorded on a scale ranging from 1 (No Conflict) to 5 (Substantial Conflict). The resulting composite measure assumed values ranging from 5 (very low conflict) to 25 (very high conflict). The alpha reliability coefficient for the measure was .85.
General Waste Knowledge	A scalar variable measuring general knowledge of hazardous waste with values ranging from 0 to 4 that indicates how many of the following statements were answered correctly. "Nearly all industries can achieve a level of zero waste production if they use available waste control and anti-pollution devices." (Yes/No)

Continued on next page

Table 5.24, continued

Variable	Description
	"The permit that allows a waste management facility to dispose of hazardous waste also allows it to store radioactive waste." (Yes/No)

"In the United States, nearly all high-level radioactive waste from nuclear power plants is now being taken to be stored in a special underground facility." (Yes/No)

"In the United States, the federal agency with the primary responsibility for enforcing pollution laws is:
a. Federal Emergency Management Administration (FEMA)
b. Environmental Protection Agency (EPA)
c. U.S. Fish and Wildlife Service (FWS)
d. Bureau of Land Management (BLM)
e. Office of Technology Assessment (OTA)"

Trust and Confidence in Science and Technology

A composite variable indicating the level of confidence in the science and technology of waste management. The measure was created by summing responses to statements about the level of confidence in scientists' ability to design a waste facility that protects public health and safety; in the ability of engineering and constructional personnel to build a facility that adequately protects public health and safety; in the ability of management and operations personnel to monitor waste conditions that might threaten public health and safety; and in the ability of management and operations personnel to correct problems or deficiencies. Responses were recorded on a scale ranging from 1 (No Confidence) to 5 (Complete Confidence). The resulting additive scale assumed values ranging from 4 (Virtually no confidence) to 20 (Virtually complete confidence). The alpha coefficient for the composite measure was .91.

Trust in Agencies and Organizations (Recreancy)

A scalar variable which indicates the level of trust in agencies and organizations with responsibility for waste management. The measure was created by summing responses to statements regarding eight institutions and

Continued on next page

Table 5.24, continued

Variable	Description
	organizations entrusted with the duty to ensure safe handling and public protection These included the U.S. Environmental Protection Agency (EPA), U.S. Nuclear Regulatory Commission (NRC), U.S. Department of Energy (DOE), State Health Department, Governor's Office, State Legislature, State Agency Responsible for Environmental Protection, and Private Waste Management Companies. Responses were recorded on a scale of 1 to 5, with 1 being "no trust" and 5 being "complete trust." The scalar variable assumes values ranging from 8 (extremely low trust) to 40 (extremely high trust). Cronbach's alpha coefficient for the index was 0.90.
Economic Impact	A scalar variable which indicates the level of agreement with statements regarding the economic impacts of hosting a facility. It was created by summing responses to 3 items, with response measured on a scale of 1 (disagree strongly) to 5 (agree strongly). The items were: a waste facility is economically beneficial to a community; the presence of a waste facility encourages other industries to locate in the surrounding area; a waste facility results in a decrease in property values in the surrounding area (inversely coded). Cronbach's coefficient alpha for the index was 0.69.
Response to Incentives	A scalar variable which measures six types of incentive/compensation approaches that a waste management company could offer to a community, and asked whether provision of such incentives would influence views about the acceptability of such a project. It was created by summing responses to the following statements which were expressed on a scale of 1 to 3 with 1 being "more acceptable," 2 being "no effect/don't know," and 3 being "less acceptable." (1) Waste company pays a higher level of taxes than other local industries; (2) waste company has a policy to hire local residents first; (3) waste company offers to pay fair market real estate values and relocation costs for any property owners and residents negatively impacted by the facility; (4) waste company provides the community with equipment such as fire trucks, ambulances, etc.; (5) Waste company provides the com-

Continued on next page

Table 5.24, continued

Variable	Description
	munity with facilities such as parks, libraries or swimming pools; and (6) Waste company adopts safety standards that exceed those required by state and federal governments.
Localized Social Interactions	A composite variable created by summing responses to six items measuring frequency of localized social interaction with parents/siblings, children, other relatives, close friends, acquaintances, and neighbors. Response values on the composite measure ranged from 0 (no localized interaction) to 30 (extremely frequent interaction).
Local Property Ownership	A composite variable created from responses indicating ownership of a home, a farm or ranch, or other land or real estate in the local area. Response values ranged from 0 (no property owned) to 3 (ownership of all three property types).
Age	Respondent's self-reported age measured in years.
Sex	A dummy variable that indicates respondent's sex; coded 1 for male.
Education	An ordinal variable that measures respondent's education using six levels, 1 = 8th grade or less; 2 = 9th-11th grade; 3 = high school or GED; 4 = some college but no degree; 5 = college degree; 6 = graduate degree.
Years Lived in Community	A variable that reports the number of years respondent has lived in the community.
Household Income	An ordinal variable that measures respondent's household income for 1993 using eight levels, 1 = <$15,000; 2 = $15,000-24,999; 3 = $25,000-34,999; 4 = $35,000-49,999; 5 = $50,000-59,999; 6 = $60,000-69,999; 7 = $70,000-79,999; 8 = $80,000+.
Child in Home	A dummy variable coded 1 if any children younger than 18 years of age are present in respondent's home.

turn our attention first to a multivariate regression analysis in which level of perceived risk is used as the dependent variable. The relationships between risk perceptions and selected independent variables are reported first for the residents-only samples, and then for all respondents (both residents and leaders).

Table 5.25 presents results obtained from the regression of risk perceptions on the key variables measuring residents' orientations toward other waste management issues along with localized social interactions, property ownership, and selected sociodemographic characteristics. These results indicate that higher levels of perceived risks associated with hazardous waste facilities occur among those respondents who expressed lower levels of trust in science and technology, lower levels of trust in agencies and organizations responsible for waste management (recreancy), and lower favorability regarding the provision of incentives to host communities. Also, higher risk perceptions were associated with residence in a nonwaste development community, while risk perceptions were significantly lower in the waste operating and waste siting community categories. Among the sociodemographic variables considered, the results indicate a tendency for risk perceptions to be significantly higher among women. At the same time, several of the other attitudinal and perceptual variables considered in earlier parts of the analysis exhibited little if any relationship with the risk perception measure in this multivariate analysis. Specifically, the measures of community conflict, levels of knowledge about waste facility siting, the measure of anticipated economic effects of waste facilities, and both the social interaction and property ownership measures did not add significantly to the ability to predict risk perception levels. Overall, the coefficient of variation (R^2) indicates that associations involving this set of independent variables jointly account for 30 percent of the variation in the risk perception measure.

When the data for the total sample of respondents (including residents plus leaders) are examined (table 5.26), the relationships are generally similar to those for the residents-only sample with the exception of two variables, the importance of knowledge about waste management and the importance of leader status. Given the substantially higher levels of knowledge among community leaders that was reported earlier in this chapter and the distinctions in resident/leader responses on most variables measuring perceptions about waste facility siting, the appearance of both of these variables as significant predictors of risk perceptions is not surprising. As with the residents-only analysis, the other variables exhibiting significant relationships with the risk perceptions measure are trust in science and technology, recreancy, favorability toward incentives, community type,

Table 5.25: Ordinary Least-squares Multiple Regression of Risk Perception Levels on Selected Predictor Variables, Residents-only Sample

Independent Variable	Regression Coefficient (b)	Standard Error
Community conflict	-.0008	.0170
Knowledge about waste management	-.0715	.0684
Trust in science/technology	-.1931***	.0223
Trust in agencies (recreancy)	-.0413**	.0126
Expected economic effects	.0463	.0342
Response to community incentives	-.1717***	.0355
Localized social interactions	.0135	.0122
Local property ownership	-.0631	.1013
Residence in waste operating community	-.6894***	.1982
Residence in waste siting community	-1.0719***	.2166
Residence in nonwaste devel. community	.3937*	.1847
Age	-.0061	.0060
Sex	-.5210***	.1469
Education	.0502	.0699
Length of residence	.0062	.0045
Household income	-.0197	.0436
Child in home	.2886	.1676
Intercept	10.4543***	.6377
N	1036	
R^2	.3009	
R^2 (adjusted)	.2892	

*$p \leq .05$ **$p \leq .01$ ***$p \leq .001$

sex of respondent, and the presence of children in the respondent household. In combination the full set of independent variables accounts for approximately one-third of the variation in the risk perception measure.

Multivariate Analysis of Favorability Toward Siting

Tables 5.27 and 5.28 present the results of the OLS and logistic regressions of favorability toward waste facility siting for the residents-only sample. Although the five-category ordinal measurement scale used for this dependent variable violates the assumption of continuous measurement for the dependent variable when using OLS regression, the general robustness of OLS-based estimates even in the face of some measurement violations and the ease of interpretation of regression coefficients compared to those produced using other multivariate procedures provide a strong rationale for

Table 5.26: Ordinary Least-squares Multiple Regression of Risk Perception Levels on Selected Predictor Variables, Residents/Leaders Combined Samples

Independent Variable	Regression Coefficient (b)	Standard Error
Community conflict	-.0082	.0161
Knowledge about waste management	-.1266*	.0621
Trust in science/technology	-.2047***	.0204
Trust in agencies (recreancy)	-.0434**	.0118
Expected economic effects	.0394	.0323
Response to community incentives	-.1499***	.0327
Localized social interactions	.0095	.0113
Local property ownership	-.0985	.0929
Residence in waste operating community	-.7421***	.1844
Residence in waste siting community	-.9994***	.1996
Residence in nonwaste devel. community	.3845*	.1706
Resident/leader status	.6397**	.2140
Age	-.0065	.0057
Sex	-.3972**	.1363
Education	.0664	.0646
Length of residence	.0056	.0042
Household income	-.0237	.0388
Child in home	.3219*	.1541
Intercept	10.2454***	.6770
N	1191	
R^2	.3396	
R^2 (adjusted)	.3295	

$*p \leq .05$ $**p \leq .01$ $***p \leq .001$

including results derived from the OLS approach. The subsequent presentation of a similarly structured multivariate analysis using logistic regression procedures provides a means of determining whether results based on the dichotomized favorability measure (favor/do not favor) reveal similar relationships with the various predictor variables.

As reported in table 5.27, the multiple regression of favorability toward waste facility siting on the array of measures addressing other dimensions of residents' responses to waste facilities and respondent sociodemographic measures indicates that several of the variables are significant predictors of favorability levels. Specifically, the results indicate that favorability tends to be higher among those who perceived low environmental contamination and health risks, who trust the science and technology of waste management as well as the agencies and organizations responsible for waste management, who anticipate that their community would experience positive economic

Table 5.27: Ordinary Least-squares Multiple Regression of Favorability Toward Waste Siting on Selected Predictor Variables, Residents-only Sample

Independent Variable	Regression Coefficient (b)	Standard Error
Level of perceived risk	-.2367***	.0149
Community conflict	.0081	.0081
Knowledge about waste management	-.0068	.0326
Trust in science/technology	.0567***	.0111
Trust in agencies (recreancy)	.0192**	.0061
Expected economic effects	.1103***	.0163
Response to community incentives	.1157***	.0171
Localized social interactions	-.0031	.0058
Local property ownership	.0624	.0482
Residence in waste operating community	.1891*	.0948
Residence in waste siting community	.4418***	.1047
Residence in nonwaste devel. community	-.0447	.0881
Age	-.0016	.0028
Sex	.1182	.0704
Education	-.0482	.0334
Length of residence	-.0001	.0022
Household income	-.0336	.0208
Child in home	-.0099	.0799
Intercept	1.6132***	.3411
N	1032	
R^2	.5276	
R^2 (adjusted)	.5192	

*$p \leq .05$ **$p \leq .01$ ***$p \leq .001$

effects from the development of a waste facility, and who respond favorably to the provision of community incentive programs by waste management firms. Higher favorability is also significantly related to residence in a waste operating or waste siting community. Perceptions of community conflict levels, knowledge about waste management, and the measures of social interaction and economic investments in the local community are not significant predictors of favorability levels. Also, none of the sociodemographic variables included in the multiple regression analysis exhibited a statistically significant relationship with the favorability measure using conventional ($p < .05$) criteria. In combination, the full set of independent variables account for about 52 percent of variation in the measure of favorability toward waste facility siting.

A parallel analysis using logistic regression procedures (table 5.28) produced generally similar results. Among the set of independent variables included in this portion of the analysis, the variables that emerged as having statistically significant relationships with the favorability measure included risk perception levels, trust in science and technology, agency/organization trust, anticipated community economic effects, and favorability toward developer-provided incentives. Thus, both the multiple regression and the logistic regression procedures identified the same set of attitudinal and perceptual factors as key predictors of favorability toward waste facility siting. The analysis also identified a tendency for respondents from waste siting communities to express higher levels of favorability, compared to the control community category. One noteworthy difference in results derived

Table 5.28: Logistic Regression of Favorability Toward Waste Facility Siting on Selected Predictor Variables, Residents-only Sample

Independent Variable	Parameter Estimate	Odds Ratio
Level of perceived risk	-.4979**	0.608
Community conflict	.0170	1.017
Knowledge about waste management	.1335	1.143
Trust in science/technology	.1170**	1.124
Trust in agencies (recreancy)	.0737**	1.076
Expected economic effects	.2222**	1.249
Response to community incentives	.1962**	1.217
Localized social interactions	-.0072	0.993
Local property ownership	.0169	1.017
Residence in waste operating community	-.0343	0.966
Residence in waste siting community	.9883**	2.687
Residence in nonwaste devel. community	-.3266	0.721
Age	-.0108	0.989
Sex	.2760	1.318
Education	-.0700	0.932
Length of residence	.0045	1.004
Household income	-.1811*	0.834
Child in home	-.0574	0.944
Intercept	-3.2931	
Pseudo R^2	.3995	

* $p \le .01$ ** $p \le .001$

from the two approaches involved the sociodemographic variables; respondent income level emerged as a significant predictor of favorability in the logistic regression, suggesting a tendency for higher favorability among persons with lower household incomes. This could reflect a tendency for persons with lower incomes to perceive waste facility developments as possible sources of improved employment and income opportunities.

Tables 5.29 and 5.30 present results of similar multiple regression and logistic regression analyses for the combined resident/leader sample, with leadership status defined as an additional independent variable. As indicated in table 5.29, the multiple regression results indicate that, as for the

Table 5.29: Ordinary Least-squares Multiple Regression of Favorability Toward Waste Siting on Selected Predictor Variables, Residents/Leaders Combined Samples

Independent Variable	Regression Coefficient (b)	Standard Error
Level of perceived risk	-.2336**	.0140
Community conflict	.0082	.0077
Knowledge about waste management	-.0202	.0299
Trust in science/technology	.0636**	.0102
Trust in agencies (recreancy)	.0152*	.0057
Expected economic effects	.1071**	.0156
Response to community incentives	.1259**	.0159
Localized social interactions	-.0010	.0054
Local property ownership	.0512	.0447
Residence in waste operating community	.2425*	.0892
Residence in waste siting community	.4752**	.0972
Residence in nonwaste devel. community	-.0779	.0821
Resident/leader status	-.1798	.1033
Age	-.0007	.0027
Sex	.1178	.0657
Education	-.0493	.0311
Length of residence	-.0014	.0020
Household income	-.0259	.0186
Child in home	-.0785	.0741
Intercept	1.7788**	.3554
N	1186	
R^2	.5514	
R^2 (adjusted)	.5441	

*p ≤ .01   **p ≤ .001

residents-only analysis, higher favorability toward waste facility siting is associated with lower risk perceptions, higher trust in science and technology and in agencies/organizations with waste management responsibilities, anticipation of positive effects on community economic conditions, favorable responses to developer-provided community incentives, and residence in communities where waste facilities have been developed or are being sited. The dummy variable for leadership status in the community suggests a slight tendency for more favorable response among leaders, net of the influence of the other independent variables, although that relationship only approaches statistical significance. The coefficient for respondent sex also approaches statistical significance, suggesting some tendency for men to respond more favorably to waste facility siting. In combination, the full set of independent variables accounts for approximately 55 percent of variation in the level of favorability toward waste facility siting.

Table 5.30: Logistic Regression of Favorability Toward Waste Facility Siting on Selected Predictor Variables, Residents/Leaders Combined Samples

Independent Variable	Parameter Estimate	Odds Ratio
Level of perceived risk	-.4724**	0.623
Community conflict	.0090	1.009
Knowledge about waste management	.0736	1.076
Trust in science/technology	.1286**	1.137
Trust in agencies (recreancy)	.0658**	1.068
Expected economic effects	.2070**	1.230
Response to community incentives	.2264**	1.254
Localized social interactions	-.0071	0.993
Local property ownership	.0213	1.022
Residence in waste operating community	.1580	1.171
Residence in waste siting community	1.0221**	2.779
Residence in nonwaste devel. community	-.4019	0.669
Resident/leader status	-.5515	0.576
Age	-.0058	0.994
Sex	.3055	1.357
Education	-.0686	0.934
Length of residence	.0009	1.001
Household income	-.1509*	0.860
Child in home	-.1318	0.877
Intercept	-2.8678	
Pseudo R^2	.4246	

*$p \leq .01$ **$p \leq .001$

The parallel logistic regression analysis (table 5.30) produced very similar results. Among the various independent variables measuring waste-related attitudes and perceptions, those exhibiting significant association with favorability toward waste facility siting included risk perceptions, trust in science and technology, trust in agencies and organizations (recreancy), anticipated community economic effects, favorability toward incentive programs, and residence in a waste siting community. The parameter estimate for the resident/leader variable approached statistical significance, reflecting the tendency for leaders to express more favorable orientations toward waste facility developments. Finally, household income level emerged in this analysis as the only sociodemographic variable with a significant association with favorability in the logistic regression analysis.

Summary

In this chapter we have attempted to provide a relatively comprehensive analysis of the major social and special impacts of waste projects as indicated by residents' and leaders' responses in the community surveys. The results suggest that while many respondents from these study areas are strongly opposed to waste facility siting in or near their communities, there are also substantial proportions of both residents and leaders who have more neutral or even positive views about the desirability of hosting such facilities in their areas. The results also suggest that some of the social and economic impacts that have been suggested as accompanying the development of hazardous waste facilities have generally been of relatively small magnitude in those study areas that have experienced waste facility siting or development.[3] Some effects such as those involving heightened community conflict levels appear to emerge in the context of waste facility siting activities, but then apparently dissipate to levels more characteristic of other nonwaste community contexts after a waste facility has been completed and begins operation.

What appears repeatedly in both the bivariate as well as the multivariate analyses is the tendency for certain residents' perceptions to be related to favorability toward siting. Perceptions of how the siting process occurred relative to equity and fairness, perceptions of the health and safety risks associated with waste projects, levels of trust in both the science and technology of waste management and the agencies and organizations responsible for implementing and managing that technology, and perceptions of economic benefits either directly resulting from the project or resulting from incentives provided by project developers are significantly related to levels of favorability toward siting. These factors appear to have a pervasive influence on residents' responses to waste facility siting. Also pervasive is a tendency for favorability toward waste siting to be especially pronounced among those who occupy community leadership positions. Given the relatively minor impact of waste siting on economic, fiscal, demographic, and public services identified in earlier chapters, and the fact that such impacts are perceived as of relatively minor importance by residents of these study areas, the results presented in this chapter strongly suggest that it is residents' perceptions and interactions that are the key factors impacted by waste project siting and operation. The results suggest as well that perceptions are the key factors affecting local responses to facility siting efforts. Attempts to increase public acceptance of waste facilities should therefore include major emphases on these types of perceptual factors.

Notes

1. Question wording varied slightly across the questionnaires used for different study areas to refer to either specific, locally relevant industrial or waste management facilities or, in the case of the control areas, to generic "local industries."

2. This part of the analysis was based on the original uncollapsed values of the conflict index.

3. Additional analyses not reported here included an examination of survey respondents' perceptions of the effects of development activities on various social groups (youth, elderly, and minority populations), the effects on local social organizations, and the effects of location specific capital and satisfaction with community involvement on responses to waste facility siting (see Murdock et al. 1997). Because respondents perceived only modest effects, and because perceptions in these areas had little relationship to orientations toward waste facility siting, discussions of these factors have been excluded from this analysis.

Chapter 6

Summary, Conclusions, and Implications

In this report we have presented the findings of a relatively comprehensive study of the impacts of waste projects in fifteen communities in five states in the Western United States. An overview of the rationale and objectives of the study, a description of the methods of data collection and analysis, and summaries of study findings relative to economic and fiscal, demographic and public service, and social and special impacts have been presented.

The study represents an attempt to identify the socioeconomic impacts of waste facility siting and operation in rural areas in the western United States using a comparative analysis of communities that are at the siting and operational phases of waste facility development compared to communities that have experienced other types of development projects and areas that have experienced only the baseline conditions that characterize rural areas in the United States. The study utilized extensive secondary data collected from federal and state sources and agencies and the results of resident and leader surveys. The study involved the completion of survey questionnaires by more than 1,800 persons in these 15 communities and the collection of extensive secondary data over a three-year time period. Although the study reflects the limitations of any such analysis that attempts to match communities that are, to varying extents, dissimilar, the results are nevertheless useful in identifying the nature and magnitude of the effects of waste facilities on rural areas. Rather than reexamining the results of the analysis reported in detail in previous chapters, we simply restate the major findings of the analysis and discuss the implications of the findings for the conceptual and empirical bases of the field of impact analysis, identify limitations of the present effort and research needs that should be pursued in future analyses, and discuss the implications of the findings for rural communities and waste facility siting in rural areas in the United States.

Major Findings

The intent of this section is not to repeat the extensive description of findings delineated in previous chapters but to simply restate what may be the most important findings relative to their implications for the base of knowledge in impact assessment in general and waste facility impacts in particular, for additional research needs, and for rural communities. These selected findings are as follows:

1. There is little indication that waste-impacted communities have experienced extensive economic growth as a result of such projects or that the fiscal conditions of the impacted areas have been substantially enhanced due to such projects. Although waste operational areas and waste siting areas showed increases in income and per capita expenditures, so did nonwaste development areas. For other economic and fiscal indicators there was little indication of waste-related impacts. At the same time, there is little indication that economic conditions have been negatively impacted due to waste facility siting or operation or that waste-impacted areas have experienced fiscal difficulties as a result of waste projects.

2. There is little evidence that waste-related projects have impacted communities either by changing patterns of population growth or by changing the characteristics of the population. Waste-impacted areas have not shown substantial increases in rates of population growth and there is little evidence of extensive inmigration of young adults or others who would alter long-term population patterns in such areas. As with the economic and fiscal impacts, the results for the demographic analysis also do not indicate that there have been negative impacts. Waste-related communities have not experienced greater rates of population decline than other communities and there is little indication that residents have been more likely to outmigrate from these areas.

3. Although the use of some services, such as welfare services, increased substantially in some waste-impacted communities, similar changes occurred in nonwaste development areas. For other services, such as police and fire services, there is little indication that there has been a substantially different pattern of change in service demands in waste-impacted communities than in nonwaste related communities. There is little indication of service-related impacts due to waste facility siting or operation.

4. Although not evident in waste-impacted communities, there is a clear indication that economic, demographic, and service growth have occurred in the nonwaste development areas with the nonwaste development projects in such areas leading to growth in income and employment, increases in populations, and growth in service needs. For baseline communities, the patterns are ones of relative stagnation in all forms of growth.

5. Relative to social and special impacts, one of the most pervasive patterns is respondents' opposition to the siting of a waste facility in their community. Although this varies in the manner noted below, it is obvious that opposition to such projects is extensive and pervasive.

6. Relative to social and special impacts, among the most persistent differences are those between leaders and residents. Leaders are older, better educated, have higher incomes, are more likely to own property, and are significantly different than residents in regard to numerous other demographic and socioeconomic characteristics. They also have very different perceptions of their communities and development projects. Leaders are more likely than residents to favor siting a waste facility in their area, likely to perceive greater equity, and lower levels of conflict in regard to the siting of such projects, likely to view service and economic impacts as having been more positive, likely to have higher levels of knowledge regarding waste storage and management, likely to view technology more positively and view risks as lower, and to view incentives as more positive. Differences between leaders and residents are evident in all four types of communities but the leaders of waste-impacted communities are substantially more likely than leaders in other community types to favor siting.

7. Differences in residents' perceptions of social and special impacts by community type show several important patterns. First, residents in waste siting and waste operational areas are more likely to favor siting than residents in other types of communities. There are few if any differences among residents in different types of waste-impacted communities relative to perceived levels of participation and equity in the siting process or levels of knowledge about waste management, but residents in waste siting areas perceive substantially higher levels of conflict than residents in other types of communities. However, perceived levels of conflict are not significantly different between residents in waste operational and those in nonwaste communities, suggesting that such conflict may not persist over time. Residents of waste siting and operational communities, especially those living in waste siting communities, tend to view the impacts on services more positively than residents in other types of communities. Residents of waste-impacted areas also perceive lower levels of risk from waste projects than residents from other communities. Finally, residents from waste-impacted areas tend to perceive incentives as more important to the acceptability of waste projects than do residents in nonwaste related areas.

8. When multivariate analyses were completed on those factors impacting levels of risk, higher trust in science and technology, higher trust in responsible agencies and organizations, more favorable responses to community incentives, residence in a waste siting or waste operating community, and sex were significantly related to lower levels of perceived risk for residents. These same factors plus knowledge about waste management and holding a leadership position were significantly related to reduced perceptions of risk for all respondents (inclusive of residents and leaders).

9. The multivariate regression analysis on favorability toward siting indicated that lower incomes, not having residence in a community with a waste facility or in a community experiencing the siting of such a facility, perceptions of greater economic benefits from such projects, higher trust in science and technology and in agencies responsible for waste management decisions and activities, perceptions of lower levels of risks, and higher levels of support for incentives increased favorability toward siting among residents and among all respondents including leaders and residents.

Overall, then, the results of this analysis suggest that waste-related facilities have not had the major impacts, either positive or negative, that are sometimes presumed to occur as a result of them. At the same time, opposition to them remains strong but there is some lessening of opposition and some increase in the proportion of respondents with positive perceptions of such projects in communities that have experienced waste-facility siting or operation. Economic as well as risk and related perceptions apparently do impact perceptions of siting and the results suggest that how the siting of such projects is managed does impact how positively they are perceived.

Implications for the Knowledge Base in Impact Assessment

The findings noted above and elsewhere in this volume have several implications for the base of knowledge in impact assessment in general and for the specific impact assessment questions included among the factors to be addressed in objectives for this study. In this section, we discuss such implications.

One of the implications of the findings is that standard socioeconomic impacts appear to largely reflect the size of the project's employment and expenditure bases. The premise long maintained in impact assessments (Murdock and Leistritz 1979) that the magnitude of the impacts is largely a product of the relative size of the project-related work forces and economic activities relative to baseline conditions appears to be supported by the findings of this analysis. The economic, demographic, public service, fiscal, and many of the social impacts of waste facility-related projects were minimal, as would be expected given the relatively small size of the waste facility workforces. This is important because there has been substantial speculation that such impacts would be different in waste facility-impacted areas (Murdock et al. 1983b; 1991). Speculation that waste-related projects would lead to substantial outmigration, to reductions in business volume as businesses leave the area, or to substantial employment growth and population inmigration are not substantiated by the results from the study communities. Rather, as noted below, some types of impacts appear to be different because of the waste-related factors involved but the standard impacts appear to reflect relative labor force size in waste-related as in other (nonwaste related) developments.

Relative to the issue of the duration of impacts, the results here are limited by the fact that differences unrelated to waste development exist between different study communities. However, the evidence from this study suggests that many of the impacts of waste siting may not be sustained. For example, the differences in levels of perceived conflict between waste siting and waste operational and nonwaste communities indicated that, although residents of waste siting communities perceived higher levels of conflict, the perceptions of residents in waste operating communities were little different than those for residents in nonwaste communities. Such findings suggest that at least some impacts may be transitory. The fact that there were few differences between sites in which siting has failed and those in which the process was ongoing suggests, however, that the siting of such a project leads to conflicts whether the process leads to a successful siting or not. The findings of this analysis suggest that the fear that the siting of such projects will result in conflict appears justified, but the fear that this siting will leave lasting residues of community distrust and division is not supported.

The findings from this effort strongly support the importance of risk perceptions and concerns related to technology management in determining residents' favorability toward siting. Throughout the analysis, it was apparent that concerns related to the failure of technology and of failure in its management were of major importance to residents in all types of communities. It appears that an abiding fear of technology failure is pervasive among residents in many different community contexts in the United States and that this fear increases resistance to siting. What also is apparent in the waste siting controversy in the United States is the truth of the sociological maxim that factors perceived as real are real in their consequences (Thomas and Znaniecki 1918-20). There is little doubt that the largest contributor to resistance to such siting lies in such perceptual factors. Therefore, if one wishes to understand social factors in waste siting one must address these key perceptual issues.

Although some of the initial analysis from our efforts (Spies et al. 1996) suggested that concerns related to perceived risks may have been so substantial that such fears could not be overcome (therefore suggesting that siting processes are doomed to failure no matter what course of action is followed), additional analysis suggests that some actions can be taken that can address some of the concerns of residents and increase the likelihood of siting. The results related to differentials in perceptions of equity as they impact favorability toward siting suggest that how the siting process is managed may impact siting. Similarly, the positive relationships between the perceived economic benefits of siting and incentives for siting and favorability toward siting suggest that the potential economic benefits of such projects may impact residents' level of acceptance of siting. In addition, the fact that the incentive receiving the strongest support was that of increasing safety standards at the facility, suggests that actions to directly alter perceptions of risk may be beneficial. Finally, the fact that leaders, particularly those in waste-impacted communities who have generally received the largest amounts of information about such projects, tend to be more favorable toward siting may suggest that making such projects more acceptable is feasible. Although our findings do not allow us to suggest that actions can be taken that are sufficient to completely overcome risk and other perceptions that limit siting, they do suggest that siting is not unaffected by the actions of those who are responsible for siting and project management.

In sum, the results of this analysis make it apparent that empirical evidence must substitute for speculation if the base of knowledge in impact assessment is to be expanded. Several of the findings noted above contradict the commonly accepted premises in impact assessments about waste siting while others tend to verify what had been expected. Only broad-based, multisite and multistage empirical information can separate speculation from fact.

Limitations Affecting and Implications for Research on Socioeconomic Impacts

The research process and the results of the research reported here also have implications for research on waste facility siting and management in rural areas in the United States. Some of these implications are discussed below.

One of the implications of this project is the need for such studies to be based on true longitudinal panel designs. Although every attempt has been made to isolate the effects of different project phases by comparing siting to operational, and siting and operational to other types of communities, it is evident that even small differences in the starting dates for projects and differences in community contexts make it difficult to presume that results from given communities at one stage of the development process are, in fact, completely comparable to other communities at that project phase. Communities must be analyzed over time so that the effects of project events can be carefully monitored and the effects of project phases more completely established.

Although the identification and collection of data at additional sites was beyond the resources available for this study, the use of additional sites would have been beneficial to the resolution of numerous issues. With the number of sites available for this analysis, the existence of even one set of extraneous events (such as the questionable Census Bureau population estimates for the Texas control community or the emergence of the Utah waste site as a distant bedroom community for a major metropolitan center) created difficulties in comparisons that can only be completely overcome by the use of additional study areas. In retrospect, the study may have been enhanced by the selection of additional communities with comparisons being made on a more limited set of dimensions.

Similarly, the study may have benefitted from focusing on a more limited set of research issues. Analyzing economic, demographic, public service, fiscal, and social and special effects across the number of communities included in this study effort with the resources available is a formidable task. Examining fewer of these dimensions for a larger number of communities or examining these dimensions in more depth for a smaller number of communities may have been advantageous.

The analysis also suggests that additional consideration must be given to the selection of areas in which the cooperation of development firms and service agencies has been obtained. Primary consideration must be given to selection of sites that allow for valid comparisons on key study parameters and study areas should only be selected if such considerations are first met. Lack of adequate cooperation on the part of developers and service providers substantially limits study efforts such as the one reported here. Although obtaining verbal commitments from local project management such as was obtained in this study may appear sufficient, obtaining written confirmation of cooperation from the appropriate levels of company management may be a necessary condition if the total impacts of such developments are to be established. Similarly, verifying the existence of needed service data at the local level for the specific study areas of interest (rather than relying on information from officials from service agencies located at the state or regional level) is essential.

The analysis also suggests the importance of additional detailed analyses of each of several key parameters. Knowing that risk perceptions related to technology and its management are of key concern to residents in potential siting areas does not establish the factors determinative of differentials in such risk perceptions. Although we have partially addressed this issue, it is evident that it must be given considerable additional attention because of its importance in decisions related to siting. Similarly, issues related to the siting process deserve additional attention. Under what conditions are the equity of participation increased and perceptions of the process enhanced? The science of the waste facility siting process must be substantially improved. The role of incentives in the siting process must also be investigated more thoroughly. Our findings suggested that residents in waste-impacted communities were those who were most likely to believe that the provision of incentives would increase project acceptability, but such perceptions were not generally evident among residents in nonwaste development areas. Do incentives only come to play a role after a community has made the decision (or had the decision made for them) to accept a waste facility? Additional examination of the conditional dimensions of incentive provision are essential.

We also believe that our assessments of the economic, fiscal, demographic, and service impacts have been less complete than is desirable. Personal interviews with specific industry and service providers should be included in future analyses. In addition, although a very difficult task, it is also necessary to examine the role of waste projects in offsetting economic and demographic decline. As noted above, problems in community selection make it obvious that consideration of simulation analyses that examine with and without project scenarios compared to actual trends should be considered for inclusion in future analyses.

Finally, we believe that this analysis shows the need for additional multisite and multistage analyses. The limitations revealed by this effort can only be overcome, and the potential opportunities inherent in such analyses sufficiently pursued, with additional efforts. The unique contexts of waste facility siting in different areas and different eras must be examined if our knowledge of waste siting is ever to be sufficient to effectively guide community decision-making processes and the processes of siting such projects in rural areas in the United States.

Implications for Rural Communities
and Waste Facility Siting

Despite the limitations noted above, we believe the results of this analysis suggest several important implications for rural communities and those involved in waste facility siting. Among the most important findings for rural communities is that waste projects are unlikely to bring either extensive socioeconomic benefits or socioeconomic ruin. The modest size of such developments means that they are likely to have limited benefits for most siting communities. At the same time, they do not appear to be deleterious to the socioeconomic health of the community. This suggests that rural community residents should view both claims of large socioeconomic benefits and those of loss (due to outmigration and business loss) with skepticism. From the standpoint of standard socioeconomic impact, the results of this analysis suggest that such projects are likely to have limited positive or negative effects. On the other hand, the results also suggest that other types of service and production industries in nonwaste development communities may have more substantial economic, demographic, and related benefits for a community. This analysis indicates that if a choice exists between the hosting of different types of facilities, nonwaste development projects are likely to be more economically and demographically beneficial for a community than waste-related facilities.

What is also evident is that waste projects are likely to be seen by residents as having substantial risks and that the siting of such projects is likely to result in increased levels of conflict within the community, at least in the short term. Communities considering such projects will need to balance the potential risks to relationships within the community against the potential benefits. The exact parameters of this balance are likely to be community specific.

The results also suggest that community leaders involved in waste siting should be aware of several characteristics about such projects and their involvement in such projects. In addition to the benefit and cost factors noted above, leaders should be aware that waste projects are likely to be accepted only if both the means by which they are obtained and their ends are acceptable to community residents. The findings here related to the importance of equity in the siting process make it apparent that community leaders must place high priority on how the process of project evaluation is completed. A deliberate, open, and broadly participatory process of project evaluation is essential. Leaders may benefit from understanding that residents must be provided with the opportunity to either accept or reject such projects in a participatory process, or their leadership on key issues related to such projects is likely to be ineffective.

Leaders should also recognize that their knowledge of waste projects and their perceptions of such projects may be quite different than those of other community residents. Leaders may be more knowledgeable and more positive toward such developments because they perceive them as part of essential community development efforts (Spies et al. 1998) but they should be aware that their levels of knowledge and positive perceptions may not be shared by community residents. It is important for leaders to extend their interactions about such projects beyond the circle of other leaders so that they obtain full knowledge of how residents perceive such projects. Concerted efforts to obtain such knowledge are important at the early stages of such a development because leaders are likely to be exposed to more polarized positions as the siting process proceeds. It will be increasingly difficult to obtain objective information from community residents, if the community becomes polarized. Such projects are likely to have considerable political risks for leaders because of their conflictual and controversial characteristics. Leaders who become involved in such projects may wish to ensure that all processes involving the project are of the participatory nature described above and that their position relative to the project is one which they can, and are willing to, defend as the intensity of community discussion regarding the project increases.

The results also have implications for those involved in waste facility siting. Although given the history of such siting efforts it may seem unlikely that any developer would be unaware of such perceptions, it is essential for those responsible for waste facility siting efforts (whether they are waste industry or governmental and regulatory officials) to be aware that residents do not evaluate such projects as they do other projects. Waste projects come with resident perceptions that these projects involve increased levels of risks relative to other types of projects. To portray them as simply another form of development, to overemphasize their likely benefits, or to fail to acknowledge that they may involve some risks (no matter what the technical probability of the occurrence of events leading to increased risks) is likely to be detrimental to the credibility of siting efforts. It is necessary to initiate the siting of such projects with the knowledge that they are uniquely perceived and their siting will likely require extraordinary measures.

The findings also suggest that developers should, like community leaders, be aware that open, broadly participatory, siting processes are essential. There can be few shortcuts in the siting of such projects because of residents' perceptions of them. Although a developer may be tempted to avoid such costly and often cumbersome processes, it appears that although completing such processes may not guarantee success, avoiding them substantially increases the probability of siting failure.

Siting entities must also recognize that educating community leaders is not enough. The finding that leaders in waste-impacted communities have substantially higher levels of knowledge than residents and that residents in waste-impacted communities show no higher levels of knowledge than residents in other areas, when coupled with the general association between higher levels of knowledge and higher levels of favorability toward siting, suggests that educational efforts of developers may have been effective but insufficiently broad based. Given that community leaders' higher levels of acceptance do not necessarily affect residents' levels of acceptance, there can be no substitute for direct educational efforts with community residents. The same type of intensive efforts often shown in informing leaders are likely to be required across the community.

The results presented here also suggest that communities are likely to want to be compensated for hosting such projects. Since such projects appear to be unlikely to bring the extensive socioeconomic benefits of other (larger-scale) projects, but are seen as bearing levels of unknown risk, it is not likely to be possible to simply suggest that the communities treat such projects like other economic development projects. Compensation for such risks is likely to increasingly be a required business expense for such projects. What is equally important to note, however, is that the most important form of incentive may be for the developer to take steps to directly address residents' perceptions of risk. Increasing safety measures was the incentive most strongly supported by respondents in all types of communities. Steps to directly address risks should be given careful consideration.

Finally, we believe the findings here suggest that the siting and development of waste projects may be more possible than is sometimes perceived but that it is clearly a formidable and uncertain process. The fact that knowledge, experience with waste facilities, equity dimensions of waste siting, and incentives, under some conditions, increased levels of acceptance suggests that there are private- and public-sector policies that may increase the probability of siting such a project. At the same time, the general society wide perceptions that such projects bring with them makes it impossible to guarantee that any specific sets of actions will increase community acceptance to the level necessary to ensure siting success. Communities have legitimate rights to choose and will exercise those rights. Developers may be able to affect only the probabilities of acceptance and cannot expect communities to necessarily agree with their perceptions of the value of waste projects for rural communities.

Conclusion

Overall, the results of this study suggest that the empirical examination of the impacts of waste facility siting, the community factors that must be considered in such siting, the impacts of the siting and operation of such facilities, and the actions that developers should take relative to waste facility siting are highly complex. This study has limited its examination to the socioeconomic effects of waste facilities while other equally important health, safety, engineering, and environmental dimensions have not been considered. However, even with its restricted scope, the results of this study indicate that waste facility siting and development require much additional examination by scientists as well as community residents and that such developments are unlikely to soon be more acceptable or less controversial in rural areas in the United States.

Appendix: Questions Used in Resident and Leader Surveys

RESIDENT SURVEY

In nonwaste development and baseline (control) communities the following letter was used:

Dear Resident:

The [name of university conducting the survey] is conducting a study of how certain types of waste development projects (e.g., hazardous, industrial and chemical, but not municipal waste and garbage storage sites) and other types of development projects may affect small communities in different parts of the nation. We are interested in how you feel about such issues and about how you and other members of this community feel about the place in which you live and the economic and social changes affecting your community. The goal of this research project is to help communities make better decisions about various development projects.

Your community has been selected because it is **not** involved in waste siting but has similar characteristics to other communities that are experiencing such projects. Your answers will be compared to those of residents in communities involved with waste projects to identify how they have been affected by such projects.

Please help us by completing this questionnaire. The information you provide is important. The overall results of this study [but no individual responses] will be provided to leaders in your community. Also, a Community Leader Handbook will be published to provide information to local officials in your community and similar communities about the effects of various types of economic development.

All your answers are confidential. The information you provide will not be identified with you in any manner. If you have any questions, please contact any of us at the address or phone number shown on the first page of the questionnaire. Thank you for your time and assistance.

Respectfully,

In waste siting and waste operating (in parenthesis) communities, the following letter was used:

Dear Resident:

The [name of university conducting the survey] is conducting a study of how certain types of waste development projects (e.g., hazardous, industrial and chemical, but not municipal waste and garbage storage sites) and other types of development projects may affect small communities in different parts of the nation. We are interested in how you feel about such issues and about how you and other members of this community feel about the places in which you live and the economic and social changes affecting your community. The goal of this research project is to help communities make better decisions about various development projects.

As you may be aware, _____ attempted to site (operates) a hazardous waste facility near _____ in _____ County. This questionnaire asks how you feel about your community and how the siting (presence) of a waste facility may have affected your community or how such facilities may affect similar communities.

Please help us by completing this questionnaire. The information you provide is important. The overall results of this study [but no individual responses] will be provided to leaders in your community. Also, a Community Leader Handbook will be published to provide information to local officials in your community and similar communities about the effects of various types of economic development.

All your answers are confidential. The information you provide will not be identified with you in any manner. If you have any questions, please contact any of us at the address or phone number shown on the first page of the questionnaire. Thank you for your time and assistance.

Respectfully,

PLEASE READ THE FOLLOWING BEFORE STARTING THE QUESTIONNAIRE

To make sure we have an even mix in our responses, we use the following method to select who fills out the questionnaire:

The person who fills out the questionnaire should be the person 18 years of age or older who has had the <u>most recent birthday</u>. This person must be a permanent resident of the household. This means the person is not a guest or someone who rents a room from you.

It is essential that only one person in the household fills out the questionnaire. This means that the person who starts the questionnaire should be the one who finishes it. It also means that all the opinions should be those of the person who completes the questionnaire. We do not want your spouse's or some other person's opinions. We need your opinions and your opinions alone. Remember, all of your answers are confidential. The information you provide will not be identified with you in any manner.

Please complete the questionnaire by circling the appropriate answer or by filling in the blanks provided. If you do not know the answer to a question, simply write DK for don't know by it and go to the next question.

A member of our research team will pick up the questionnaire within 48 hours. If you do not plan to be home, a plastic bag is provided so that you can hang the questionnaire on the outside of your door.

This survey is being conducted by (name of university doing survey). If you have any questions about the questionnaire, please call or write (researchers at the university on the research team) at:

(Address and telephone number of university)

COMMUNITY

This group of questions deals with your community ties. It asks about friends, relatives, and neighbors and how you feel about your community.

1. Indicate how often you see or meet on an informal basis with the following types of people if they live in your community.

1=More than once a week; 2=Once a week;
3=A few times a month; 4=Once a month;
5=A few times a year; 6=Never; 7=Does not apply

a. Mother, father, brothers or sisters not living in your household	1	2	3	4	5	6	7
b. Children not living in your household	1	2	3	4	5	6	7
c. Other relatives	1	2	3	4	5	6	7
d. Close friends	1	2	3	4	5	6	7
e. Acquaintances	1	2	3	4	5	6	7
f. Co-workers	1	2	3	4	5	6	7
g. Neighbors	1	2	3	4	5	6	7

2. Using the scale below, how would you describe your feelings toward your neighbors? Would you say you are:

1	2	3	4	5
Very Close	Somewhat Close	Neutral	Somewhat Distant	Very Distant

3. Do you have any plans to move away from this community in the next five years?

1 Definitely will not move
2 Probably will not move
3 Probably will move
4 Definitely will move

Why? _____

4. On average, about how many hours do you ordinarily spend in a normal <u>month</u> attending or taking part in any kind of organized or planned group activity or event (not associated with your work or job) that involves other members of this community?

   1 More than 10 hours per month
   2 5-10 hours per month
   3 1-4 hours per month
   4 Less than one hour per month

5. Please indicate how satisfied you are with the following factors in this community.

1=Completely Dissatisfied; 2=Somewhat Dissatisfied; 3=Neither Sat. or Dissat.; 4=Somewhat Satisfied; 5=Completely Satisfied

a.	Public schools	1	2	3	4	5
b.	Housing	1	2	3	4	5
c.	Medical services	1	2	3	4	5
d.	Fire protection	1	2	3	4	5
e.	Law enforcement	1	2	3	4	5
f.	Streets and roads	1	2	3	4	5
g.	Utilities	1	2	3	4	5
h.	Recreation facilities	1	2	3	4	5
i.	Opportunity to earn an adequate income	1	2	3	4	5
j.	Employment opportunities to keep youth in the area	1	2	3	4	5

6. Using the scale below, please circle the response that best indicates how satisfied you are with this community as a place to live.

1	2	3	4	5
Completely Dissatisfied	Somewhat Dissatisfied	Neither Dissatisfied nor Satisfied	Somewhat Satisfied	Completely Satisfied

WASTE AND WASTE MANAGEMENT

The next set of questions asks what you think and how you feel about certain aspects of the waste management industry. Please remember we are asking about hazardous, industrial, and chemical waste—not municipal waste and garbage.

7. Please indicate whether you disagree or agree with the following statements.

1=Disagree Strongly; 2=Disagree Somewhat;
3=Neither Agree nor Disagree;
4=Agree Somewhat; 5=Agree Strongly

a.	A waste facility is economically beneficial to a community	1	2	3	4	5
b.	The presence of a waste facility encourages other industries to locate in the surrounding area	1	2	3	4	5
c.	A waste facility results in a decrease in property values in the surrounding area	1	2	3	4	5
d.	A waste facility poses health risks for future generations living in the surrounding area	1	2	3	4	5
e.	Environmental contamination is likely to occur as a result of a waste facility being in an area	1	2	3	4	5
f.	The current methods of transporting wastes to storage and disposal sites do not adequately protect the public from contamination	1	2	3	4	5
g.	Agencies responsible for public health and safety are capable of responding to waste accidents in ways which will ensure public safety	1	2	3	4	5

8. Using the scale below, indicate how close you would be willing to live to certain types of facilities. Please look at the list and for each facility circle the number that represents the closest acceptable distance between the facility and your home.

Number of Miles

		less than 1 (1)	1 to 5 (2)	6 to 10 (3)	11 to 20 (4)	21 to 50 (5)	51 to 100 (6)	more than 100 (7)	not at any dis- tance (8)	Don't know (DK)
a.	Shopping Mall	1	2	3	4	5	6	7	8	DK
b.	Chemical Disposal or Incinerator Facility	1	2	3	4	5	6	7	8	DK
c.	Nuclear Power Plant	1	2	3	4	5	6	7	8	DK
d.	Radioactive Waste Storage Facility	1	2	3	4	5	6	7	8	DK
e.	Hazardous Waste Incinerator	1	2	3	4	5	6	7	8	DK
f.	U.S. Air Force Base	1	2	3	4	5	6	7	8	DK
g.	Large Airport	1	2	3	4	5	6	7	8	DK
h.	Minimum Security Prison	1	2	3	4	5	6	7	8	DK
i.	Municipal Waste Landfill	1	2	3	4	5	6	7	8	DK
j.	Hazardous Waste Landfill	1	2	3	4	5	6	7	8	DK

9. Nearly all industries can achieve a level of zero waste production if they use available waste control and antipollution devices.

    1   Yes   2   No   DK   Don't Know

10. The permit that allows a waste management facility to dispose of hazardous waste also allows it to store radioactive waste.

    1   Yes   2   No   DK   Don't Know

11. Using a scale of 1 (NO TRUST) to 5 (COMPLETE TRUST), please circle the number that best indicates how much trust you have in the ability of each of the following to make appropriate decisions about the siting and operation of a waste facility.

		NO TRUST				COMPLETE TRUST
a.	State Health Department	1	2	3	4	5
b.	State Agency Responsible for Environmental Protection	1	2	3	4	5
c.	Governor's Office	1	2	3	4	5
d.	State Legislature	1	2	3	4	5
e.	County Government	1	2	3	4	5
f.	City or Town Government	1	2	3	4	5
g.	Private Waste Management Companies	1	2	3	4	5
h.	U.S. Environmental Protection Agency (EPA)	1	2	3	4	5
i.	U.S. Nuclear Regulatory Commission (NRC)	1	2	3	4	5
j.	U.S. Department of Energy (DOE)	1	2	3	4	5
k.	Local Volunteer Citizen Groups	1	2	3	4	5
l.	Environmental Groups	1	2	3	4	5

12. In the United States, nearly all high-level radioactive waste from nuclear power plants is now being taken to be stored in a special underground facility.

1 Yes   2 No   DK Don't Know

13. In the United States, the federal agency with the primary responsibility for enforcing pollution laws is:

    1   Federal Emergency Management Administration (FEMA)
    2   Environmental Protection Agency (EPA)
    3   U.S. Fish and Wildlife Service (FWS)
    4   Bureau of Land Management (BLM)
    5   Office of Technology Assessment (OTA)
    DK Don't Know

14. Using a scale from 1 (NO CONFIDENCE) to 5 (COMPLETE CONFIDENCE), please indicate your level of confidence concerning the following statements.

		NO CONFIDENCE				COMPLETE CONFIDENCE
a.	Scientists can design a waste facility that adequately protects public health and safety	1	2	3	4	5
b.	Engineering and construction personnel can build a waste facility that adequately protects public health and safety	1	2	3	4	5
c.	Management and operations personnel can monitor waste conditions that might threaten public health and safety	1	2	3	4	5
d.	Management and operations personnel can correct problems or deficiencies that might threaten public health and safety	1	2	3	4	5

15. Listed below are various incentives that a waste management company might offer a community. Suppose a waste management company proposed to place a waste facility in your community. Please read each statement and circle one number to show whether or not that incentive would make the proposed facility more or less acceptable to you or would not affect your opinion.

1=More Acceptable; 2=No Effect;
3=Less Acceptable; DK=Don't Know

a.	Waste company pays a higher level of taxes than other local industries.	1	2	3	DK
b.	Waste company had a policy to hire local residents first.	1	2	3	DK
c.	Waste company offers to pay fair market real estate values and relocation costs for any property owners and residents negatively affected by the facility.	1	2	3	DK
d.	Waste company provides the community with equipment such as fire trucks or ambulances, etc.	1	2	3	DK
e.	Waste company provides the community with facilities such as parks, libraries, or swimming pools.	1	2	3	DK
f.	Waste company adopts safety standards that exceed those required by state and federal governments.	1	2	3	DK

16. If an election were held today, most people in my community would vote in favor of having a waste facility located in our area.

STRONGLY DISAGREE				STRONGLY AGREE
1	2	3	4	5

17. If an election were held today, I would vote in favor of having a waste facility located in our area.

STRONGLY DISAGREE				STRONGLY AGREE
1	2	3	4	5

In nonwaste development and control communities, the following questions were asked about economic development and community involvement.

ECONOMIC DEVELOPMENT
AND COMMUNITY INVOLVEMENT

This part of the questionnaire asks about economic change and development, community involvement, and other changes and events in your community and other communities like it. Economic development refers to the creation, expansion, operation or contraction of commercial businesses. At this point we **do not** want you to consider changes in locally financed public facilities such as public schools, county government, or city government.

18. This question asks about involvement in matters that are important to the economic development of your community. Please read the list below and indicate whether you have done any of the following activities concerning any community, local government, or local business issues.

    a. Attended a public meeting or hearing   1   YES   2   NO

    b. Contacted a government official   1   YES   2   NO

    c. Signed a petition   1   YES   2   NO

    d. Written a letter to a newspaper   1   YES   2   NO

    e. Joined, donated money, or volunteered
        time to an organization involved in
        local issues   1   YES   2   NO

    f. Other activities that are not listed above   1   YES   2   NO

        If you answered YES to question **f**, please list the activities below.

        _____

    g. If you answered YES to any of **a-f** above, please indicate when you <u>first</u> did any of the activities listed above and indicate the type of issue that was involved.

        month _____   year _____

        type of issue _____

In waste siting and waste operating (in parenthesis) communities, the following question was asked about the facility.

18. Please read the following list of statements concerning the proposed (the word proposed deleted from waste operating) _____ facility, and circle YES if the statement is true or NO if the statement is false.

a.	I know where the _____ facility would have been (is) located.	1	YES	2	NO
b.	I have visited the site location for the _____ facility.	1	YES	2	NO
c.	1 was hoping to work for (I work for) _____.	1	YES	2	NO
d.	A member of my immediate family (i.e., husband/wife; son/daughter; father/mother; brother/sister) was hoping to work (works) for _____.	1	YES	2	NO
e.	I lived in this community when _____ first decided to locate here	1	YES	2	NO
f.	I own or work for a company that would have provided (provides) materials, goods, or services to the _____.	1	YES	2	NO

In waste siting and waste operating (in parenthesis) communities, the following question was asked about the proposed facility.

19. How close do you live to the _____ site (name of facility)?

```
1    Less than 1 mile
2    1 to 5 miles
3    6 to 10 miles
4    11 to 15 miles
5    16 to 20 miles
6    21 to 25 miles
7    More than 25 miles
8    Don't Know
```

In waste siting and waste operating communities, the following question was asked:

20. Do you own any other property (other than the house you live in) that is located within five miles of the _____ site?

    1   YES   2   NO   DK   Don't Know

    If you answered Yes, then please indicate what type of property you own.

In waste siting and waste operating (in parenthesis) communities, the following question was asked:

21. Please indicate whether you disagree or agree with the following statements.

                                        1=Disagree Strongly; 2=Disagree Somewhat
                                        3=Neither Agree nor Disagree; 4=Agree
                                        Somewhat; 5=Agree Strongly

---

a.	The majority of the construction workers at the _____ facility would be (are) current residents.	1	2	3	4	5
b.	The majority of the employees who would have operated (who operate) the _____ facility would have been (are) current residents.	1	2	3	4	5
c..	State government officials have provided the public with complete and accurate information about the safety of waste disposal.	1	2	3	4	5
d.	Officials representing _____ have provided the public with complete and accurate information about the safety of waste disposal.	1	2	3	4	5

In waste siting and waste operating (in parenthesis) communities, the following question was asked:

22. Which of the following types of facilities best describe what _____ would have been (is)? (Note: You may circle more than one number)

    1. A landfill facility (wastes are buried in the ground)
    2. A landspread facility (waste are spread and mixed into the soil)
    3. An above ground containment facility (wastes are stored in barrels or other portable containers)
    4. An incinerator facility (wastes are burned at high temperatures)
    5. An injection well facility (wastes are placed underground by a well)
    6. A recycling facility (recovers material resources from waste)
    DK Don't Know

In waste siting and waste operating communities, the following question was asked:

23. Please read the list below and indicate whether you have done any of the following activities.

    a. Attended a public meeting or hearing
        about _____ facility.   1   YES   2 NO

    b. Contacted a government official
        about the _____ facility.   1   YES   2 NO

    c. Signed a petition about the
        _____ facility.   1   YES   2 NO

    d. Contacted _____ .   1   YES   2 NO

    e. Written a letter to a newspaper
        about the _____ facility.   1   YES   2 NO

    f. Joined, donated money, or volunteered
        time to an organization that supports
        the _____ facility.   1   YES   2 NO

    g. Joined, donated money, or volunteered
        time to an organization that opposes
        the _____ facility.   1   YES   2 NO

    h. Other activities concerning the
        _____ facility that are not
        listed above.   1   YES   2 NO

If you answered YES to question **h**, please list the activities below.

---

i.   If you answered YES to any of **a-h** above, when did you <u>first</u> participate?

month _____ year _____

The following question was asked in the alternative forms shown in all communities:

24. The following is a list of community factors that can be affected by development. Please indicate what kind of effect you think that _____ (name of facility in waste-impacted or recent economic changes for nonwaste and baseline [control] communities) would (has had for waste siting, nonwaste development and baseline communities) have on each aspect of your community.

1=Very Positive Effect; 2=Positive Effect
3=Neither Positive Nor Negative;
4=Negative Effect; 5=Very Negative
Effect; DK=Don't Know

a.	Employment	1	2	3	4	5	DK
b.	Income	1	2	3	4	5	DK
c.	Funds for schools or public education	1	2	3	4	5	DK
d.	Local public revenues (taxes, fees, etc.)	1	2	3	4	5	DK
e.	Local public expenditures (funds spent in service provisions)	1	2	3	4	5	DK
f.	Housing costs	1	2	3	4	5	DK
g.	Police protection	1	2	3	4	5	DK
h.	Fire protection	1	2	3	4	5	DK
i.	Young people	1	2	3	4	5	DK
j.	Elderly residents	1	2	3	4	5	DK
k.	Ethnic minorities	1	2	3	4	5	DK

		1=Very Positive Effect; 2=Positive Effect 3=Neither Positive nor Negative; 4=Negative Effect; 5=Very Negative Effect; DK= Don't Know					
l.	Crime	1	2	3	4	5	DK
m.	Family life	1	2	3	4	5	DK
n.	The physical health of community members	1	2	3	4	5	DK
o.	The reputation of your community	1	2	3	4	5	DK
p.	Quality of life	1	2	3	4	5	DK
q.	Social organizations such as churches, civic groups, and business groups	1	2	3	4	5	DK
r.	Levels of stress, anxiety, fear, or worry among members of the community	1	2	3	4	5	DK

25. Of all the factors listed in question 24 above, which two or three do you think have been most significantly affected by recent economic changes (name of facility in waste-impacted) in your community and why do you think this might be so? Please use the space below for your answer.
    1. _____
    2. _____
    3. _____

In nonwaste development and control communities, the following question was asked:

26. Of all the types of businesses that are now operating in your community, please indicate which type has had the most significant impact on economic change in your community and please indicate why you think this is so. (Please remember, do not include public employers such as the school district or county government.)

    I think that_____ has had the greatest impact on my
                    (Type of business)
    community because:_____

In waste siting and waste operating (in parenthesis) communities, the following question was asked:

27. What kinds of waste would have been handled (are handled) at _____?
    Please circle at least one of the numbers below. (Note: You may circle more than one number)

    1. Municipal solid wastes
    2. Industrial solid wastes
    3. Medical or biological wastes
    4. Debris from hazardous waste clean-up activities
    5. Industrial liquid wastes
    6. Low level radioactive wastes
    7. High level radioactive wastes
    DK Don't know

In waste siting and waste operating (in parenthesis) communities, the following question was asked:

28. Are you satisfied with the level of participation your community has had in matters concerning the siting (operation) of _____?

    1 YES   2 NO   DK Don't Know or Have No Opinion

    If you answered YES or NO, please use the space below to explain why you think this is so.

The following question was asked in the alternative forms shown in all communities.

29. Using a scale of 1 (SUBSTANTIAL CONFLICT) to 5 (NO CONFLICT AT ALL) please indicate how much conflict you think there has been among each of the following groups due to (name of facility for waste impacted or recent economic changes for nonwaste communities) in your community

		Substantial Conflict				No Conflict At All
a.	The level of conflict between people in your community and the owners, operators, or managers of local businesses.	1	2	3	4	5

	Substantial Conflict				No Conflict At All
b. The level of conflict between people in your community and state government agencies.	1	2	3	4	5
c. The level of conflict between people in your community and the local government.	1	2	3	4	5
d. The level of conflict between people in your community and other communities.	1	2	3	4	5
e. The level of conflict among members of your community.	1	2	3	4	5

In nonwaste and control communities, the following question was asked:

30. In your community, have the overall effects of recent economic changes been positive or negative?

   1   Positive   2   Negative   DK   Don't Know or Have No Opinion

   If you answered Positive or Negative, please use the space below to explain why you think this is so.

In waste siting and waste operating (in parenthesis) communities, the following question was asked:

31. Do you think that the economic benefits to your community of the _____ facility would have been (have been) greater than the economic costs?

   1   YES   2   NO   DK   Don't Know or Have No Opinion

   If you answered YES or NO, please use the space below to explain why you think this is so.

In nonwaste development and control communities, the following question was asked:

32. Are you satisfied with the level of participation your community has had in decisions affecting recent economic changes in your community?

    1   YES   2   NO   DK   Don't Know or Have No Opinion

    If you answered YES or NO, please use the space below to explain why you think this is so.

    _____

In waste siting and waste operating communities, the following question was asked:

33. Looking back on this area's experiences with _____, is there anything you think that should be done differently the next time such a company chooses to locate in your community or a similar community?

    1   YES   2   NO   DK   Don't Know or Have No Opinion

    If you answered YES or NO, please use the space below to explain why you think this is so.

    _____

In nonwaste development and control communities, the following question was asked:

34. Overall, do you think that recent economic changes have affected all community members similarly?

    1   YES   2   NO   DK   Don't Know or Have No Opinion

    If you answered YES or NO, please use the space below to explain why you think this is so.

    _____

In waste siting and waste operating communities, the following question was asked:

35. Overall, do you think that the siting of the facility was fair to all parties involved? Using a scale of 1 (COMPLETELY UNFAIR) to 5 (COMPLETELY FAIR) please indicate your answer below:

COMPLETELY				COMPLETELY
UNFAIR				FAIR
1	2	3	4	5

Please use the space below to write any comments you may wish to make about the fairness of the siting process.

The following questions were asked in all communities:

BACKGROUND

36. How old were you on your last birthday? _____Years

37. What is your sex?

     1 Male   2 Female

38. Please indicate if you are:

    1 White   3 Native American, Alaskan Native, or Aleut
    2 Black   4 Asian or Pacific Islander
              5 Other: _____
                 (please describe)

39. Are you of Spanish or Hispanic origin?

     1 Yes   2 No

40. Including yourself, how many people live in this household? _____

41. How many in your household are less than 18 years of age? _____

42. How many in your household are 65 years of age or older? _____

43. What is your current marital status?

    1 Married   4 Divorced
    2 Living as married   5 Separated
    3 Widowed   6 Never married

44. Please indicate the highest level of school that you have completed:

    1   8th grade or less
    2   9th through 11th grade
    3   High school graduate or GED
    4   Some college but no degree
    5   College degree
    6   Graduate degree

45. Are you the primary wage earner in your household?

    1 Yes   (if Yes, then go to question 46)
    2 No ⎯⎯⎯⎯⎯⎯⎯⎯⎯⎯↓

The primary wage earner is my:

    1 Husband or wife   7 Nephew or niece
    2 Unmarried partner   8 Uncle or aunt
    3 Natural born or adopted   9 Grandparent
        son or daughter   10 Grandchild
    4 Stepson or stepdaughter 11 Housemate or roommate
    5 Brother or sister   12 Other _____
    6 Father or mother   (please describe)

46. Please circle your current employment status.

1   Unemployed ---------------------------------- (please go to question 47)
2   Retired -------------------------------------- (please go to question 47)
3   Employed by someone else ------------(please go to question 46a and 46b)
4   Self-employed --------------------------- (please go to question 46a and 46b)

46a. What is your occupation? (Examples: Manager, Health Technician,
     Secretary, Waiter, Teacher, Laborer, Heavy Equipment Operator,
     Police Officer, Engineer, Carpenter, Farmer, Rancher, Salesperson)

     _____

     (Please write your occupation in the space above.)

46b. Which of the following best describes the industry you work in; that is,
     the main kind of activity that is done by the place where you work?

     1   Agriculture, Forestry, or Fishing
     2   Mining, Oil, and Gas Extraction
     3   Construction
     4   Manufacturing
     5   Transportation, Communication, or Public Utilities
     6   Wholesale Trade
     7   Retail Trade
     8   Finance, Banking, Insurance, or Real Estate
     9   Services (Business, Professional, Household, Personal, Social,
         Educational, or Health)
     10 Public Administration or Government (all government services
         including police and fire protection)

---

47. If you are married and living with your spouse (or living as married with
    someone), please circle your husband or wife's (or partner's) current
    employment status.

1   Unemployed ---------------------------------- (please go to question 48)
2   Retired -------------------------------------- (please go to question 48)
3   Employed by someone else -----------(please go to questions 47a and 47b)
4   Self-employed --------------------------- (please go to questions 47a and 47b)

47a. What is his or her occupation? (Examples: Manager, Health
   Technician, Secretary, Waiter, Teacher, Laborer, Heavy Equipment
   Operator, Police Officer, Engineer, Carpenter, Farmer, Rancher,
   Salesperson)

   _____

   (Please write your spouse's occupation in the space above.)

47b. Which of the following best describes the industry he or she works in;
   that is, the main kind of activity that is done by the place where he or
   she works?

   1 Agriculture, Forestry, or Fishing
   2 Mining, Oil, and Gas Extraction
   3 Construction
   4 Manufacturing
   5 Transportation, Communication, or Public Utilities
   6 Wholesale Trade
   7 Retail Trade
   8 Finance, Banking, Insurance, or Real Estate
   9 Services (Business, Professional, Household, Personal, Social,
      Educational, or Health)
   10 Public Administration or Government (all government services
      including police and fire protection)

48. How long have you lived in this community?
   _____Years (If less than 1, then put <1.)

49. How long have you lived in your current residence?
   _____Years (If less than 1 year, then put <1.)

50. Which of following describes the house in which you currently live?

   1   Owned outright (that is, no mortgage payment)
   2   Buying
   3   Renting
   4   Occupying at no cost but do not own

51. Do you own or operate a farm or ranch?

    1 No   (if No, then go to question 52)
    2 Yes _____

    > 51a. What is the total acreage of your farm or
    >   ranch operation (including land that is
    >   owned, leased, and rented)?
    >   _____ Total Acres
    >
    > 51b. How many of these acres do you own?
    >   _____ Owned Acres

52. Excluding the house that you now live in and excluding farmland, do you own
    any other land or real estate in this area?

    1   Yes   2   No

53. Please circle the number below that is closest to your household's 1993 total
    income. (Include income from all sources before any deductions or taxes. This
    includes income from wages, salaries, self-employment, interest, rents, royalties,
    Social Security, other retirement income, child support, disability income, public
    assistance payments, and welfare income.)

1	Under $15,000	5	$50,000 to $59,999
2	$15,000 to $24,999	6	$60,000 to $69,999
3	$25,000 to $34,999	7	$70,000 to $79,999
4	$35,000 to $49,999	8	$80,000 or more

Community Leader Addendum

Now we would like to ask you some questions about your activities as a community leader. In particular, we would like to ask you about the impacts resulting from the siting (operation for waste operating) of the _____ facility [or the impacts resulting from recent economic changes and development activities in your community for the nonwaste development and control communities].

First, however, let me ask you some general questions about your community.

1. What have been the major economic changes or developments in your community in recent years? _____

2. What do you see as the major strengths of your community in regard to such changes and developments? _____

3. What do you see as the major weaknesses of your community in regard to such changes and developments? _____

4. Do you think that a community should offer incentives to attract businesses?

                                        yes   no
    [Why or why not?] _____

5. Do you think that a company should offer incentives to a community in which it wishes to locate?

                                        yes   no
    [Why or why not?] _____

6a. Has your community made efforts to attract businesses or industries into this area?

                                        yes   no
    [If yes] What kinds of efforts has it made and what have been the results?

    _____

b. Does your community have a specific group (e.g. a community development committee or agency) designated to recruit new businesses or industries?

                                        yes   no
    [If yes] What is the name of this group?_____

c. Does this group have any paid employees (e.g. a director, secretary, etc.)?

                                        yes   no
    [If yes] What are these positions?_____

The following questions were asked in the alternative forms shown in all communities

Now I would like to ask you about events associated with recent economic changes and developments in your community (events associated with the siting and operation of the facility for waste-impacted communities).

7. In regard to potential economic changes or developments in your community (during both the siting and operation for waste-impacted counties), did you obtain information from:

    a. Any industrial groups/companies?

                                        yes   no

        What type of information did you attempt to obtain?_____

        _____

        How adequate was this information for decision-making purposes?

        _____

        Was there any other information that you would like to have obtained from such groups?

                                        yes   no

        [If yes] What type of information was that?_____

    b. Did you obtain information from state/federal or other governmental agencies?

                                        yes   no

        What was this information? _____

        How adequate was that information for decision-making purposes?

        _____

        Was there any other information that you would like to have obtained from these agencies?

                                        yes   no

        [If yes] What type of information was that?_____

c. Did you obtain information from any other sources/groups?

                                                    yes   no

[If yes] What was the group/source and the information you obtained?
_____

How adequate was this information for decision-making purposes?
_____

d.   What types of information do you think communities such as yours need in relation to economic development projects or such projects?
_____

What groups/agencies should provide that information?_____

8. What types of information do you think residents want about potential economic development (waste siting or waste operating facilities in waste-impacted communities)?
_____

Do you believe they obtained this information?

                                                    yes   no

[If yes] Where did they obtain it?_____

[If no] Why not? _____

9. Have there been any occasions when you wanted additional information to disseminate to citizens about potential economic development projects?

                                                    yes   no

[If yes] What was the major limitation you faced in obtaining and disseminating that information?
_____

Now we would like to ask you about the impacts of recent economic changes and developments in your community (or the impacts of the facility for waste-impacted communities) on your community.

10. What aspects of your community have been most impacted by recent economic changes and developments in your community (or by the facility in waste-impacted communities).
_____

11. Have recent economic changes and developments (or the waste facility in waste-impacted communities) had impacts on:

a. Police services   yes   no

    If yes, what have the impacts been?_____

b. Fire and other safety services   yes   no

    If yes, what have the impacts been?_____

c. Health services   yes   no

    If yes, what have the impacts been?_____

d. Education services   yes   no

    If yes, what have the impacts been?_____

e. Water utilities   yes   no

    If yes, what have the impacts been?_____

f. Sewer and related utilities   yes   no

    If yes, what have the impacts been?_____

g. Housing   yes   no

    If yes, what have the impacts been?_____

h. Real estate   yes   no

    If yes, what have the impacts been?_____

i. Retail sales   yes   no

    If yes, what have the impacts been?_____

j. Recreational or other services   yes   no

    If yes, what have the impacts been?_____

k. Public expenditures   yes   no

    If yes, what have the impacts been?_____

l. Tax revenues   yes   no

    If yes, what have the impacts been?_____

m. Economic growth   yes   no

    If yes, what have the impacts been?_____

n. Job opportunities   yes   no

    If yes, what have the impacts been?_____

o. Residents' incomes   yes   no

    If yes, what have the impacts been?_____

p. Specific groups of people such as the young or old?   yes   no

    If yes, what have the impacts been?_____

In nonwaste development and control communities, the following question was asked:

12. How would you characterize the relationships of your community with potential developers who have expressed interest in your community in recent years?

_____

In waste siting and waste operating (in parenthesis) communities, the following question was asked:

12. During the siting (operation) of the _____ facility how would you characterize the relationship between the groups you represent and _____?

_____

In nonwaste development and control communities, the following question was asked:

13. How would you characterize the relationship of your community with local, state and federal governmental bodies during your attempts to deal with potential developers who have expressed interest in your community in recent years?

_____

In waste siting and waste operating (in parenthesis) communities, the following question was asked:

13. During the siting (operation) of the _____ facility, how would you characterize the relationships between the groups you represent (are a leader of) and local, state and federal governmental bodies?_____

In waste siting and waste operating communities, the following questions were asked:

14. In relationship to the _____ facility, I am going to ask if you and other local leaders were involved in certain processes. If you or other leaders were involved, please describe when you or other leaders became involved and the nature and extent of your involvement for each of the following:

In nonwaste development and control communities, the following questions were asked:

14. During recent economic development projects, were you and other local leaders involved in certain processes? If you or other leaders were involved, please describe when you or other leaders became involved and the nature and extent of your involvement for each of the following:

    a. Site selection   yes   no

          When and how? _____

    b. Facility location   yes   no

          When and how? _____

    c. Facility design   yes   no

          When and how? _____

    d. Hearings or other public meetings   yes   no

          When and how? _____

e. Decisions regarding the provision of services to the facility

                                                              yes   no

   When and how? _____

f. Decision regarding incentives or other trade-offs   yes   no

   When and how? _____

g. Monitoring or regulation of facility   yes   no

   When and how? _____

h. Other decisions or activities regarding the facility   yes   no

   When and how? _____

Are any of these processes ones in which you feel you should have had greater
involvement?   yes   no

Which ones? _____

What type of involvement? _____

**In nonwaste development and control communities, the following question was
asked:**

15. What groups or organizations have been involved in the recent economic
    development projects and what has been the nature of their involvement?

    Local government _____

    State government _____

    Local citizens _____

    Groups with membership or headquarters located outside your community
    _____

In waste siting and waste operating (in parenthesis) communities, the following question was asked:

15. What were the groups or organizations involved in the siting (operation) of the _____ facility and what was the nature of their involvement?

   Local government _____

   State government _____

   Local citizens _____

   Groups with membership or headquarters located outside your community

---

In nonwaste development and control communities, the following questions were asked:

16. Overall, how do local residents view recent development projects?

   What do they see as the major benefits of recent development projects?

   What do they see as the major problems and/or costs of recent development projects?

In waste siting and waste operating communities, the following questions were asked:

16. Overall, how do local residents view the _____ facility?

   What do they see as the major benefits of the facility?

   What do they see as the major problems and/or costs of the facility?

In nonwaste development and control communities, the following question was asked:

17. Have local residents' views about economic development projects changed over time?

                                          yes   no

Why? _____

In waste siting and waste operating communities, the following question was asked?

17. Have local residents' views about the facility changed over time?

                                          yes   no

Why? _____

In nonwaste development and control communities, the following question was asked:

18. Overall, as a community leader, what do you see as the major benefits of recent economic changes and/or potential developments?

_____

In waste siting and waste operating communities, the following question was asked:

18. Overall, as a community leader, what do you see as the major benefits of the _____ project? _____

In nonwaste development and control communities, the following question was asked:

19. Overall, as a community leader, what do you see as the major problems associated with recent economic changes and/or potential developments?

_____

In waste siting and waste operating communities, the following question was asked:

19. Overall, as a community leader, what do you see as the major problems associated with the _____ project?

In nonwaste development and control communities, the following question was asked:

20. As a community leader, would you rate recent economic development projects (or potential projects) as having an overall positive or negative impact on your community?

    positive   negative

    Why do you feel that way?_____

In waste siting and waste operating communities, the following question was asked:

20. As a community leader, would you rate the _____ project as having an overall positive or negative impact on your community?

    positive   negative

    Why do you feel that way?_____

In nonwaste development and control communities, the following question was asked:

21. Finally, thinking about recent economic development projects (or potential projects) that you have been involved in, can you think of any things you believe leaders of other communities need to know or that you would advise them to do?

In waste siting and waste operating communities, the following question was asked:

21. Finally, thinking about other communities that may be impacted by similar facilities in the future, can you think of any things you believe their leaders need to know or that you would advise them to do?

In nonwaste development and control communities, the following question was asked:

22. Is there anything else that you would like us to know about your community, recent economic development projects, or other factors?

_____

In waste siting and waste operating communities, the following question was asked:

23. Is there anything else that you would like us to know about your community, the _____ facility, or the relationship of the two?

_____

References

Albrecht, S. L. 1995. Equity and Justice in Environmental Decision Making: A Proposed Research Agenda. *Society and Natural Resources* 8:67-72.

Albrecht, S. L., R. G. Amey, and S. Amir. 1996. The Siting of Radioactive Waste Facilities: What Are the Effects on Communities? *Rural Sociology* 61(4):649-73.

Albrecht, D. E., S. H. Murdock, F. L. Leistritz, J. M. Halstead, and S. L. Albrecht. 1985. The Impacts of Energy-Resource Projects on Rural Communities in the Western United States. *Research in Rural Sociology & Development* 2:109-23.

Bailey, C., C. E. Faupel, and S. F. Holland. 1992. Hazardous Wastes and Differing Perceptions of Risk in Sumter County, Alabama. *Society and Natural Resources* 5:21-36.

Benford, R. D., H. A. Moore, and J. A. Williams, Jr. 1993. In Whose Backyard?: Concern About Siting a Nuclear Waste Facility. *Sociological Inquiry* 63:30-48.

Bourke, L. 1994. Economic Attitudes and Responses to Siting Hazardous Waste Facilities in Rural Utah. *Rural Sociology* 59 (3): 485-96.

Brown, R., R. Geertsen, and R. Krannich. 1989. Community Satisfaction and Social Integration in a Boom Town: A Longitudinal Analysis. *Rural Sociology* 54:568-86.

Bullard, R. D. 1990. *Dumping in Dixie: Race, Class and Environmental Quality*. Boulder, CO: Westview Press.

Bureau of the Census. 1994. *Intercensus Estimates of Population 1994*. Washington, DC: U.S. Government Printing Office.

Bureau of the Census. 1990. *Census of Population 1980 and 1990*. Washington, DC: U.S. Government Printing Office.

Bureau of Economic Analysis. 1995. *Personal Income by Place of Residence 1994.* Washington, DC: U.S. Department of Commerce, Regional Economic Information Service.

Cerrell Associates, Inc. 1984. *Political Difficulties Facing Waste-to-Energy Conversion Plant Siting.* Los Angeles: California Waste Management Board.

Cotgrove, S. F. 1982. *Catastrophe or Cornucopia: The Environment, Politics, and the Future.* New York, NY: John Wiley.

Desvousges, W. H., H. Kunreuther, P. Slovic, and E. A. Rosa. 1993. Perceived Risk and Attitudes Toward Nuclear Wastes: National and Nevada Perspectives. In *Public Reactions to Nuclear Waste: Citizens' Views of Repository Siting,* ed. R. E. Dunlap, M. E. Kraft, and E. A. Rosa, 175-208. Durham, NC: Duke University Press.

Easterling, D. and H. Kunreuther. 1995. *The Dilemma of Siting a High-level Nuclear Waste Repository.* Boston, MA: Kluwer Academic Publishers.

Edelstein, M. R. 1988. *Contaminated Communities: The Social and Psychological Impacts of Residential Toxic Exposure.* Boulder, CO: Westview Press.

Erikson, K. 1994. *A New Species of Trouble: The Human Experience of Modern Disasters.* New York: W. W. Norton and Co.

Feldman, D. L., J. H. Peretz, and B. D. Jendrucko. 1994. Policy Gridlock in Waste Management: Balancing Federal and State Concerns. *Policy Studies Journal* 22:589-603.

Fitchen, J. M. 1991. *Endangered Spaces, Enduring Places: Change, Identity, and Survival in Rural America.* Boulder, CO: Westview Press.

Fitchen, J. M., J. S. Heath, and June Fessenden-Raden. 1987. Risk Perception in Community Context: A Case Study. In *The Social and Cultural Construction of Risk: Essays on Risk Selection and Perception,* ed. B. B. Johnson and V. T. Covello, 31-54. Boston, MA: D. Reidel.

Flynn, J., P. Slovic, and C. K. Mertz. 1994. Gender, Race, and Perception of Environmental Health Risks. *Risk Analysis* 14:1101-1108.

Freudenburg, W. R. 1992. Nothing Recedes Like Success? Risk Analysis and the Organizational Amplification of Risks. *RISK—Issues in Health and Safety* 1:1-35.

―――. 1988. Perceived Risk, Real Risk: Social Science and the Art of Probabilistic Risk Assessment. *Science* 242:44-49.

―――. 1986. Social Impact Assessment. *Annual Review of Sociology* 12:451-78.

Freudenburg, W. R. and R. Gramling. 1992. Community Impacts of Technological Change: Toward a Longitudinal Perspective. *Social Forces* 70:937-55.

Freudenburg, W. R. and R. E. Jones. 1991. Criminal Behavior and Rapid Community Growth: Examining the Evidence. *Rural Sociology* 56(4):619-45.

Gerrard, M. 1994. *Whose Backyard, Whose Risk: Fear & Fairness in Toxic & Nuclear Wastes*. Boston, MA: MIT Press.

Gervers, J. H. 1987. The NIMBY Syndrome: Is It Inevitable? *The Environment* 29:18-29.

Gilmore, J. S. and M. K. Duff. 1974. *The Sweetwater County Boom: A Challenge to Growth Management*. Denver, CO: Denver Research Institute.

Gilmore, J. S., D. Hammond, K. Moore, J. Johnson, and D. Coddington. 1981. *Socioeconomic Impacts of Power Plants*. Denver, CO: Denver Research Institute.

Halstead, J. M., A. E. Luloff, and S. D. Myers. 1993. An Examination of the NIMBY Syndrome: Why Not in My Backyard? *Journal of the Community Development Society* 24:88-102.

Halstead, J. M., R. A. Chase, S. H. Murdock, and F. L. Leistritz. 1984. *Socioeconomic Impact Management: Design and Implementation*. Boulder, CO: Westview Press.

Kasperson, R. 1990. Social Realities in High-level Radioactive Waste Management and Their Policy Implications. Paper presented at the First Annual International High Level Radioactive Waste Management Conference. Las Vegas, NV, April 9.

Kasperson, R. E., D. Golding, and S. Tuler. 1992. Social Distrust as a Factor in Siting Hazardous Facilities and Communicating Risks. *Journal of Social Issues* 48(4):161-87.

Kraft, M. E. and B. B. Clary. 1993. Public Testimony in Nuclear Waste Repository Hearings: A Content Analysis. In *Public Reactions to Nuclear Waste: Citizens' Views of Repository Siting*, ed. R. E. Dunlap, M. E. Kraft, and E. A. Rosa, 89-114. Durham, NC: Duke University Press.

Krannich, R. S. and S. L. Albrecht. 1995. Opportunity/threat Responses to Nuclear Waste Disposal Facilities. *Rural Sociology* 60:435-53.

Krannich, R. S. and A. E. Luloff. 1991. Problems of Resource Dependency in U.S. Rural Communities. In *Progress in Rural Policy and Planning*, ed. A. Gilg, D. Briggs, R. Dilley, O. Furuseth, and G. McDonald, 5-18. London: Belhaven.

Krannich, R. S., E. H. Berry, and T. Greider. 1989. Fear of Crime in Rapidly Changing Rural Communities: A Longitudinal Analysis. *Rural Sociology* 54:195-212.

Krannich, R. S., K. Wrigley, J. D. Wulfhorst, S. Murdock, S. Spies, S. White, F. L. Leistritz, R. Hamm, R. Sell, and J. Thompson. 1997. In Search of Local Support for Hazardous Waste Facility Siting: Resident Responses to Alternative Community Compensation and Incentive

Programs. Paper presented at the 1997 Annual Meeting of the International Association for Impact Assessment, New Orleans, LA, May 28-31.

Kroll-Smith, J. S. and S. R. Couch. 1992. Social Impacts of Toxic Contamination. In *Social Impacts of Hazardous and Nuclear Facilities and Events: Implications for Nevada and the Yucca Mountain High-level Nuclear Waste Repository*, 1-59. Carson City, NV: Nevada Nuclear Waste Project Office.

————. 1991. Technological Hazards, Adaptation and Social Change. In *Collective Response to Technological Hazards*, ed. S. R. Couch and J. S. Kroll-Smith, 293-320. New York, NY: Peter Lang Publishing, Inc.

————. 1990. *The Real Disaster Is Above Ground: A Mine Fire and Social Conflict*. Lexington, KY: University Press of Kentucky.

Leistritz, F. L. 1994. Economic and Fiscal Impact Assessment. *Impact Assessment* 12(3):305-17.

Leistritz, F. L. and B. L. Ekstrom. 1986. *Socioeconomic Impact Assessment and Management: An Annotated Bibliography*. New York, NY: Garland Publishing Company.

Leistritz, F. L. and R. R. Hamm. 1994. *Rural Economic Development, 1975-1993: An Annotated Bibliography*. Westport, CT: Greenwood Publishing.

Leistritz, F. L. and S. H. Murdock. 1988. Financing Infrastructure in Rapid Growth Communities: The North Dakota Experience. In *Local Infrastructure Investment in Rural America*, ed. T. Johnson, B. Deaton, and E. Segarro, 141-54. Boulder, CO: Westview Press.

————. 1981. *The Socioeconomic Impact of Resource Development: Methods for Assessment*. Boulder, CO: Westview Press.

Leistritz, F. L., S. H. Murdock, and A. G. Leholm. 1982. Local Economic Changes Associated with Rapid Growth. In *Coping with Rapid Growth in Rural Communities*, ed. B. Weber and R. Howell, 25-61. Boulder, CO: Westview Press.

Leistritz, F. L., J. M. Halstead, R. A. Chase, and S. H. Murdock. 1983. Socioeconomic Impact Management: Program Design and Implementation Considerations. *Minerals and the Environment* 4:141-50.

Little, R. L. and R. S. Krannich. 1989. A Model for Assessing the Social Impacts of Natural Resource Utilization on Resource-dependent Communities. *Impact Assessment Bulletin* 6(2):21-35.

Manning, P. K. 1992. Managing Risk: Managing Uncertainty in the British Nuclear Installations Inspectorate. In *Organizations, Uncertainties, and Risk*, ed. J. F. Short, Jr. and L. Clarke, 255-73. Boulder, CO: Westview Press.

Margolis, H. 1996. *Dealing with Risk: Why the Public and the Experts Disagree on Environmental Issues*. Chicago, IL: The University of Chicago Press.

Mazmanian, D. and D. Morell. 1992. *Beyond Superfailure: America's Toxics Policy for the 1990s*. Boulder, CO: Westview Press.

Molotch, H. 1976. The City as a Growth Machine: Toward a Political Economy of Place. *American Journal of Sociology* 82:309-32.

Murdock, S. H. and F. L. Leistritz. 1979. *Energy Development in the Western United States: Impact on Rural Areas*. New York, NY: Praeger Publishers.

Murdock, S. H., F. L. Leistritz, and R. R. Hamm. 1986. The State of Socioeconomic Impact Analysis in the United States: Limitations and Opportunities for Alternative Futures. *Journal of Environmental Management* 23:99-117.

————. 1983a. Socioeconomic Impacts of Large-scale Developments: Implications for High-Level Nuclear Waste Repositories. *The Environmental Professional* 5:183-94.

————. 1983b. *Nuclear Waste: Socioeconomic Dimensions of Long-term Storage*. Boulder, CO: Westview Press.

Murdock, S. H., R. R. Hamm, E. Colberg, and F. L. Leistritz. 1991. The Waste Management Problem. In *Rural Policies for the 1990s*, ed. C. B. Flora and J. A. Christenson, 281-91. Boulder, CO: Westview Press.

Murdock, S. H., F. L. Lesitritz, R. R. Hamm, and S. S. Hwang. 1982. An Assessment of Socioeconomic Assessments: Utility, Accuracy, and Policy Considerations. *The Environmental Impact Assessment Review* 3:333-50.

Murdock, S. H., S. Spies, K. Effah, S. White, R. Krannich, J. D. Wulfhorst, K. Wrigley, F. L. Leistritz, R. Sell, and J. Thompson. 1997. *Final Report on Socioeconomic Impacts of Waste Facility Siting and Management in Rural America*. Washington, D.C.: U.S. Department of Agriculture, National Research Initiative Project No. 93-37401-8973.

Nuclear Regulatory Commission (NRC). 1996. Radioactive Waste Disposal. Washington, DC: Office of Nuclear Reactor Regulation.

Perrow, C. 1986. Risky Systems: The Habit of Courting Disaster. *The Nation* October 11(329):247-56.

————. 1984. *Normal Accidents: Living with High-risk Technologies*. New York, NY: Basic Books.

Piller, C. 1991. *The Fail-safe Society: Community Defiance and the End of American Technological Optimism*. New York, NY: Basic Books.

Portney, K. E. 1991. *Siting Hazardous Waste Treatment Facilities: The NIMBY Syndrome*. New York, NY: Auburn House.

Reich, M. R. 1991. *Toxic Politics: Responding to Chemical Disasters*. Ithaca, NY: Cornell University Press.

Reiss, A. J., Jr. 1992. The Institutionalization of Risk. In *Organizations, Uncertainties, and Risk*, ed. J. F. Short, Jr. and L. Clarke, 299-308. Boulder, CO: Westview Press.

Renn, O., W. J. Burns, J. X. Kasperson, R. E. Kasperson, and P. Slovic. 1992. The Social Amplification of Risk: Theoretical Foundations and Empirical Applications. *Journal of Social Issues* 48(4):137-60.

Rocky Mountain Social Science. 1992. Boyd County Sociocultural Assessment: Final Report. Logan, UT.

Shrader-Frechette, K. S. 1993. *Burying Uncertainty: Risk and the Case Against Geologic Disposal of Nuclear Waste.* Berkeley, CA: University of California Press.

Segal, H. P. 1994. *Future Imperfect: The Mixed Blessings of Technology in America.* Amherst, MA: The University of Massachusetts Press.

Slovic, P., M. Layman, and J. Flynn. 1993. Perceived Risk, Trust, and the Politics of Nuclear Waste: Lessons from Yucca Mountain. In *Public Reactions to Nuclear Waste: Citizens' Views of Repository Siting*, ed. R. Dunlap, M. Kraft, and E. Rosa, 64-86. Durham, NC: Duke University Press.

Slovic, P., M. Layman, N. Kraus, J. Flynn, J. Chalmers, and G. Gesell. 1991. Perceived Risk, Stigma, and Potential Impacts of a High-level Nuclear Waste Repository in Nevada. *Risk Analysis* 11:683-96.

Smith, F. L., Jr. 1995. Risks in the Modern World: What Prospects for Rationality? *The Freeman* 4 (3): 140-44.

Smith, M. H., L. J. Beaulieu, and A. Seraphine. 1995. Social Capital, Place of Residence, and College Attendance. *Rural Sociology* 60(3):363-80.

Spies, S., S. H. Murdock, S. White, R. Krannich, J. D. Wulfhorst, K. Wrigley, F. L. Leistritz, R. R. Hamm, R. Sell, and J. Thompson. 1998. Support for Waste Facility Siting: Differences Between Community Leaders and Residents. *Rural Sociology* 63(1):65-93.

———. 1996. Waste Facility Experience and Perceptions of Waste-Related Health and Safety Risks. Paper presented at the Sixth International Symposium on Society and Resource Management, University Park, PA, May 18-23.

Stoffle, R. W., M. W. Traugott, C. Harshbarger, F. Jensen, M. Evans, and P. Drury. 1988. *Perceptions of Risk from Radioactivity: The Superconducting Supercollider in Michigan.* Ann Arbor, MI: Institute for Social Research, University of Michigan.

Takahashi, L. M. and S. L. Gaber. 1998. Controversial Facility Siting in the Urban Environment: Resident and Planner Perceptions in the United States. *Environment and Behavior* 30 (2): 184-215.

Thayer, R. L., Jr. 1994. *Gray World, Green Heart: Technology, Nature, and the Sustainable Landscape.* New York, NY: John Wiley & Sons, Inc.

Thomas, W. I. and F. Znaniecki. 1918-1920. *The Polish Peasant in Europe and America.* 5 volumes. Boston, MA: Richard G. Badger. Volumes I and II originally published by the University of Chicago Press, 1918.

Tierney, T. F. 1993. *The Value of Convenience: A Genealogy of Technical Culture.* New York, NY: State University of New York Press.

U.S. Environmental Protection Agency. 1997a. The Preliminary Biennial RCRA Hazardous Waste Report (Based on 1995 Data). Washington, DC: U.S. Environmental Protection Agency.

———. 1997b. Final National Priorities List (NPL) Sites. Washington, DC: U.S. Environmental Protection Agency, Office of Emergency and Remedial Response.

Walsh, E. J., R. Warland, and D. C. Smith. 1997. *Don't Burn It Here: Grassroots Challenges to Trash Incinerators.* University Park, PA: Penn State Press.

Weinberg, A. M. 1987. Science and its Limits: The Regulator's Dilemma. In *De Minimis Risk*, ed. C. Whipple, 27-38. New York, NY: Plenum Press.

Wilkinson, K. P. and M. J. Camasso. 1987. The Energy Boom and Juvenile Delinquency. Paper presented at the 1987 Annual Meeting of the Rural Sociological Society, Madison, WI, August 11-15.

Winner, L. 1977. *Autonomous Technology: Technics-out-of-Control as a Theme in Political Thought.* Cambridge, MA: The MIT Press.

Wulfhorst, J. D. 1997. Technological Risk and Community Development in Tooele County, Utah. Ph.D. diss., Utah State University.

Index

About the Authors

Steve H. Murdock is Professor and Head of the Department of Rural Sociology and Regents Professor at Texas A&M University. Richard S. Krannich is Professor of Sociology at Utah State University. F. Larry Leistritz is Professor of Agricultural Economics and holds the title of Distinguished Professor at North Dakota State University. Sherrill Spies is a Training Specialist with VALIC Corporation. J. D. Wulfhorst is a Research Associate with the Rural Sociology Section of the School of Human Environmental Sciences at the University of Arkansas. Krissa Wrigley is an Information Services Analyst with the Division of Economic Development in the Idaho Department of Commerce. Randy Sell is a Research Scientist in the Department of Agricultural Economics at North Dakota State University. Steve White is an Assistant Research Scientist in the Department of Rural Sociology at Texas A&M University. Kofi Effah is a Research Associate in the Department of Rural Sociology at Texas A&M University.

The three senior authors have conducted extensive analyses of the socioeconomic impacts of a wide variety of industrial, energy and waste-product storage and disposal facilities in rural America for more than two decades. Their research programs and those of the other authors are intended both to provide a base of empirical information about the actual, rather than the presumed, impacts of such facilities and to provide information necessary for rural community residents and leaders to make informed decisions about the types of projects which they may wish to develop and host within their communities.